Selling Real Estate

Without

Selling Your Soul

Volume 1

My Best to You!

Jennifer Allan-Hagedorn

Oct 2013

Jennifer Allan-Hagedorn, GRI

Bluegreen Books
publisher@bluegreenbooks.com

ISBN: 978-0-9816727-8-6

Edited by Barbara Munson, Munson Communications www.munsoncommunications.com

Cover design by Sheryl Evans, Evans Studios, www.evans-studios.com

Interior design by Jonathan Gullery, RJ Communications, www.selfpublishing.com

First Printing 2013

Printed in the United States of America

To the friend, confidante and right-hand woman,
without whom none of this would have been possible.
Sue Gabriel...thank you. Just...thank you.

Contents

Kind Words for Jennifer Allan-Hagedorn and
Selling with Soul 13

Introduction 16
    About This Blog-to-Book 18
    What is a Blog? 18
    How This Blog-to-Book Is Organized 19

The Sell with Soul Glossary 21

About the Author 22
    The Life & Times of Jennifer Allan
    (now Allan-Hagedorn) 1996 – 2009 23

DECEMBER 2006 25
    Selling with Soul for Real Estate Professionals 25

JANUARY 2007 27
    Real Estate Is Not a Numbers Game
    (at least, it doesn't have to be) 27

FEBRUARY 2007 30
    Being Up-Front with Our Sellers 30

MARCH 2007 31
    "I'm a Listing Specialist so I Don't Work with Buyers" 31
    What Does a Listing Agent DO for All that Money? 32

APRIL 2007 34
    Okay, so I Lied...Real Estate
    IS a Number's Game...Sort of... 34
    Introverts—Stay IN Your Comfort Zone! 35
    What's the Best Way to Ask for Referrals? Don't. 36

MAY 2007 38
    Using Reverse Psychology with Your FAMILY SOI 38
    Introverts—Always Offer Your Hand First 39

A Great Niche for Introverts! 40

JUNE 2007. . . . . **42**
Doctors and Lawyers...and Real Estate Agents? 42

JULY 2007 . . . . **44**
Just Say NO to Price Reductions! 44
SOI—It's More Fun with a Friend! 45
Give (Referrals) and Ye Shall Receive! 46

AUGUST 2007 . . . . **48**
Announce Your Website with a Scavenger Hunt! 48
Introverts—Show up When It's the Right Thing to Do 48
Do I Deserve Your Loyalty? 49
Introverts—Pick up that Phone! 50

SEPTEMBER 2007. . . . .**52**
What Your Home Sellers May Not Know...but Need to 52
Jake's New Real Estate Career 53
The Saga of Jake Continues.... 54
Jakes Sells a House...or Two 55
Announcing Our Rookie of the Year...Jake! 57
Life Is Good...Says Jake 60
Reflections on Jake's Success 60
Was Jake Lucky? 61
Is SOI Right for You? 63

OCTOBER 2007. . . . . **64**
Real Estate Agents: Get Good...or Get out 64
My Friday SOI Success Story 65
Hey! What Happened to the Real Estate Market? 66

NOVEMBER 2007 . . . . **68**
Preview Ten Listings Today and Report Back 68
Where'd My MoJoGo? 69

DECEMBER 2007 . . . .**71**
Found My MoJo! How About You? 71

An Excuse to Contact Your Past Clients—
for Old Fogies Only! 72

ANOTHER Excuse to Contact Past Clients—
Use that Camera! 73

Does Your Spouse Refer Business to You? 74

JANUARY 2008 76

Farewell, Alabama the Beautiful. I Will Miss You. 76

Denver is.... 77

What I've Missed About Denver 78

Should New Real Estate Agents Focus on Buyers
or Listings? And Why? 80

Newbies, Don't Be Intimidated...You Can Do It 80

FEBRUARY 2008 82

You Won't Win 'Em All with Your SOI...and that's Okay 82

My Dear Sphere of Influence,
"Thanks, But I Don't Want Your Loyalty!" 83

I Was Cold-Called This Morning...and I Was Rude 83

No Wonder Houses Aren't Selling.... 84

MARCH 2008 85

Surviving the Inspection...I Love This Stuff 85

More Tips to Survive the Inspection 86

Pay for Non-Performance? I Really Don't Wanna... 87

"Advertising" to Your Sphere of Influence 88

Always Look for the Negative...Yeah, That Works
(she says sarcastically) 89

APRIL 2008 90

Sales Pitched at 24-Hour Fitness...
and I WON'T Be Joining! 90

What's Your Angle? Do You Really Need One? 91

Back and Forth, Back and Forth—
Just Make the Date Already! 92

Does Arguing with Your Clients Sound like a Good Idea? 93

Arguing Will Get You Nowhere! Try This Instead.... 94

My New Buyer Calls at 7:30am on Sunday Morning...
Do I Jump? You Betcha! 96

MAY 2008. . . . . **98**

Helloooooooooo??? Are You out There, SOI?
Yes, Jennifer, We're Here! 98

I'll Be Happy to Refer You as Long as It's My Idea...
(that is, please don't ask me to) 99

Gas Prices Too High to "Waste" My Time with Buyers? Oh,
Puh-leeeaze! 100

Please Tip in Cash (an alternative to Referral-Begging) 101

"So, What Is a GOOD Real Estate Agent?" 102

JUNE 2008. . . . .**103**

There's GOLD in Them Thar SOI! 103

It's All About ME (a rant)! 104

My Four-Month Anniversary Back in Biz:
Eight Lessons from the Trenches 104

Asking for Referrals Versus NOT Asking for Referrals—
Which Is More Risky? 105

Thanks for the Referral—Here's Your Toaster! 106

JULY 2008 . . . .**108**

My "Waste of Time" Listing Appointment
This Holiday Weekend 108

Wasting Time Again...Will I Ever Learn? 109

My Dear Home Seller: What's Your Plan B? 110

Y'think Your Current Clients Are Talking About
Their Real Estate Agent? Uh, Yeah! 111

AUGUST 2008 . . . . **112**

When Scripts Suck 112

Can a New Agent Make It in Today's Market? 113

Pretending to Be a Democrat—That'll Teach Me! 114

SEPTEMBER 2008. . . . . **116**

Aspiring Real Estate Agents—Can't Go Full-Time Yet?
Consider This..... 116

I Still Love My Guardian Angel
(she mutters thru clenched teeth) 117

Can a Single Woman Expand Her Sphere of Influence Without
Sending the Wrong Message? 118

Is Walking Away the Financially Responsible Thing to Do? 119

OCTOBER 2008. 120

PUH-LEEEEEAZE Don't Use Your Office Email Account!! 120

Is a Sphere of Influence Approach
Enough in Today's Market? 121

Yes, a Sphere of Influence Approach
IS Enough in Today's Market, if You... 122

Dave Ramsey Sez: In a Tough Market, Work
Twice as Hard. JA Sez... 123

NOVEMBER 2008 124

Breaking up Is Hard to Do...
but It Doesn't Have to Be Ugly 124

To Expand Your Sphere of Influence—Be in the Right Place at the
Right Time...More Frequently! 125

DECEMBER 2008 127

Phooey on Prospecting...I Just Wanna Do My Job! 127

All I Want for Christmas Is.... 127

The Realities of Today's Less-than-Vibrant
Real Estate Market 128

Today's Market Realities, Part I: When to Venture
out of Your Comfort Zone...and When to Stay in... 129

Seriously, Is It Time to Hit PAUSE on Your Real Estate Career? 131

Christmas Card Lemons...to Lemonade 132

To Present or Not to Present...I Have My Answer 132

Now THIS Is a Non-Dorky Business Card!
(Well, it's dorky, but I love it!) 134

JANUARY 2009. 135

Average "Days on Market"? Who CARES? 135

In Today's World...Sales Pitchee's Just Say No 135

Sales-y or Service-y? 136

FEBRUARY 2009. 138

SOI 101—What Exactly Is an SOI (Sphere of Influence)
Business Model? 138

SOI 102—The SECRET to a Successful Real Estate
Sphere of Influence Business Model 139

SOI 103—"My Daughter's Best Friend's Parents
Just Hired Another Real Estate Agent!" 141

SOI 104: "I Think I've Blown It with My Sphere
of Influence. Can I Recover Their Support?" 143

MARCH 2009 145

I'm Sure She Didn't Mean It This Way...or Did She? 145

Introverts, Always Ask "What's in It For Me?"
(and no, that's not a typo) 145

The Rookie Agent Learning Curve...Elongated? 146

New Real Estate Agents—Get Help if You Need It...
Yes, Even if.... 147

Real Estate Agents—A Better Approach to:
"I Return Calls Between x and y..." 148

APRIL 2009 149

The Rookie Series—Ten Secrets to Looking as
if You've Done This Before! 149

The Confident Rookie Series—SECRET ONE:
Master Your Systems BEFORE You Need Them! 150

The Confident Rookie Series—SECRET TWO:
Practice with Your Printer! 151

The Confident Rookie Series—SECRET THREE:
Don't Wing It with Your New Buyer! 152

The Confident Rookie Series—SECRET FOUR:
Drive Your Route Ahead of Time 153

The Confident Rookie Series—SECRET FIVE:
Cheerfully Waste Your Time 154

The Confident Rookie Series—SECRET SIX:
Find Your Handyman 155

The Confident Rookie Series—SECRET SEVEN:
Let Your Seller Prospect Talk! 156

The Confident Rookie Series—SECRET EIGHT:
Get Comfy with Your Commission 157

The Confident Rookie Series—SECRET NINE:
Admit that You're New 158

The Confident Rookie Series—SECRET TEN:
What to Say When You Don't Know the Answer 159

Getting Busy? Seize This Opportunity
to Care for Your Clients! 160

"How Can I Compete with a Minimum
Service Real Estate Company?" 161

MAY 2009 . . . . **163**

Where the Heck Do You Live (and Work)? 163

UNSUBSCRIBED! Some Utterly Random Thoughts
on the Matter... 163

Do You Take Control? Please Do! 165

"Mismatched" Spouses—Introverts & Extroverts 166

Always Be Closing...? 167

What if My Seller Asks for a 'Listing Exclusion'? 168

June 2009 . . . . **169**

Does Your Friend Owe You a Courtesy Call
when She Hires Someone Else? 169

"Dear Real Estate Professional,
I'd Like to See a House, Please" 170

High School Dating Versus Real World Dating...
and Yes, It Relates to Real Estate 171

Lessons from The Bachelorette 172

Any Idiot Can Give Their House Away...
If Price Is All that Matters, What Do They Need Us for? 173

July 2009 . . . . **175**

Okay, Miss Smarty-Pants, HOW Do You Get Your
Sellers on Board to Get Their Home Ready for Market? 175

Persistence Pays Off...? Eh, Maybe There's a Better Way 176

Making New Friends to Sell Real Estate to—a Guide
for Introverts & Other Reluctant Networkers 177

Reluctant Networkers—Your Next
Biggest Client May Be at Walmart! 179

"Good for You, Let Me Know if You Need Anything." 180

JA Thru the Years...in Pictures 181

Do You Use an Autoresponder?
Please Be Careful with It! 183

Should You Price to Ward off Appraisal Problems? 184

August 2009 . . . . **187**

Is Shaking Hands Too 20th Century
in Today's Germophobic World? 187

What You Can Do TODAY to Ensure
a Sweeeet Tomorrow 187

Just What a Rookie Agent Needs—CHARM SCHOOL! 188

Call Me Mercenary...But a Personal Crisis

Can Be Good for Business 189
Can You "SOI" in a Resort Community (that is, can
you depend on your sphere of influence for business)? 190

September 2009. . . . .**193**
WHY Don't We Care About Training for Rookie
Real Estate Agents? Seriously, I'm Asking! 193
Ten Tips to Being a Good Refer-ree (that is—
one who receives referrals from other real estate agents) . . . 194
Attracting Real Estate Business by Being
a Master of Your Market 195
Becoming a Market Master—Here's How... 197
Nurturing Your Relationships TODAY
for Business Tomorrow 198
AVOID BURNOUT! Stop Taking Responsibility for Stuff
that's Not Your Responsibility to Take! 199
Declining the Monkey Without Being
Snotty About It—Part II 200
How to Decline the Monkey, Part III 202
What to SAY (or not say, as the case may be)
to Respectfully Decline the Monkey! 203
A Perfect Example of Keeping the Monkey...
Agents Bickering over Commission to Keep
the Buyer and Seller in the Deal 205
Even if They Don't Complain...Sellers Notice 206
Sixteen Ways to Keep Your Seller Happy with You 207

October 2009 . . . . **209**
Why Did My Friend Hire Someone Else?
Oh, Let Me Count the Reasons... 209
Ten Ways to Show Your Seller You Don't Care 210
"Jennifer, What Do You Think of
Client Appreciation Parties?" 212
Adventures in Pricing—Historic Homes
in Urban Neighborhoods 213
Pricing Historic Homes in Urban Markets—
Step One: Make like a Boy Scout... 214

November 2009 . . . .**216**
Pricing Historic Homes in Urban Markets—
Step Two: Preview, Preview, Preview! 216
Playing Detective...Pricing Historic Homes in

Urban Neighborhoods: Step 3 217

Pricing Historic Homes in Urban Neighborhoods,
Step Four: Analyzing the SOLDs—Dealing with the Outliers . 219

"Real Estate Is a Relationship Business"—
Not Exactly (a rant) 220

It's That Time of Year Again...Doo-Dad Time! 221

A Real Estate Career Is NOT for the Liability-Phobic* 222

Greatness Doesn't Inspire Me Nearly as
Much as Mediocrity Does 224

"I'm Your Friend, so I'll Be Honest with You...!" 225

Real Estate Prospecting—Turning Cheese into Soul 226

Real Estate Prospecting—Turning Cheese into Soul:
Expired Listings & FSBO's 227

December 2009 . . . . **229**

Real Estate Prospecting—Turning Cheese into Soul:
Newsletters 229

Real Estate Prospecting—Turning Cheese into Soul:
Newsletters, Part Deux 230

Turning Cheese into Soul—Send(ing)
Out Cards the Soulful Way 232

A New "Game" Plan for 2010 235

Appendix **237**

Additional SWS Resources 237

Index by Category. 239

Kind Words for Jennifer Allan-Hagedorn and Selling with Soul

I have been blessed with a fanatically loyal following and they have been kind enough to share their appreciation for how Selling with Soul has changed their careers. Following are some of the sweet notes and reviews I've received over the years from real estate agents who are actually out there in the trenches, practicing what we preach!

"Your books are all I can ever imagine needing. I've read a lot of books, articles, blogs, etc. and your advice is the simplest, most respectful I've seen. Your personality and mine are similar and I am so anxious to put your principles to work. You are unlike any real estate agent I've ever met and I'll be snatching up every book and tool you put out there for the rest of my real estate career."
Lee Ann Davisson, Real Estate Agent in Pittsburgh, Pennsylvania

"I think you just saved my career (if not my sanity). I've been battling coming out of my shell to door knock, cold call and chase FSBOs. I was beginning to think that I really wasn't cut out for this career that I moved 200 miles from home and family for, but after reading your book, I really feel like I can do this, because someone else like me made it."
Joshua Sherman, REALTOR® in Philadelphia, Pennsylvania

✦

"I just wanted to write and tell you how excited I am about your view on being a real estate agent! I was hesitant to even consider going into real estate when my husband first suggested it until I found YOU. I too, am an admitted introvert, and although I enjoy spending time with people, I've never been one who wants to stand out, talk big or take all the credit. I don't feel like a salesperson and don't want or need any sales tactics. What I have is honesty and integrity, and to find a line of thought in the real estate world that interweaves that into a successful career EXCITES me beyond belief!"
April Tsotsos, Aspiring Agent in North Port, Florida

"I am so very grateful that a colleague told me about you when I got my real estate license in 2009. It is because of you that my clients love me. They see that it is about them and NOT about me. I love this line: "Because selling real estate well is a lot of fun and can be extremely satisfying, but when you're desperate for a paycheck, your focus shifts and your attitude changes. People can tell when it is just about the paycheck."
Marlene Dufresne-Smith, REALTOR® in Potomac, Maryland

✦

"A colleague recommended I read *Sell With Soul*, and it changed my life! By page four I was in tears...of joy! I recently completed a grueling 6-week sales/script induction class at my company, and I was miserable about my new career choice. The thought of making those calls made me physically sick to my stomach. I couldn't speak words that were not mine nor were they spoken from a place of integrity for me. And then you saved the day! I now feel energized and ready to tackle the world...in my own soulful way!"
Jeanne Ramsay, Broker Associate in Denver, Colorado

✦

"I just wanted to let you know that since I got my real estate license last fall, I have read a little snippet from you every morning and night. Your approach to real estate resonates so clearly with who I am, not only as a professional, but as a human being as well. My business has been going gangbusters with fantastic sellers and buyers right out of the gate and every buyer and seller I've worked with has referred me to at least one client that I'm working with now. Thank you for your inspiring thoughts, direction and guidance."
Annalie Glazen, REALTOR® in Cleveland, Ohio

✦

"I've just finished reading your book *Sell With Soul* and wanted to drop you a quick line to let you know how useful and entertaining I've found it. I only bought it a couple of weeks ago and have been reading it every spare moment I've had since.

I'm in the early stages of planning a career transition into real estate from my current career in marketing and project management. Your book has been really useful in giving me a realistic overview of what it will involve and shown me I can do it in a way that suits my personality and values without feeling I have to become the stereotypical real estate agent.

Thank you for writing such an inspiring book and one I know I'll be coming back to again and again for reference in the coming years!"
Simon Edwards, Aspiring Agent in Pasadena, California

"I just had to take a moment from my real estate studying to tell you how you MADE MY DAY! I am SO happy I found your website and your books.

I have wanted to go into real estate for years, but I was turned off by the image of what I thought of as the typical real estate agent. I wanted a career where I could be creative, authentic and allow my heart to take the lead, not just a pushy and aggressive sales agent. So when I read your book, I was beyond excited! It was a sign from the Universe that I am heading in the right direction. If all you have to do is be respectful, knowledgeable, responsive, reliable and efficient, then I can do this and I know I will be a very GOOD agent. Thank you so much for what you do."
Kelley Anderson, REALTOR® in St. Louis, Missouri

Introduction

You have a choice to make. Today. And tomorrow. In fact, you will make a very important decision every day you work as a real estate agent, from today until the day you retire from the business.

Each and every day, you'll have to choose between Right and Wrong. Fair or Unfair. Respectful or Disrespectful. Every time you meet with or talk to a client...a prospect...a buyer...a seller...every time you make a judgment call or "executive decision" on a matter with no clear cut answer...you'll need to choose on which side to hang your hat. The side with Soul...or No Soul.

I'd like to tell you that if you make too many un-soulful choices you will fail miserably in your real estate career. I'd like to tell you that, but I'd be lying (and that would be un-soulful!). Unfortunately, thousands of real estate agents have experienced wild financial success treating their clients and associates disrespectfully and, well, like dirt.

This has not gone unnoticed by the general public; real estate salespeople "enjoy" a Top Five ranking in a recent list of the nation's most un-trusted professions. Ouch! We're up there (down there?) with car salesmen and politicians, a fact largely due (in my humble opinion) to what I call the "Old School" of real estate thought and training.

You may already be familiar with the Old School philosophies. According to the Old School, the way to succeed selling real estate is to treat it like a numbers game. To use condescending sales scripts, hard-core prospecting techniques and high-pressure closing strategies. Old School agents are frequently depicted in the movies as greedy, self-serving creeps. Unfortunately, these characters weren't invented by screen-writers; they are alive and well and working in your neighborhood. And some are even making a pretty good living.

But I'm guessing that if you purchased a book with the words "Selling with Soul" in the title, you're hoping there is a better way. A way to succeed without sacrificing your soul to do so. While you may freely admit that you want to make lots of money (and there's nothing wrong with that!), you'd prefer not to make it at the expense of your integrity or dignity.

Or, let's be blunt here, maybe you don't consider yourself particularly soulful, but you doubt your ability to use the methods you've been taught by Old

School trainers because they're just too "salesy" for you. You cringe when you imagine yourself making 100 cold calls a day, or putting those tired old closing techniques into play. You might even feel inadequate that you aren't overly enthusiastic about pestering strangers for business.

Quite simply, you know in your heart (and soul) that something is wrong with the advice of the Old School masters, yet you worry that you might not be successful unless you follow it.

Well, take heart—I have terrific news for you! You absolutely, positively can succeed in real estate sales without resorting to Old School methodology! And when I say succeed, yes, I mean you can make a ton of money, but oh, so much more.

A successful career selling real estate can be a beautiful thing. An extraordinary thing. If you are a great real estate agent, that's something to be proud of. And chances are, if you are great, you will love your job. Can you imagine bouncing out of bed in the morning, every morning, eager to get to work? Or not dreading the end of your vacation because you're so excited about getting back to your business? Itching to check your voicemail messages because you can't wait to find out who called you while you were in the dentist's chair? If you've never experienced the euphoria of doing a job you love, and being well paid to do it, ahhhh, you have something wonderful to look forward to.

I wrote these words back in 2008 as the introduction to my first book, *Sell with Soul: Creating an Extraordinary Career in Real Estate Without Losing Your Friends, Your Principles or Your Self-Respect*. Little did I know at the time how dramatically the concept of Selling Real Estate with Soul would change my life forever, and far more importantly, the lives of the thousands of real estate agents who have since embraced the Sell with Soul philosophy. Hmmmm, let me rephrase that...how dramatically the concept of Selling Real Estate with Soul would change the lives of the thousands of real estate agents who nearly fainted with relief when they learned they did NOT have to annoy strangers, pester their friends or otherwise embarrass themselves in order to succeed.

Because, contrary to what you might have heard, read or observed thus far in your own career in real estate, you CAN enjoy a wildly successful career without becoming someone you don't recognize or even much care for – yes, without even Selling Your Soul.

About This Blog-to-Book

Hi, I'm Jennifer Allan-Hagedorn and I'm a real estate broker, a published author and an obsessive blogger.

I started blogging in late 2006, so since blogging became mainstream in 2004 (according to Wikipedia), I guess I'm comfortable calling myself a semi-early adopter. My blog platform of choice was (and is) ActiveRain (www.ActiveRain.com), which is a real estate-specific website where agents and others affiliated with the real estate industry create their own blog and enjoy not only the company of thousands of other real estate professionals, but also take advantage of some phenomenal SEO (Search Engine Optimization).

But lest you are tempted to contact me and pick my brain about the aforementioned SEO power of blogging on ActiveRain, please don't! I have no idea how it all works, *I just know that it does.* I can honestly say that ActiveRain has been one of the biggest factors in the successful spread of the Sell with Soul message, and for that I am eternally grateful to, as we old-time ActiveRainers call them, the AR Gods—who created the platform for us to blog, blog, blog (and comment, comment, comment) to our heart's content.

What is a Blog?

As I write this introduction in mid-2013, I wonder if it's even necessary to include a little "What is a Blog?" section. Is the term "blog" now as mainstream as the terms "website" or "thread" or "forum"? Maybe so, but just in case, here is one definition of a blog, courtesy of www.blogger.com:

"**Blog**: In simple terms, a blog is a website where you write stuff on an ongoing basis. New stuff shows up at the top, so your visitors can read what's new. Then they comment on it or link to it or email you. Or not."

I like that definition, although I'll expand it to be more specific to the reason many "write stuff on an ongoing basis" in a blog. They want to attract potential clients—their blog is a business development tool. Because what they blog about is related to their business (be it real estate sales, real estate training, mortgage brokering, home staging or whatever), the goal is that their potential customers are out there on the www searching for the stuff they're writing about and stumbling onto them.

So, what you hold in your hands is a collection of blogs I wrote between the years of 2006 and 2009. Not all of them, but enough to keep you busy for a while. When you've finished this blog-to-book, I hope you'll move onto Volume 2 of the Soulful Collection, which picks up in early 2010 and goes through the end of 2012. Will there be a Volume 3? We shall see...

How This Blog-to-Book Is Organized

When I set out to put this blog-to-book together, I fussed and fretted for all of ten minutes (maybe even fifteen) as to how to organize the 300+ blogs I'd chosen to include.

Chronologically? By Topic? Random Order?

I polled the audience (my mailing list) who responded nearly unanimously: "By Topic!"

With that clear and obvious feedback, I opted for..."Chronologically." Not that I intentionally dismissed the preferences of my beloved readers (well, I guess I did), but rather because the process of sorting through more than 300 blogs and assigning each and every one to A Topic was a task I suspected I simply wasn't up to. For example, one of the blogs in this book is called: *"Just Say No to Price Reductions."* What one topic would it fall under? Pricing? Listing Presentations? Working with Sellers? Maybe even Professionalism & Competence?

Or how about *"Back and Forth, Back and Forth; Just Make the Date Already!"* which isn't really "about" anything in particular, or at least nothing that would fit tidily into a category name or chapter title.

And, frankly, I was pretty sure that the process of copying and pasting blocks of text around in a 200+ page document would cause me to lose my mind, or worse, abandon the project all together.

That said, I feel pretty good that the decision to organize the book chronologically really WAS the right decision, both for me and for you, my reader, and not just as a way to maintain my sanity and get the silly project finished. But to appease everyone who suggested the book be organized By Topic, I have included a handy-dandy index that lists the blogs under the various categories to which each belongs. So if you're looking for help putting your listing presentations together, just flip to the Index in the back of the book and explore the blogs listed under the Listing Presentation category. If you're in the mood for a good rant or two or three, explore the blogs listed under the Rants & Ridiculousness category. Compensation? Yep, there's a category for that, too.

And with that, I welcome you to Volume 1 of *Selling Real Estate Without Selling Your Soul*. If you'd like to see the original blogs which include (often spirited!) reader commentary and discussion, you can do that here: www.ActiveRain.com/blogs/sellwithsoul.

The Sell with Soul Glossary

Here are a few SWS-specific terms you'll see scattered throughout the blogs.

Sell with Soul (SWS)
To enjoy a wildly successful career in real estate by treating clients and prospects respectfully, as you yourself would like to be treated. Basically, following the Golden Rule in your practice of real estate while staying true to yourself. Read more about Selling with Soul in the very first blog of this book, just a few pages away.

SWS'er
One who follows Sell with Soul principles and philosophies. SWS'ers consider themselves to be just a little bit smarter and a little bit more creative than the average real estate agent.

Sphere of Influence (SOI)
Everyone who knows you and knows that you sell real estate. We talk A LOT about Sphere of Influence around here.

Sphere of Influence (SOI) Business Model
A business model where a significant percentage of an agent's clients comes directly or indirectly as a result of their personal relationships, as opposed to their marketing-to-strangers activities.

SOI'er
One who has implemented a Sphere of Influence business model.

Reasonably Competent Human Being (RCHB)
One who comes across to the people he or she knows and meets as a generally competent, reliable and ethical guy or gal. *Antonym*: Flaky

Old School
Traditional real estate thought and training that emphasizes the pushy, cheesy and predictable over the respectful, intelligent and creative.

About the Author

This being my fourth book, I've already written several "About Me's" that appear in the introductory material of the previous three books I've published—*Sell with Soul, If You're Not Having Fun Selling Real Estate, You're Not Doing it Right* and *Prospect with Soul*. So, if you'd like to refresh your memory of who I am or why you'd care, I'll refer you to any of those books, at least one of which is surely gracing the shelves of your personal library☺.

For the purposes of THIS book, however, I'm going to take a different approach to the obligatory About Me section of the introduction, one which coincides with my decision to organize my Blog-to-Book Chronologically.

Because this book covers a specific period of time in the real estate industry, many of the blogs you'll read reflect the economic reality of the time period in which they were written.

However, since a blog is also somewhat of a personal journal, much of what you will read was influenced by what was going on in my life at the time of writing. The years between 2006 and 2010 were a tumultuous time for me, both personally and professionally. I lived in six different houses in three different states. During that period I went from being the broker/owner of a real estate company to a non-practicing real estate licensee who generated referrals for others back to being a full-time broker associate—and then leaving the practicing side of the industry in 2009 for good (at least to date!).

Of course, every opinion I have about how a real estate business ought to be run is heavily influenced by my own Denver-based real estate career which began in mid-1996 and continued, as noted above, until 2009.

So, here is a little timeline in the life of Jennifer Allan (now Allan-Hagedorn) starting with the beginning of my career in August of 1996 through the end of 2009.

The Life & Times of Jennifer Allan
(now Allan-Hagedorn) 1996 – 2009

August 1996 – Quit my "real" job and obtained a real estate license in the state of Colorado. Went to work selling real estate full-time at a Coldwell-Banker office in the foothills west of Denver.

October 1997 – Got married. In Mexico. On the beach. It was cool.

Late 1997 – Received the Rookie of the Year runner-up at the annual Coldwell-Banker awards dinner. Quite a pleasant surprise.

1998 – Left Coldwell Banker to work at a boutique real estate firm in Central Denver.

Late 1999 – Concerned about the end of the world (Y2K), took a sabbatical from real estate to prepare. Yeah, seriously.

January 1, 2000 – Peeked out the first morning of the new millennium, realized the world had not come to an end, and went back to work.

Early 2000 – Moved my license to RE/MAX.

2001 and 2002 – Kicked some butt selling real estate; was the top agent in my RE/MAX office both years. When asked about my secret of success, quipped *"the phone rings, I answer it and I have a great new client."*

Late 2002 – Separated from my husband, the divorce was final in mid-2003.

Sometime in 2003 – On a lark, began writing the first chapters of the first edition of *Sell with Soul*.

October 2003 – Moved to Steamboat Springs, Colorado; went to work as a licensed assistant for a top-producing agent.

April 2005 – Moved back to Denver, opened my own real estate company with a partner. Called ourselves New Precedent Real Estate of Denver and provided real estate services at a "lower-than-typical" fee.

December 2005 – Moved to Alabama for love; managed New Precedent from my southern country home. Purchased three Alabama properties (at the peak of the market unfortunately. They just seemed like such a deal compared to Denver!).

April 2006 – My partner in New Precedent called it quits; the company dissolved.

May 2006 – Decided to finish *Sell with Soul* and become a rich and famous writer.

Late 2006 – Started blogging at ActiveRain.

January 2007 – Released the first (extremely amateurish) edition of *Sell with Soul* (thankfully now out of print!)

Early August 2007 – The Mortgage Meltdown

November 2007 – Exhibited at the National Association of REALTORS© Convention. Unbelievably frustrating and expensive undertaking. Vowed to never do it again. Financially disastrous, therefore...

January 2008 – Moved back to Denver to revive my real estate career while continuing to be the Author of *Sell with Soul*. Re-joined my former RE/MAX office and achieved RE/MAX Hall of Fame status.

Mid-2008 – Released the second (much improved) edition of *Sell with Soul*.

Fall 2008 – One of the most stressful periods of my life. You may notice my blog reflected my mood ☹

May 2009 – Realizing I couldn't do both effectively, I hung up my real estate license and moved back to the South to focus on being the Author of *Sell with Soul*.

Fall 2009 – Released my second book, *If You're Not Having Fun Selling Real Estate, You're Not Doing it Right*.

End of *Selling Real Estate without Selling Your Soul, Volume 1*. Volume 2 picks up in early 2010 with my move to the BEACH (just in time for the BP Oil Spill, and yes, I blogged about it).

So...now that you know a little bit more about me...let's begin!

Selling with Soul for Real Estate Professionals

Selling with Soul has nothing to do with new age philosophies, holier-than-thou attitudes or even learning to dance. It's really just a catchy phrase for following the Golden Rule in your day-to-day practice of real estate. That you treat your clients and prospects respectfully, as you would like to be treated. That you are competent, reliable and fair. That you appreciate the commissions paid to you directly by your sellers, and indirectly by your buyers. That you don't take these hefty paychecks for granted. That you truly want to earn your commission, not just show up at closing with hand outstretched.

But there's more! If you Sell with Soul, not only will you be a breath of fresh air to the home-buying and -selling public, you can also make a great living while sleeping soundly at night. You make all this money because you're good at your job. You are a Good Real Estate Agent! You find your buyers the right homes, not just because you know your market, but also because you listen to your clients and strive to meet their needs for a home, not just your need for a commission. Your seller's homes sell, not just because they're priced right, but because you've helped them recognize and correct any obstacles to sale...instead of simply bullying them for a price reduction.

Soulful real estate agents know how to hold their transactions together. They usually get through the inspection period, even a difficult one, not just because they are good negotiators, but also because they have great resources for getting repairs made. Their listings appraise because they are prepared for the appraiser and know how to defend their sales price. Throughout the transaction, they strive for a win/win whenever possible and they don't antagonize the other team just because they're sitting on the other side of the closing table.

And of course, an agent who Sells with Soul will be rewarded with plenty of repeat business and referrals. She won't have to spend thousands of dollars on personal promotion, or to pester strangers to ask for their business; no, her friends and past clients will be her own personal marketing department. She'll be proud of the business she's developed and will have no problem promoting herself at listing appointments or holiday parties.

But lest you believe that soulful real estate agents are simply nice guys and gals who smile sweetly and then get trampled over by the rest of the real estate community, that just ain't so. No, your natural instincts to protect your client will ensure that you are not a pushover. But instead of protecting that client by blustering and posturing and setting up unnecessary confrontations, you do it with creativity, good negotiating skills and old-fashioned good manners. Oh, and throw in a healthy serving of competency.

This all sounds pretty rosy, doesn't it? As in, Be Nice and They Will Come? Real Estate in Utopia? I read over the above and smiled...because, well, it's not that easy of course. Real estate is a tough business and the staggering failure/drop-out rate can attest to that. Every client, every sale, every situation is unique and it's not always easy, or even possible (for us human-types, anyway) to play by the Golden Rule perfectly, every time.

But it's not impossible or even difficult to be a soulful real estate agent most of the time. If you are a basically decent person who wants to make a fantastic living, sleep well at night and respect yourself in the morning, then I salute you. And wish you the best in your real estate career.

JANUARY 2007

Real Estate Is Not a Numbers Game
(at least, it doesn't have to be)

You've heard the cold-caller's philosophy...for every 100 phone calls you make, you'll get five appointments; for every five appointments you go on, you'll get one listing. Therefore, if you make 500 phone calls, you can count on five listings as a result. If your average listing commission is $5,000, then every phone call is worth $50 since it takes 100 phone calls to get a listing. Supposedly you will actually start to enjoy each rejection, because you realize that every 99 "no's" equals a "yes," which leads to a paycheck, since every "no" means you are one step closer to a "yes."

Sound fun?

Not to me. In fact, it sounds like an awful way to make a living. Pestering people three hours a day asking the poor sap who answers the phone if he "knows anyone who's thinking of buying or selling real estate?" Being rejected 99 times out of a hundred? Ick. Phooey. Blech.

So tell us how you really feel, Jennifer!

Okay, thanks for asking, I will.

The State of Colorado's Division of Real Estate did not grant me a real estate license so that I could be a professional prospector. I have to assume that The Division intended for me to spend a significant amount of my time serving the clients I am honored to have today instead of tracking down the ones I hope to have tomorrow. Taking good care of my listings and my buyers. As my first priority. Not as an afterthought when I can squeeze them in around my prospecting and networking efforts.

But, but, but....!

Yeah, I know. As self-employed types, we have to ensure ourselves a steady stream of business to keep the home fires burning in the style to which we intend to become accustomed. Hey, believe me, I never took a vow of poverty and I didn't sell real estate out of the goodness of my heart.

But you know what? I never cold-called, I never knocked on a stranger's door...

in fact, I never even asked a stranger for business. Ever. No, not even FSBO's or expireds.

Throughout my career, I depended on my Sphere of Influence (SOI) for the vast majority of my business. And they generously delivered. Sure, I picked up the odd client here and there from floor time or open houses; maybe two or three a year, which is nothing to sneeze at. But the vast majority of my business always came directly or indirectly from the people I knew or met.

And every client was special to me. Even precious. Okay, admittedly some were a pain in the a$$, but I still appreciated their business and the juicy commission checks I got as a reward for putting up with them. But most of my clients were pleasant people with a real estate need who simply want to be treated as if their business was valuable to me. Not like a number.

When you depend on your SOI for business, you bow out of the numbers game. And it's wonderful. No more dragging yourself to the phone for your daily cold-calling session. No more searching the real estate ads for your next FSBO target. No more beating yourself up because you'd rather take a nap than finish up your 10 HouseValues CMAs that are due today.

When your pipeline is running low, you have a little Super Bowl party. Or send out some friendly personal emails. Or ratchet up your "go-to-lunch-with-a-friend" campaign. You don't need 20 more clients today; just two or three good ones will restore your mood. And pad your bank account.

SOI business is good business. It's loyal business. It's fun business. The success ratios are more like 50%-75%, compared to 5%-10% from traditional lead generation (and that's being optimistic!). So if you get 100 leads from your SOI, that will result in 50-75 closings for you.

So how does it work exactly? Glad you asked.

SOI business comes in one lead at a time. But the leads are good leads, leads that will likely result in a closing. And, depending on your market and your broker split, each lead-that-will-probably-result-in-a-closing is worth thousands of dollars to you.

So let's say you have 20 close friends. If you have implemented a respectful, consistent SOI campaign, you, obviously, are the agent of choice for most of them if any happen to need a real estate agent this year. Maybe that will only get you one or two sales; or maybe your friends are a restless bunch and you'll get five or six.

You should also get the family business of your 20 nearest & dearest. Katie's grandma moves to town to be closer to her grandchildren. Fred's brother-in-law needs a referral to a Las Vegas agent. Maria's sister gets engaged and needs to sell her condo. Her fiancé wants to sell his too. There's a good chance you'll get first dibs on this sort of business. So let's say you pick up three family members.

Let's not forget everyone else your 20 friends know. If just half of your friends refer you to just one person, that's 10 more clients for you. What if all of your friends refer you to one other person? Or if 3 of your friends each refer you to 5 of their friends? What if you have 30 friends? 50?

Oh, and what about everyone else in your SOI? The other 150 people you know and stay in touch with? Your husband's assistant? Your dog trainer? Your massage therapist? Depending on the strength of your SOI campaign, you might see 5-15 sales a year from these folks.

And we haven't even talked about the NEW friends you're going to make over the next 12 months! If you're out there in the world, with your antenna up, you will run into people who happen to be in need of real estate services. If you approach them right, that business is yours. Maybe that's another five sales for you.

So add it all up and you're selling some real estate! All without treating anyone like a number.

Unless you're striving to be a mega-producer with 10 buyer agents scurrying around underfoot, you really don't need to go after every buyer and seller in town. This is what I mean when I say that Real Estate is Not a Numbers Game. The business that you can generate from your SOI and from your own social encounters really ought to be enough.

And the best part? If you spend a few years building a strong cheering section (i.e., your SOI), you can coast through the rest of your real estate career. NO prospecting, NO marketing budget, NO sleepless nights worrying about where your next closing is coming from. Now, that's a lifestyle I could get used to (and I have).

FEBRUARY 2007

Being Up-Front with Our Sellers

We real estate agents should have strong opinions. We should be willing and able to share these opinions with our clients, especially our seller clients. We are not hired for our looks, so to speak, rather we are hired because we are experts in the field of marketing, selling and closing the homes of those who honor us with their business.

What if you visited with an attorney who said you had a strong case when in fact, you did not? Or if your physician told you that the little mole on your shoulder was nothing to be concerned about when indeed, it was cancerous? If your CPA assured you that you were getting a tax refund when in fact you owed $5,463.75?

While you might leave your doctor's, lawyer's or accountant's office in a good mood, that good mood would fade once you realized that you were misled. You would self-righteously proclaim that these professionals lied to you! Or that they were incompetent! Or that they didn't have the balls to tell you the truth...and you might be right.

It's the same in our industry. When sellers talk to us about selling their home, they deserve to know the truth. Even if the truth is difficult to hear...even if it's ugly. Our job is not to make friends with our clients because we tell them what they want to hear, no, our job is to tell them the cold hard facts. Nicely, of course.

MARCH 2007

"I'm a Listing Specialist so I Don't Work with Buyers"

If you don't work with buyers on a regular basis, you don't have the expertise to accurately price homes for market. Many experienced agents snottily declare that they Don't Work With Buyers—they only handle listings and hire buyer agents to show homes. I knew a few agents in my area who were huge listers and never showed or previewed any of my listings. I never understood how they could claim to be a neighborhood expert when they didn't know the competition and didn't have an understanding of how buyers think.

Because I worked with both buyers and sellers equally, I could help a seller look at his home through the eyes of a buyer...and the buyer's agent. I knew what was currently in vogue with the local buyers. I knew what would WOW a buyer as he walked in the door...and what would immediately turn him off.

I could advise my seller client on the upgrades and improvements that truly mattered in OUR market, even specific to his particular neighborhood. I knew how important a walk-in closet was...or wasn't. I knew if buyers would overlook a dated kitchen...or if they wouldn't. I knew if buyers would balk at the lack of a garage...or if they would be tickled just to have off-street parking.

I knew how much value to add for being close to a popular coffee shop...or how much to subtract for being on a bus route. I knew how to price an asbestos-sided house so that buyers would consider it over the vintage brick Tudor they really wanted.

Other things I knew because I worked with buyers...

I understood why a 1,200sqft Bungalow was far more valuable than a 1,000sqft Bungalow (aside from the difference in square footage).

I understood why a main floor master bedroom was undesirable for many buyers.

I knew that in certain neighborhoods, one-story Bungalows were selling far more quickly than two-story Victorians. And I knew why.

The real estate market changes on a daily basis and data from the MLS tells only part of the story. What you knew about the market six months ago is irrelevant to the market conditions today. To truly be a "listing specialist," you must also be committed to knowing the inventory...and to knowing the buyer.

What Does a Listing Agent DO for All that Money?

I was cleaning out old files this morning and came across this little blurb I wrote years ago and used in my listing presentations. If you like it, feel free to use it!

What does a Real Estate Agent DO for all that money?

Many people think that the main reason you hire a real estate agent is for MLS exposure. And, unfortunately, in some cases that may appear to be the primary service some real estate agents provide. However, a GOOD agent provides much more than simply a For Sale sign and a listing on an online database.

Connections

A good real estate agent has great connections in the real estate world. She has a readily available list of home improvement contractors (heating, roofing, structural, electrical, painting, plumbing, etc.), one or two good handymen, a cleaning service, legal referrals and lawn service providers. You should never have to go to the phone book to find help during the marketing process.

Systems

A good real estate agent has systems in place to sell homes far more efficiently than a homeowner ever could. Selling or buying a home within the established real estate system is incredibly efficient compared to selling or buying a home outside of the system. Real estate agents have (or should have) a 7 day/week showing service, MLS access, a contracts library, lock boxes, signs and Internet sites.

Expertise

Obviously, one important reason you hire a real estate agent is because you expect him to know more about selling homes than you do. Selling real estate professionally requires a license and continuing education, but in reality, 99% of a real estate agent's expertise comes from on-the-job experience. And, the more experienced the real estate agent, the more expertise he has. Every real estate transaction is a little different, with its own little quirks, glitches and special circumstances. The best way to get in trouble is when you don't know what you don't know!

Time

Your real estate agent will spend a lot of time managing the sale of your home. There is far more going on behind the scenes than holding open houses and attending closings, although due to the above factors (connections, systems and expertise), a good real estate agent will be pretty efficient at her job. The time your agents spends handling the sale of your home will save YOU lots of time...and money!

Okay, so I Lied...Real Estate
IS a Number's Game...Sort of...

Earlier, you read a rather opinionated blog about how Real Estate is NOT a Number's Game. And, I will stand by that statement, in principal. However, I later realized that, unfortunately, it kinda is (a numbers game).

I'm a big fan of Sphere of Influence (SOI) business. I mean, why pester strangers when you can pester your friends? (Just kidding. Actually, you should never, ever pester anyone for business). I built a very successful real estate business that depended nearly 100% on my SOI from Day One. Which, as an introvert and "not the friendliest person in the world" (a direct quote from a client), that was quite an achievement.

I left the business of selling real estate exactly one year ago (today), yet my Outlook Express inbox still jingles with business and referrals from my loyal SOI, which I happily refer to my referral partner in Denver. So, even in this crummy market, I know that an SOI business model works.

But here's where I lied.

In the first blog, I implied that you can have a successful SOI business with as few as 20 "friends." As long as those 20 friends know you're a real estate agent, you'll be just fine.

That's not exactly true. What I should have said was that with a **strong cheering section** of 20, you'll be just fine. Here's why:

Most people in this world are not "referrers." It simply doesn't occur to them to generate referrals for people they know. Or perhaps they've had bad experiences in the past referring their friends to others and refuse to do it anymore. Have you heard the expression "No good deed goes unpunished"? That's how we feel sometimes when a referred relationship goes bad!

So there's a big difference between simply having 20 friends and having a strong cheering section of 20. It's not that all 20 of your friends don't think you're wonderful; it's just rare that all of them will take on the role of being your marketing department. Even if every single one of them thinks you're the most awesome real estate agent on the planet, most simply won't be the type to hand out your business cards. Maybe one or two of them will be. That's the truth.

Therefore, in order to create a cheering section of at least 20, you need to know (and impress) a whole lot more.

How many more? I don't have anything solid to go on with this opinion except my own anecdotal experience with my personal business and with the businesses of agents I've coached, but I think the magic number is around 200.

With 200 people in your SOI, you have a good shot at ending up with 20 people who are, or will become your biggest fans (and I guarantee that you have NO idea today who those 20 will be). You also have enough people in your sphere—who know your name and know you sell real estate—to generate another significant handful of sales throughout the year.

So, is real estate a numbers game or isn't it?

Yes and No.

Yes: When it comes to your SOI, size matters. The more people who know you and know that you sell real estate, the more real estate you will sell.

No: The people on your SOI are special and deserve to be treated as such. Every single one of them. Not like a number.

Introverts—Stay IN Your Comfort Zone!

(note: if you haven't read any of the About Me's from my previous books, you might not know that I am an introvert...and proud of it. Many of my readers are introverts as well; maybe you are! Just know that around here we consider introversion to be a positive attribute, not something to apologize for or overcome.)

The sales gurus tell you to step outside your comfort zone. Take that first painful step. Push yourself to do the things you'd rather not.

Makes sense, I s'pose.

But is it really necessary? Maybe not.

Frankly, I think I'm pretty darn cool just the way I am, without stepping out of my zone. I think that I can be me, and succeed just fine.

Don't wanna cold-call? So don't. If you don't wanna, you'll probably suck at it anyway. Call your mother instead.

Don't wanna hunt for FSBO's? Join the club. Meet three friends for brunch or bang out a few personal emails.

Don't wanna spend the weekend handing out cards from your company's Peanut Festival booth? Me neither. But I might stop by and say hi!

So what DO you wanna do?

Make a list of the things you're good at, the things you enjoy, things that don't give you the jitters. Chances are, hidden in that list are plenty of ideas to generate business for yourself. I'll bet you're creative enough to come up with some great ones.

You got this far in life being YOU. Just 'cause you're in real estate doesn't mean you have to change. You're already terrific!

What's the Best Way to Ask for Referrals? Don't.

Whatchu talkin' 'bout, Jennifer? You can't be serious!

Yes, I am.

If you're asking the question "What is the best way to ask for referrals?" that tells me that something about doing it bothers you.

And if it bothers you, don't do it. Your discomfort will be crystal clear to the person you're asking, which is probably worse than not asking at all.

Do YOU like being asked for referrals? I don't.

When a friend asks me to refer business to her, I feel uncomfortable. What was five minutes ago a friendship suddenly feels like an obligation. If she asks me twice, our friendship may very well be in danger. I don't want to have to explain to her why I haven't referred anyone to her lately (or ever). I don't want to listen to her sales pitch...again. And, frankly, if I haven't referred anyone her way, there may be a reason I'd rather not share with her, but I'd hate to lose a friendship over it.

When a business professional asks me for referrals, it lowers my respect for them a notch. Right or wrong, I assume everyone is as successful as they wanna be. So when I receive a marketing letter from my insurance agent or my accountant asking for referrals, I suddenly question their level of success... and therefore, just a teeny bit, their competence. Where five minutes ago, I perceived them to be a prosperous, crazy-busy professional...now they're just another salesperson.

Don't get me wrong, I love to refer. I'm a referring madwoman when I find someone I believe in. You don't have to ask me to refer, I'm all over it! Aren't you the same way? If you have the world's best hairdresser, dog trainer, chiropractor—don't you tell everyone you know? Do these people have to constantly ask you for your referrals?

Here's a better way.

Be a friend first. If not a friend, then a reasonably competent human being. Be happy, excited and enthusiastic. Act as if your career is everything you always dreamed of. Practice saying "I'm a real estate agent and it's the coolest job in the world!" with a huge smile on your face. Or how about, "I had no idea how much I would enjoy selling real estate, I'm having a blast!" Followed up by a sincere, "How are YOU doing?"

To ensure that every potential referrer in your life knows you're a reasonably competent human being, make sure your self-promotion materials are professional and error-free. Return phone calls promptly, even social phone calls. Show up on time for appointments and lunch dates. Do what you say you're going to do, when you say you're going to do it. No excuses. Dress appropriately. Watch your language.

It really is that simple.

Using Reverse Psychology with Your FAMILY SOI

As the self-proclaimed Master of All Things SOI, I encourage everyone to respectfully seek business from their friends and family. If done right, it works. And works beautifully.

Lots of agents argue with me. They claim to "hate to work with friends or family," for a variety of reasons. Most of their reasons don't hold much water, but I'm not here to argue that opinion right now (be happy to, later though, if you like!).

But I'm realizing something—friends...and...FAMILY are two different animals.

Generating business and referral from your friends is pretty easy. Family? Not so much.

I read a post yesterday on a different forum about how the Original Poster (OP) was furious with a relative for not hiring him to sell her home. OP said *"THIS is why I hate working with family!"* It made me think. Many agents bemoan the fact that they're getting very little support from their families. Their **friends** are gung-ho about the agent's real estate venture, but not their blood relatives. Weird, huh?

Maybe—I dunno.

But anyway (finally getting to my point), how about trying out this solution?

Howzabout you send out a personal letter to your family members telling them the following:

1. You are a real estate agent (if they seem to have forgotten).

2. You love your job (show your enthusiasm).

3. You have made the decision not to work with family members because of possible conflicts of interest.

4. However, you would truly appreciate the opportunity to counsel with your beloved relatives and help them find the perfect agent for their situation (referral fees are cool!), and would be available to them throughout their

transaction for advice.

Here are some of the benefits I see in this strategy:

1. People want what they can't have. You might find your relatives actually begging you to be their agent.

2. By showing your willingness to help your family without the possibility of a paycheck, you demonstrate your professionalism, which will probably result in referrals.

3. If a relative does take you up on your offer for help finding the right agent, you can always change your policy if it seems appropriate.

4. A lot of stress is relieved among family members that you aren't going to be bugging them for business.

What do you think?

Introverts—Always Offer Your Hand First

Any extrovert reading this is gonna go, "HUH? Well, DUH" (extroverts can be so well-spoken—said with a smile).

However, I bet some of you introverts are going to relate.

Have you ever been introduced to someone...who didn't offer their hand in greeting...and you didn't offer yours...and the relationship went downhill from there?

It happens to me all the time and I hate it. Maybe I just wasn't versed in the social graces as a child, but I really think that it's due to my personality. I almost always wait for the other person to initiate a handshake and usually they do.

Great! Onward!

But...sometimes, the other person is also an introvert and waits for ME to get the social ball rolling. And when I don't, oooooh...it's painful. Awkward. Uncomfortable. And it doesn't get any better with time.

So, the obvious simple solution is to remind yourself to always extend your hand in greeting until it becomes a habit.

Great! Onward!

A Great Niche for Introverts!

When I was a full-time real estate agent, I found myself with an unusual niche...Vacant Homes!

I was "Denver's Vacant Home Specialist!"

I LOVED it! I could do (or not do) an open house whenever I felt like it. Show up when it suited me, leave when I wanted, no worrying about small-talking with the homeowner who was trying to get her toddler ready, her dog penned up and her lunch dishes washed at 2:20 (for my 2-4 open house). I could show my listing at any time, without calling ahead. No dealing with seller complaints about agents who showed up early...late...or not at all.

Is marketing vacant homes brain surgery? Nope. But believe it or not, marketing vacant homes IS a valid specialty!

Here are just a few of the problems I offered solutions to:

~ Vacant homes don't photograph well (bring in the home stager!)

~ Light bulbs burn out with astonishing frequency

~ Who's gonna shovel the snow?

~ Mow the lawn?

~ Clean up the dead bugs?

~ Unused toilets get nasty, fast!

If you have a vacant listing, you'll be dismayed by how quickly things deteriorate into chaos. Shower curtains fall down, lockboxes jam, sprinkler systems mis-fire. Strange smells permeate the home from any number of mysterious sources. SOMEONE has to solve these problems...why not YOU?

I fell into my niche because of all the fix-n-flip investors I worked with in the late 1990's. In response to the fix-n-flip craze, I started one of the first full-service home staging companies (www.stagingdenver.com) and offered free staging to my investor clients. Ahhhh, the good old days.

But, I digress. If you're an introvert and looking for a niche suitable to your personality, think about the vacant home market. Hook up with a home-stager, pack a little tool kit (lightbulbs, dusting clothes, trash bags, etc.) for your car and put your antenna up for vacant home sellers.

They're out there...and maybe they're looking for YOU!

JUNE 2007

Doctors and Lawyers...and Real Estate Agents?

We real estate agents long to be respected by the general public. We ache to be considered as worthy of acclaim as our CPA, MD and JD friends. We fuss among ourselves when our clients appear to disrespect our time, our knowledge or, worse, our gasoline.

We claim that even though doctors and lawyers and accountants (oh my!) may have a few more years of education compared to our month (or maybe two) of real estate school, that doesn't mean they are any smarter, more dedicated or more qualified to practice their craft than we real estate agents are to handle one of the most important financial transactions most people will ever make.

We encourage our new agents to charge a full commission "because they're worth it!" even though they've yet to hold an open house, prepare a market analysis or successfully negotiate a low offer.

Wander through any real estate forum...peruse the conference schedule of the NAR National Convention—most of what you see is advice on how to PROSPECT! More Customers! More Referrals! More Leads!

Apparently, that's what our business is all about. At least, as far as I can tell from the topics that seem to interest our industry. In fact, most trainers come right out and say that Prospecting is Your Number One Duty as a professional real estate agent. Hmmmmmm. Is that really why it's a licensed profession? Because our JOB is to be great prospectors?

But back to my opening statement. We want to be respected just like doctors and lawyers and such. But I'll venture a guess that the professional journals, the annual conventions and the online forums of these industries aren't focused on cold-calling techniques, farming campaigns and web-lead generation. I'll bet that their memberships' interests lie more in being BETTER physicians, more KNOWLEDGEABLE lawyers and more COMPETENT veterinarians. While there may be an article or a seminar or a thread devoted to business development on occasion, something tells me that it's a wee bit more, dare I say it, RESPECTABLE than what we tend to obsess over.

Where are the sexy seminars on being an effective Buyer Agent? (And no, I don't mean the ones telling you How to Sell a Buyer a House in One Trip or Less or How to Convince Your Buyer to Offer Full Price so You Don't Waste Your Time). I mean the ones that actually teach you how to be a GOOD buyer agent. Where's the article on how to successfully negotiate a tough inspection, or prepare for an appraisal on a unique home? How to properly price a custom home in a tract home neighborhood?

Hey, we all know that doctors and accountants and veterinarians are business people, too. They, just like us, need a steady stream of business to keep their doors open and their Beemers gassed up. They, like us, need to promote themselves and their services to the public. But somehow, they've managed to do it without being called a salesperson. They are "Professionals."

We real estate agents need to make a choice. Either we're salespeople and we accept our role as such. Our job is to prospect, prospect, prospect. We'll leave the details to our assistants, who actually care about the clients we bring in.

Or, we can leave the salesperson persona behind and strive to become professionals who attract business by being competent, knowledgeable and, most of all, RESPECTABLE!

Just Say NO to Price Reductions!

I don't believe in price reductions. Never have. I believe that just about any home can sell in 30 days or less, in any market, if it's priced properly on Day One. And no, by "properly" I don't mean "under" although that may very well be the case in many markets. If a home sells in the first month of marketing, it WILL sell for market value and the seller will almost certainly obtain the highest possible price. We all know that extended marketing times do nothing positive for the eventual sales price, not only due to the perceived stigma of a high Days on Market (DOM) statistic, but also because the seller is darn tired of cleaning the litter box every day and wiping up his toothpaste spit in the morning!

My goal was always a 30-day sale.

However, lest you think I'm Miss Perfect Smarty-Pantz who never let her sellers take the upper hand, au contraire! I've been convinced more than once, more than twice, more than 100 times to "Try my price for a while, we can always reduce it later." But, as we all know, this clever little strategy doesn't usually work. It almost always backfires on the seller AND his agent. The seller walks away with less money in his pocket and the agent...well, we know all the pitfalls of having an overpriced home languishing on the market. Ugh.

But we do it. We agree to "try" a price for a while, against our better judgment. Lotsa reasons for this, some good, some not-so. And on paper, it makes sense, doesn't it? Especially to sellers who don't mess in the real estate market on a daily basis as we do. In fact, when you sell your very own home, you'll have a tough time convincing yourself to price aggressively from Day One. The words "I don't want to leave money on the table, let's try this price for a while and reduce it later if necessary" will flow effortlessly from your mouth. Or better yet, the classic "Buyers can always make an offer!"

Ah well, we're not perfect either.

A lot of agents recommend adding an automatic price reduction provision to listing contracts, stating that the price will be reduced by a nice tidy percentage at pre-determined intervals. I never used this provision; it just sounds unprofessional to me. A market can dramatically change in 30 or 60 days. In

90 days, we may have an entirely new market. It seems to me that our sellers deserve a little more personal attention than that. As real estate professionals, doesn't it make more sense to actually review the market and provide real DATA to our sellers instead of relying on the convenience and expediency of a built-in price reduction?

So let's look at the pricing pickle in a different way. Howzabout if you, during your pricing discussion, explain to your seller that you will review the market every 30 days and provide an updated CMA to him. Then, CASUALLY mention that due to the unstable market (or even declining if that's the case), the seller needs to be prepared that your 30-day CMA may show a lower market value. That your 60-day CMA may show an even lower value. You just want him to know this ahead of time so that he isn't surprised or blindsided.

Then BE QUIET.

Don't draw any conclusions for him, or try to summarize your pricing strategy. Your seller is no dummy; if you respect his intelligence, he may just come to the right conclusion himself. In fact, he probably will. However, if he feels you are beating him over the head with your agenda, he may dig in his heels and start throwing out those objections we've heard over and over. BAM! You and your seller are suddenly adversaries.

But if HE asks YOU how to avoid the price reduction game...suddenly YOU'RE the expert in his eyes! It's a beautiful thing. If he asks, feel free to demonstrate your expertise and brilliance. Talk about the 30-day sale, the market value death spiral, how the DOM statistic affects buyer perception of appeal. But again, let him draw his own conclusions. If you LET HIM, he will almost always choose the right path.

SOI—It's More Fun with a Friend!

Real estate agents aren't the only people in the world who can benefit from an SOI (Sphere of Influence) business model. In fact, many other professions would do well to consider this method of business-building.

Let's help them...and in return, they can help you.

Mentally review your list of friends. Are any self-employed? Why not introduce them to the concept of generating business from the Very Important People Who Know them?

How can this help you? Well...your self-employed friend has friends. Probably even friends you don't know. Might be nice to get YOUR smiling face in front of those friends, no? In exchange, you can return the favor, that is, give your friend the opportunity to charm the Very Important People in your world.

I'm sure you realize that this is not an opportunity to "market to" (i.e., pester) anyone. Don't simply exchange mailing lists and bombard your new "friends" with all your marketing material.

No, it's much more fun than that! Co-sponsor an impromptu happy hour with your friend. You invite a few of your friends, she invites some of hers. Hold a joint fondue party at your house or an Anti-Super-Bowl protest at hers. If either of you have outside interests or endeavors, find a way to include the other.

Not every week, not even every month. Maybe just once or twice. If all goes well, it will take on a life of its own. You'll have some new friends! If not, don't sweat it and keep your antenna up for another friend to co-SOI with.

Don't have any self-employed friends? How about a mortgage broker who seems fun & friendly? A financial planner? An insurance agent?

If you can't think of anyone at all, just keep this idea in the back of your mind. Someone will come along soon.

Give (Referrals) and Ye Shall Receive!

A great way to receive referrals is to give them. Become a referring machine. Be on a constant look-out for people who need referrals to other people.

Do you have the world's best hairdresser? Dog-sitter? Handyman? Spanish tutor? Knock yourself out building THEIR businesses through your referrals!

How does this help you?

Oh, let us count the ways.

- You become known as a resource among your SOI. Not simply as a fabulous real estate agent, but also as the Keeper of the Referral Directory. As they say, "no publicity is bad publicity"; every time your name crosses the mind of another person on this planet, the potential for receiving a real estate referral just increased, if only a wee bit. If the person actually contacts you to get the name and number of your dog-sitter, BAM! A rapport-building opportunity is delivered to you on a silver platter.

- Think about how wonderful it feels to receive a referral yourself. Don't you feel incredible warm fuzzies toward the person who thought enough of you to send their friend your way? Evoke those feelings in others and they WILL return the favor.

- What goes around...comes around. It just does.

There's not much to it. Simply keep your antenna up for people who are deserving of your referrals...as well as people who need your referrals.

Casually gather business cards of the people you feel good about referring, or simply memorize their website or phone number. BONUS! That way you can write down THEIR contact information on the back of YOUR business card!!

Get in the habit of sending business to others and they will quickly get in a habit of sending business to you!

AUGUST 2007

Announce Your Website with a Scavenger Hunt!

Got your new website all fired up and ready to go? YAY!

Waiting anxiously for the inquiries, leads and, admit it, the compliments to start pouring in?

Waiting...waiting...waiting...

Don't worry, this is NOT a blog about SEO (I'm not even sure what that means), key words or google rankings.

It's about how you can generate interest in your cyber-baby among the people you know.

Have a Cyber Scavenger Hunt!

It's pretty simple, really.

Go through your website page by page and find interesting little tidbits and factoids. (If you can't find any, you might wanna hit the drawing board again).

Formulate questions around these tidbits and factoids.

Send out an email to everyone you know announcing the scavenger hunt. Offer fun prizes, preferably ones that will give them ongoing warm fuzzies about you. Such as...I dunno...Starbuck's gift cards, a local magazine sub-scription, a year membership at the zoo....? Be creative...you'll come up with something cool.

I'll be waiting for MY invitation to YOUR scavenger hunt...

Introverts—Show up When It's the Right Thing to Do

There's nothing we introverts like more than a wedding, a funeral, a Christ-mas party or a baby shower...right?

Uh, no. Not so much. Just the sight of a wedding invitation puts a panicky feeling in the pit of my stomach that just gets bigger as the big day draws near. A whole afternoon and maybe evening of small talk with strangers? Not my cup of tea. I dread it.

But here's the thing. You, as a self-employed real estate-type, need to go. Now if you were a writer or a computer programmer or a 911 operator, you could probably get away with sending a nice gift and spending that Saturday curled up on the sofa with your cats. But...nope.

Do I mean that you should go to this wedding and hand out your business cards to every poor sap you meet there? Gawd, NO. NO NO NO NO NO! Leave those cards in the car! (You can always go grab one if absolutely necessary.)

You go because it's the right thing to do. You were obviously special enough to the hosts (the bride & groom) to be included on the guest list. Showing Up will let them know that you think they're special enough to honor with your presence.

And making people feel special is a super way to build your business. Will the bride and groom buy a house from you because you showed up at their wedding? I dunno. But I guarantee you have a much better shot at it than if you didn't. And then there are all those people that the bride & groom know...

The same thing goes for funerals, housewarming parties, birthday parties, baby showers and such. Good opportunities to prospect? No. Good opportunities to show someone you care? Yes.

I'm really bad at this actually. I'll come up with any excuse under the sun to get out of attending a social function. Not because I don't care about my friend, really, but can we be brutally honest for a moment? I don't show up because I care more about my social discomfort than about my friend. There, I said it.

So, in this instance...do as I say, not as I do!

Do I Deserve Your Loyalty?

You just read a blog called "Introverts—Show up When It's The Right Thing To Do," which advised us introvert-types to GO to weddings, GO to housewarmings, GO to, yes, funerals, to show the people in our lives that we care about them...and we appreciate that they think enough of us to include us on their special day(s). It's good for business.

But here's what that blog was/is really about.

Last Sunday, a friend of mine lost her six week old baby boy to SIDS. Being childless (by choice) but having lost a couple of dogs over the last six months and knowing how devastated I was, I can't even IMAGINE the devastation of losing a child. My heart aches for her.

But here's my point. The funeral was today. I didn't go. Why? Because, as an introvert, it would be too hard on me, socially. Small talk is tough enough for me under the best of circumstances, but small talk at such a heart-wrenching affair seemed beyond my capabilities. Frankly, I chickened out.

I was selfish. I am selfish. I put my own need for personal comfort ahead of my friend's need for support at this awful time.

It really made me think about what it means to be a friend, especially a friend who is self-employed and expects loyalty and support from her friends in her business.

Today, I didn't earn my friend's loyalty. I don't deserve it. I chickened out and didn't Show Up When it was the Right Thing to do.

Introverts—Pick up that Phone!

Okay—calm down. I'm an introvert thru and thru, so trust me, I won't ask you to do anything I wouldn't do myself.

We introverts like our email. It's safe, it's efficient and we know we aren't hassling anyone with our attempts at communication. Our prospects can choose to read it...or not. They can choose to read it NOW...or later. We're oh-so thoughtful that way. We don't want to impose our friendship on anyone who isn't open to it.

(As in my earlier post about hand-shaking, the extroverts are now saying "HUH?" But the introverts know what I'm talking about.)

But here's the thing, unfortunately for us...

It's hard to establish a professional relationship via email. Oh, yes, it can be done, but at a risk. A risk of losing the prospect to a more aggressive agent. A risk of drifting into a never-ending cyber-chat with your online prospect, during which you become complacent and, frankly, afraid to break the ice and make the call. It's so much more comfortable to continue your online relationship; it seems to be working fine!

But if you get on the phone, right away, and establish that voice-with-an-email-address rapport, you have a much better chance of:

1. Creating a personal relationship with your prospect, which encourages loyalty

2. Getting on your prospect's calendar (very important!)

3. Truly understanding your prospect's situation and knowing whether or not you can help

And you know what? Once you've broken the voice-to-voice ice, you'll feel SO MUCH more comfortable with this person. (Or not, as the case may be, which is good to know also.)

Several years ago, I contacted five real estate agents in the Wilmington, NC area, via email. Two responded—one via email, one on the phone. I chatted with both for the next several weeks, but my loyalty was 100% with the one who called me. Yeah, I'll admit I led the emailer on, picked her brain and took advantage of her offer to send me a daily update of new listings. But when I arrived in Wilmington, who showed me around? Yep. The one who called me.

When you get an Internet inquiry, pick up that phone. Be assured that your hot new prospect is emailing agents all over town, although the good news (for you) is that the vast majority of these agents won't respond at all. But if you make the call, right away, with a big smile on your face, and in your voice, you'll get that cyber-prospect, if you want them!

SEPTEMBER 2007

What Your Home Sellers May Not Know...but Need to

A few weeks ago, my referral partner in Denver put a sweet little Bungalow on the market. The seller is one smart cookie and he's sold several homes on his own. We didn't want to insult his intelligence by boring him with all the details of having a home on the market; we figured if he had a question about the process, he'd ask.

Oops.

Well, now he's asking. In a rather annoyed tone of voice, as if he feels blind-sided by what is happening to him.

And I realize that no matter how smart, how experienced, how cooperative a seller may be, we can never assume that he has a clue what is about to happen to him. And more importantly, what his role will be in the home-selling process.

It's our job to make sure that our sellers understand...

1. What it means to their lifestyles to be On the Market (basically, it sucks)

2. What they should expect from us (particularly the frequency of communication)

3. What we are expecting from them (see below)

4. How showings and feedback work

5. Why we won't be attending most showings (the buyer has his own agent)

If your seller has to call you to ask these questions after the fact, he'll likely have that annoyed tone-of-voice with you, too!

It's also our job to be upfront with our sellers, no matter how unpleasant what we have to say may be for either of us.

Topics such as:

1. Why they need to SCRAM for showings

2. Why they need to accept short-notice showings and allow a lockbox

3. Why the market will not overlook toothpaste spit in the sink or eau d'Chef Boyardee in the air

4. Why they need to be pleasant to buyer agents who show up early or late

5. Why it's not okay to have barking dogs locked up in the laundry room

When your home is on the market, you talk about the experience with everyone you know. Especially if you're confused by the process, which will translate into dissatisfaction with your agent. Uh, oh.

Jake's New Real Estate Career

Say Hello to Jake!

One fine day, Jake entered the wonderful world of real estate. He went to school at night, passed his test and found an office to bless with his presence.

On his first day as a licensed salesperson, his new broker greeted him heartily and said, "Welcome aboard! Here's your desk, here's your phone, best of luck to you!"

Jake was a little befuddled by this, but he did his best to do as he was told. He spent the first few months of his real estate career learning about cold-calling strangers, door-knocking neighbors, holding open houses for other agents and convincing For Sale by Owners (FSBO) sellers that they couldn't possibly succeed without him.

By Jake's third month in the business, he was working with two marginally qualified buyers who refused to commit to him exclusively, one FSBO who said he'd be happy to pay Jake a co-op if he brought a buyer, and a seller who planned to list his home "sometime next year." He was farming his neighborhood and half-heartedly calling a few expired listings every week.

Jake was discouraged, to put it mildly. His bank account was dwindling, his enthusiasm was fading and he didn't see anything fun about being self-employed. In fact, the daily drudgery of the 9-5 was looking pretty good to him right about now (and, frankly, to his wife as well who was having a hard time putting on her happy face every day).

In short, Jake was on the verge of failure.

Stay tuned...

The Saga of Jake Continues...

When we last saw Jake, he was three months into his real estate career and pretty darn close to quitting. He wasn't having any fun or making any money.

So, one day, Jake Googled the phrase "How not to become discouraged in real estate" and stumbled upon an article by Jennifer Allan, author of *Sell with Soul*. The article was about something she called an "SOI" which, upon further reading, Jake discovered stood for "Sphere of Influence" and meant "The people who know you."

Jennifer claimed that if you devote your business-building efforts toward the people who know you instead of the people who have never heard of you, not only will you have a heck of a lot more FUN, but you'll stand a much better chance of success.

"How can this be?" Jake asked himself. *"I don't know anyone who wants to buy or sell a house right now! How could I possibly generate enough business from my friends to pay the bills and keep the wife's toenails polished? This doesn't make any sense!"*

Well, Jake kept digging and reading and found a whole bunch of articles Jennifer had written on the topic. As he read, he realized that what he was seeing contradicted almost everything he'd ever heard about promotion and marketing for a self-employed person.

Jennifer advised against pursuing strangers for business...against offering incentives for referrals...against, even, ASKING for referrals at all!

Jake felt a tug deep inside as he continued to read. He felt a glimmer of hope. Even though her approach was "wrong," according to his corporate training, it felt very very right. It made sense to Jake. Bothering strangers and mailing out hundreds of postcards never felt right to him, but his broker insisted that it the best way. And Jake believed him.

But he was starting to have his doubts. Maybe, just maybe...this SOI stuff was the magic bullet he'd been hoping for.

So Jake began his own SOI Seduction campaign. He made a list of everyone he knew, grouped them into two categories, and sent out a respectful, interesting, non-salesy letter to them all. He started reaching out to his friends and acquaintances, not as a real estate agent, but as a genuinely nice guy with a good head on his shoulders...who happened to sell homes for a living.

Stay tuned, we'll check back in with Jake soon to see how it's going.

Jakes Sells a House...or Two

Let's see how Jake is doing.

About a week after Jake sent out a respectful, interesting, non-salesy letter to his SOI, he got a call from Sam, his old boss's assistant. Sam's grandmother was moving to town and would be looking to purchase a one-story, ground-level condominium near Sam's house. Could Jake help?

"*Heck yeah!*" Jake exclaimed. And he did. He helped Grandma find the perfect handicapped-accessible condominium, negotiate a good price for it and get her to the closing (literally—Grandma doesn't drive!). Grandma loves Jake—he's such a nice young man.

Sam was also thrilled with Jake. Sam knows a lot of successful real estate agents, but was afraid his grandma would get lost in the shuffle of a Top Producer's busy schedule. He was pleasantly surprised at how attentive Jake was to Grandma. He treated her like a queen.

Sam told everyone he knew what a good job Jake did.

Six weeks after he received the call from Sam, he has his first commission check in hand for $4,236. Jake and the Missus celebrated in style.

During this same time period, Jake and his wife met a young couple (Jim and Patricia) at the wedding of a mutual friend. Jake was riding high that day, due to the successful negotiation of Grandma's condo inspection. Enthusiasm was oozing from every pore.

They found themselves chatting comfortably with Jim and Patricia about this and that. Of course, the conversation naturally turned to careers and when Jim asked what Jake did for a living, Jake beamed and said:

"*I'm a real estate agent!*"

Well, wouldn't you know it, Jim and Patricia were just starting the process of looking for an investment property; maybe two! They had been working with an agent, but the guy was...well...kind of blowing them off. They weren't happy with him and hadn't signed any exclusive agreement.

A week later, Jake took Jim and Patricia out to look at investment properties. No luck, so they went out again. Didn't find anything this time either, so they kept at it. It took ten trips to find the perfect investment property. They put it under contract and closed 30 days later.

Jim and Patricia commented that most agents would have given up after the first three trips with no offers made, but Jake hung in there.

Two months later, Jim and Patricia contracted for a second investment home, one they found themselves online. But because they were so impressed with the effort Jake made in helping them the first time around, they called him in to represent them in the sale.

Jim and Patricia told everyone they knew how awesome Jake was.

One day, Jake received a call from Kenny, his wife's massage therapist, who knew about Jake's new career from his casual conversations with Jake's wife during her massages. Kenny's lease was almost up and he had just been pre-qualified to purchase a home. He asked if Jake could help him out.

"Of course!" said Jake. And he did. They found Kenny a wonderful little Tudor home on the fringes of a killer neighborhood.

It was a struggle at first because Kenny's eyes were bigger than his pocket-book and he insisted on looking smack in the middle of one of his city's most expensive areas. Jake did his best to find homes that met Kenny's needs for location, features and price, but it simply wasn't possible.

However, Jake waited patiently for Kenny to realize the truth on his own... that Kenny couldn't afford the location he wanted just yet. As soon as Kenny figured this out (without Jake beating him over the head with it), he happily shifted his focus to other, more affordable neighborhoods. (Jake, by the way, was happy to take this opportunity to improve his knowledge of the market, always a good thing for a new real estate agent.)

Kenny really appreciated the fact that Jake hung in there with him while Kenny did his own soul-searching, which allowed him to reach his own conclusions on what he could afford.

Kenny told everyone he knew what a great real estate agent Jake was.

Meanwhile, Grandma isn't feeling so good. Unfortunately, it looks as if she may have to consider moving to a nursing home in the near future. Sam calls Jake for advice. Jake immediately does some research and determines that the market in Grandma's area hasn't appreciated much since she purchased her condo. Jake is honest with Sam and advises him to consider renting out the condo for a few years until the market improves.

Sam told everyone how honest and responsive Jake was.

Patricia's brother, Paul, has fallen in love with a woman he met online and is moving to Las Vegas. Patricia urges him to call Jake to discuss selling his bachelor pad. Jake lists the loft, and also arranges to refer Paul to an agent in Las Vegas. Ka-Ching! A $1,200 referral fee for a simple phone call!!!

One sunny Sunday afternoon, Jake and his wife take the pups to the dog park. Jake strikes up a conversation with a fellow dog-owner (Steve) and finds out that Steve just moved to town and is living at an extended stay hotel until he buys a home. And he doesn't have a real estate agent yet...AND...he fancies the neighborhood that Kenny couldn't quite afford! Since Jake had spent the last month looking at homes in that neighborhood for Kenny, he was able to speak intelligently to the buyer prospect about the inventory there. Eleven weeks later, Jake received a commission check for the purchase of Steve's $800,000 house.

How do you think Jake is feeling about his real estate career these days???

Announcing Our Rookie of the Year...Jake!

Fast forward to year-end...

Jake was the rookie of the year in his rookie "class" of nearly 100 agents. He sold 25 homes; 22 with people he knew or people he met socially. His other three clients came from floor duty and an open house. All three of these people have since referred him to their friends and family.

Here's where Jake's first 25 sales came from:

Grandma—Referral from his old boss's assistant

Jim and Patricia (2 sales)—Met at the wedding of a mutual friend

Kenny—Wife's massage therapist

Paul (1 sale and 1 referral)—Patricia's brother

Steve—Met at the dog park

Amanda—Referral from Jake's wife

Deanna—Referral from Jake's wife

Mrs. Palmer—The mother-in-law of a vendor from Jake's past life, pre-real estate

Grandpa Palmer—The grandfather of the same vendor

Stan and Colleen—Referral from Amanda

Mary—Referral from Patricia

Frank (3 sales)—Referral from an agent Jake met in a GRI class

Don & Cindy (2 sales)—Met at an open house

Catherine—Referral from Jake's insurance agent

Wayne—Met on floor duty; turns out they had a mutual friend

Joan & Marie (2 sales)—Referral from Frank

Rachel—The office receptionist at Jake's real estate office!

Cari—Met at a housewarming party for Stan and Colleen

Cindy—Referral from a new home on-site salesperson Jake met while showing homes to Deanna

Fast Forward two years...

Jake's real estate career is rocking. He was rookie of the year his first year, doubled his income the next, and is well on his way to doubling it again. Does he prospect to FSBO's and Expireds? Nah, not often.

Does he send out Just Listed! and Just Sold! cards to his farm area? Nope. Too much trouble.

Does he advertise in the newspaper or on bus benches? No. He tried it for a while, but quickly realized that he was throwing his money away.

No, Jake focuses on his ever-growing SOI. He's up to around 250 people, and adds more every week. The vast majority of his business comes directly or indirectly from his contact database, through the people he actually knows, or the people he meets through the people he knows or in the course of his daily travels.

Jake loves his career as a real estate agent. He's perplexed when he hears other agents complaining about disloyal buyers, unproductive open houses and deadly boring floor duty. He's really too busy to worry about such things.

He has an investor he works with who keeps him hopping. He was introduced to the investor toward the end of his rookie year by an out-of-town real estate agent he met at a GRI class. Over lunch, the out-of-town agent mentioned that he was working with an investor who was becoming increasingly frustrated with the market the agent specialized in. Jake jokingly offered to take the investor off the agent's hands and introduce him to the market in Jake's town.

Long story short, that's exactly what happened, and this investor (Frank) has turned into a gold mine of business and referrals for Jake. To date, Frank has bought 7 properties and listed and sold 3 of them. Frank is currently looking at multi-family apartment buildings to convert to condominiums for sale. We're talking Big Bucks here.

Frank has also referred three other people to Jake, one of whom has referred two more. During the course of listing one of Frank's properties, Jake met Danielle, who owns an upscale construction company and has used Jake to market two of her $1M spec homes. She uses other agents too sometimes, but Jake is her favorite.

A few weeks ago, Jake called Patricia just to say hello, as he does periodically with all of his social SOI. Patricia told Jake that she and Jim are splitting up, so they'll be putting their home on the market soon. Jake scheduled an appointment to meet with the unhappy couple and now has their home on the market. Both Jim and Patricia will be purchasing smaller replacement homes, and Jake will be their buyer's agent.

Remember Kenny? The massage therapist who couldn't afford his dream neighborhood quite yet? Well, Kenny is getting married in a few months to a local celebrity and they'll be buying a home in an even BETTER neighborhood than the one Kenny was earlier priced out of! Not only that, but Kenny's current home has appreciated nicely and when Jake lists it for sale next summer, Kenny is gonna thank Jake for introducing him to his "affordable" neighborhood.

And, of course, continue to tell everyone he knows what an awesome guy Jake is.

We're not finished with Jake yet...tune in tomorrow.

Life Is Good...Says Jake

Fast Forward another three years, into Jake's fifth year selling real estate.

Jake is the perennial top producer in his office and is considering going out on his own. He works about 30 hours a week and sells around 70 properties a year. Last year his gross commissions topped $300,000 and it looks as if he'll do it again this year.

His expenses? Not bad at all. Because his business is almost 100% SOI, his marketing budget is quite low, perhaps only 5% of his gross. And that 5% is spent mostly on entertainment (lunch dates and dinner parties, afternoon BBQ's and impromptu happy hours.) The rest of his marketing budget goes toward business cards, newsletters, annual calendars and postage. He spends no money on geographic farming, newspaper advertising or even web leads. Yeah, he has a website, but it's not a big source of business for him. He doesn't need it to be.

Let's look at Jake's sales statistics thru the years:

Year One: 25 homes sold (22 to SOI) Gross Commission: $71,000

Year Two: 38 homes sold (32 to SOI) Gross Commission: $138,000

Year Three: 47 homes sold (40 to SOI) Gross Commission: $215,000

Year Four: 57 homes sold (51 to SOI) Gross Commission: $305,000

Year Five: YTD in July: 33 closings, 12 active listings, 5 in escrow, 5 active buyers

Projected gross commission: well over $300,000

So, do you think Jake is a BELIEVER in the power of SOI?

Reflections on Jake's Success

I'm glad so many of you enjoyed the Jake Series. I, myself, have become attached to him, so you'll probably see him around occasionally.

As you may have figured out, Jake is me. Jake's story is my story. SOI came naturally to me; in fact, it wasn't until I discovered the online real estate community that I realized most agents didn't have a strong SOI business model. I was stunned that agents were beating the streets the way they were, when plenty of business was surely just sitting there, waiting to be plucked! Thus began my passion for spreading the word.

SOI was natural to me BECAUSE I was/am an introvert, not IN SPITE of that fact. Confused? Well, my fellow introverts will understand this better than the extroverts, probably. We introverts tend to overanalyze everything before we do it. We always look at the situation from the other guy's perspective (it can be paralyzing sometimes, but often it works to our benefit). We ask ourselves "What's in it for HIM?" before asking "What's in it for ME?" Yeah, seriously, we do!

So, before we implement a marketing strategy or even make a phone call, we ask ourselves how the other person might receive us (our farming post-card or phone call, etc.). For example, my very first broker handed me a stack of Dorky Announcement Cards and told me to mail them out to everyone I knew. I looked at that dorky announcement and was puzzled. It was a glossy, flashy, "professionally" done postcard extolling the virtues of Coldwell Banker and, of course, the professionalism and dedication of the real estate agent whose business card was enclosed.

I thought it was silly. I mean, what would I do if I received this card? Toss it, probably, with barely a second glance. So, I wrote my own announcement letter. Seemed like a no-brainer.

But a friend of mine who has been following the Jake series wrote to me privately yesterday playing Devil's Advocate. Here's what she asked:

"Is Jake running on a stream of good luck? Say, he started in the mid-90s and had his 5 years into early 2001? I do not deny that Jake probably work very hard. But do you feel that a good momentum for an agent also depends on timing of when he enters into real estate? Would you say that in a down market, that it is probably harder to get the gears rolling? Even for an experienced agent, getting 25 transactions is not easy. What say you?"

Do you have the same question?

I'll answer it, from my perspective anyway...

Was Jake Lucky?

In my last blog, I left you with the question about Jake's success:

"Is Jake running on a stream of good luck? Say, he started in the mid-90s and had his 5 years into early 2001? I do not deny that Jake probably worked very hard. But do you feel that a good momentum for an agent also depends on timing of when he enters into real estate? Would you say that in a down market, that it is probably harder to get the gears rolling? Even for an experienced agent, getting 25 transactions is not easy. What say you?"

Here is my response:

The market is certainly different now compared to 1996 (when my own real estate career began). Perhaps selling 25 homes will be difficult in a world where mortgages are harder to get and far too many homeowners are upside down in their mortgages to price their homes competitively. In Denver in 1996, homes appreciated 15%-20% a year and any home with a pulse could sell with multiple offers.

However, I distinctly remember rookie agents complaining loudly about how hard it was for newbies to break into the business because all we could get were buyers and there was nothing to sell them. Old fogies, remember those times? Where you checked the MLS hourly to stay on top of the new listings and then fought like hell to get an offer accepted? That wasn't fun either (although it sure kept us busy)!

Also, remember that in 1996 we didn't have 100% loans, FHA was king and buyers didn't qualify for nearly the loan they could qualify for later. Investors typically had to put 20% down, too. Back then, you actually had to be able to afford a home before you could buy it!

Anyway, I digress from my point which was that it MAY be harder to SELL 25 homes in one's first year simply because homes aren't moving. But you should be able to drum up enough business from your SOI to at least put you in the position of potentially making those sales! In other words, you should be able to find 25 motivated sellers and serious buyers to work with. Actually making it to closing might be more difficult (although I'm not convinced—it was tough back then, too, for different reasons).

Besides, if not SOI, then what? Are there other methods that you believe will produce a more consistent, reliable stream of business? As you are choosing your prospecting strategies and building a foundation for your future success, do you think that you'll do better with strangers? Whether you sell 10 houses your rookie year or 70, what prospecting techniques FEEL RIGHT to you?

It's not a matter of SOI being a luxury for a strong market. It's a strategy that works, period.

Will you, as a rookie, sell 25 homes this year? Probably not. Remember, Jake was the Rookie of the Year with 25 sales, in a stronger market. So don't fret over that number.

Will an SOI strategy assure every agent who uses it success? Nope. The question is...is it right for you?

I'll answer that next time.

Is SOI Right for You?

I'll bet you're thinking this is going to be a looooong blog, full of sappiness, self-serving propaganda and holier-than-thou pronouncements.

Nope. Not in the mood to be sappy, self-serving or even holier than y'all today.

So, I'll cut to the chase.

SOI might be right for you if:

- You are willing to put the needs of your clients first. This means that you have the TIME and DESIRE to go above and beyond what's expected, not just provide "good customer service."

- Your real estate career is your priority career (see above).

- You know your stuff. You aren't just a friendly and responsive party-animal, you are an excellent real estate agent.

- You know people and are willing to make an effort to meet more (and yes, we introverts can excel at this, too. In fact, we're a step ahead of the social butterflies in that we're good at keeping track of the people we know and meet!)

So, is SOI right for YOU?

Real Estate Agents: Get Good...or Get out

Yep, that means exactly what you think it means. If you are not a good real estate agent, get out of the business now before you spend one more dime or dollar on your personal marketing or MLS dues. Give your overpriced listings to someone else who will price them right and market them intelligently. (That way you might actually see a few dollars from your efforts down the line when the referral fee comes due after closing.)

Gone (for now) are the days where being a good real estate agent meant you were a Good Prospector. NO ONE IS IMPRESSED with your listing inventory or even with the number of marginally qualified buyers you're driving around.

All that matters are closings.

And you know what? You don't create closings with expert real estate prospecting. You create closings with expert real estate advising.

I don't care how good of a salesperson you are, you cannot sell a house **to** anyone. You cannot sell a house **for** anyone. Your new job description is to use the brain and creativity God gave you to best advise and serve your client.

If you don't know how to sell a house, other than to plop it in the MLS, create a brochure and put a sign in the yard (and oh, yes, enter it on Craigslist), then you have no business tying up a seller's valuable marketing time and energy.

Let a GOOD agent handle the listing...one who:

- Knows how to properly price a home and absolutely refuses to over-price;

- Has the balls to be direct with sellers about any obstacles to sale and insist that they be corrected or priced for;

- Has the manpower connections to help the seller prepare his home and/ or get through inspection;

- Is willing to risk upsetting a seller by insisting that he allow short-notice showings and that he vacate the house during showings;

- Knows how to take good digital photos and post them online;

- Knows how to explain the marketing process to the seller so that the seller feels involved, committed and included (and therefore cooperative!);

- Keeps the seller updated on local market activity and trends;

- Ensures that the brochure box is always full OR pulls the damn box off the sign;

- Ensures that the key works in the lock and doesn't accept the excuse that "there's a trick to it";

- Is pleasant, respectful and responsive to buyer agents who express interest or have questions;

- Is a respectful, creative and effective negotiator;

- Insists on a home staging consultation;

- Offers 7 day/week showing service;

- And CARES almost as much about selling that home as the seller himself!

THE PUBLIC DESPERATELY NEEDS US RIGHT NOW. It's not all about us and our needs. Our clients need us to do our jobs exceptionally well to give all those FOR SALE signs a chance to be SOLDs. If and when that happens, the perception could possibly turn this mess around. WE OWE IT TO OUR ADORING FANS!!

My Friday SOI Success Story

I had a little SOI fun yesterday. Didn't mean to, just worked out that way.

I have a rental property in Denver that needs, well...a renter. I no longer live in Denver, so it's kinda inconvenient for me to show the place. But I don't want a property manager, don't need one. I just need someone reliable and presentable to talk to pre-screened applicants on the phone, make (and keep) appointments, open a lockbox, hand over an application and lock up.

I couldn't think of a soul who might want the job.

So, I get the bright idea ask my SOI for help. BINGO! I was flooded with offers. My email inbox ding-ding-dinged and my phone started ringing off the hook (more on that below).

Apparently my SOI got the message out! Most of the people who wrote or called were NOT in my SOI; they were people my SOI knew. See where I'm going with this.....???

Now, granted, I wasn't trying to drum up business; I was offering to PAY someone to help me out. But literally within one hour, my SOI came to the rescue. And took a huge load off my mind.

Am I saying that you should bludgeon your SOI with pleas for business and referrals? Of course not. Do that, and I guarantee you'll be disappointed with the results. But when you need help—outside of begging for business—your SOI (if properly nurtured) will come thru for you.

Imagine if I were an active real estate agent, how many valuable contacts I'd have made with this little project?

Anyway, people ask me all the time HOW they should "respectfully" communicate with their SOI. This is just one example. For the record, I sent out 126 emails and got at least 30 responses (and counting). Not a bad ROI!

One additional observation...Some respondents called me, some emailed. I feel the strongest sense of "loyalty" and even obligation to those who called me. Just something to think about when you're responding to your own web prospects.

I'm screening the applicants right now. Such nice people. I have the best SOI...

Hey! What Happened to the Real Estate Market?

Unless you've been hiding under a rock since August of 2007, you know that the real estate market in most areas of the country has sustained a massive blow to its ego. Not that things were booming before August, no, we were all a little nervous about and frustrated with our slow-moving inventory, but we figured we'd snap out of our doldrums soon enough.

BAM!

Along comes the mortgage crisis and, just like that, a good chunk of the home-buying public is suddenly un-mortgage-worthy. Crap.

So here we are.

As I write this, it's late 2007. Sellers are slashing prices, buyers are making ridiculous offers and closings are canceled without warning when the lender closes its doors two hours before. Sheesh.

Not fun.

So, what's a nice real estate agent to do?

1. Cry

2. Quit

3. Adjust

I'm going to assume that anyone reading this has decided to Adjust. And you know what? If you make it through this crisis, you'll never look at the career of real estate the same way again.

Because, in order to survive, you're going to have to Get Good. Really, really good. Forget about prospecting, forget about networking, forget about lead generating. You need to focus on Selling Houses.

Yeah, Selling Houses. You know, that activity for which you are licensed?

Trouble is, Selling Houses in a Sucky Market is a lot of work. You're going to have to do things you've never had to do before. You're going to have to solve problems that, at first glance, seem unsolvable. You're going to have to communicate difficult concepts to people who don't want to hear them.

In short, you're going to EARN your commissions. And you'll be a much better agent because of it.

And...when the good times return (and they will), you'll have set a higher standard for yourself...and for your business...and you will be an exceptional real estate agent. Not just good...Exceptional.

NOVEMBER 2007

Preview Ten Listings Today and Report Back

Let's have some fun. In the next 48 hours, go out and preview ten listings in your area. Any ten you want. Make it easy on yourself and preview the ten homes closest to your home. It'll take you an hour or two.

Then report back. Of those ten properties, how many are being competently marketed? How many are not?

To my way of thinking, here's what "competently marketed" means:

- The home is easy to show

- The sellers know to be gone for the showing

- The home is clean, tidy and smells good

- It is, of course, priced well

- If there's a brochure box, it's full

- The MLS description is enticing and intriguing, not to mention accurate

- The MLS listing includes great photos

- There are no barking dogs locked up in the laundry room

- There is no lingering odor of Football Game Chili in the air

- The lockbox and key work smoothly

(If you're saying that many of these are seller responsibilities and beyond your control, you're wrong! It's our job to make sure our sellers know THEIR jobs as partners in the home-selling process.

See, here's the thing. Our job, as real estate agents, is not to prospect prospect prospect until our fingers go numb. The reason we have a license for what we do is because we provide an important service to those people who honor us with their business. We owe it to our sellers to give their listings our full attention and commitment...instead of fitting in our home-selling activities around our prospecting efforts.

I'll betcha that out of the ten listings you preview, very very few will meet the above standard of competent marketing. I'll betcha most will fail miserably. I'll bet it will be clear to you which homes are marketed by someone who gives a damn about selling their listings...and which ones are marketed by someone who has better things to do.

Imagine if we all cared about selling our listings. I mean, really really cared. Imagine if we all had the guts to tell our sellers what's what and why. And how. If we all spent just one hour a day making sure our listings are being properly marketed and presented to the market.

We could turn this mess around.

Where'd My MoJoGo?

I have writer's block. Oh, I can bang out a blog or two without much angst, but anything more labor-intensive seems beyond my capacity right now.

Unfortunately, I'm working on a brand new book and I've set some aggressive goals for myself (2,000-3,000 words a day, which will have the book finished up in two months if I stick to it), so this disinterest in writing has me a bit concerned. And frustrated. Even a little scared. I'm sure you can relate.

So, I'm taking a mental break, quietly trying to remember what inspired me to write my first book, *Sell with Soul* in the first place. How was I feeling when I began the project? I mean, writing an 80,000-word book is a big undertaking! What on earth made me want to take that on back in 2003?

Well, let's see. In 2003, I was a full-time real estate agent, making plenty of money. I was newly divorced with extra time on my hands. A friend of mine, who had just gotten her real estate license, casually mentioned to me that I should write a book about how to be a good real estate agent, since she hadn't gotten any such instruction in real estate school, or in her Big Name company training.

So, I figured, what the heck? I'll write a book about how to be a good real estate agent! And *Sell with Soul* was born.

I didn't write *Sell with Soul* to make money. I didn't need to make money writing—I had plenty from my real estate business. I didn't write *Sell with Soul* to get famous. I didn't write *Sell with Soul* to inspire a revolution or even to change anyone's mind. I had no real goals or expectations at all, other than to help new agents succeed selling real estate.

Fast forward to today. I no longer sell real estate and I'm a full-time writer. It's my job. It's how I make my living. To eat, I need to write. I now have goals, I now have expectations, heck, I wouldn't even mind starting a little soulful revolution.

In short, it's different now. I look at writing as a means to an end—that is, a financial end. As I write, I wonder how "sellable" the message is, not how "helpful" my words might be to those who need to hear them. I've shifted from wanting to create something useful to needing to create something marketable.

Thus...my writer's block.

Old Fogies (those of you who sold real estate during happier times), do you remember the feeling of looking at your prospects and clients as people you could help, rather than deals that would (fingers crossed) pay your mortgage? Remember when making that mortgage payment wasn't dependent on your buyer buying or your listing closing? When you could truly put the needs of your clients FIRST because, frankly, your life wouldn't change significantly if this or that deal didn't close?

Selling real estate was a joy back then and for our beloved rookies—I hope you get to experience that joy of HELPING your clients reach their goals, without fussing too much over whether or not you get a juicy paycheck for your efforts. It's a beautiful way to make a (good) living.

Because selling real estate well is a lot of fun and can be extremely satisfying. But when you're desperate for a paycheck, your focus shifts and your attitude changes.

Can we recapture the servant's attitude we had in days gone by? Can you? Can I?

Here's MY plan. Every morning I'm going to sit quietly and clear my head of all the noise that's accumulated there over the last 24 hours. I'm going to think about how my words might inspire, motivate or otherwise rev up a REAL person who needs my help. I'll ask for guidance, direction and most importantly, a servant's attitude.

If I do this, I think the rest will fall into place. Do you think this could work for you?

DECEMBER 2007

Found My MoJo! How About You?

Since writing my last blog "Where'd My MoJoGo?" I spent some time away from the computer and waited patiently for new inspiration to strike.

During the time I was away from the computer, I did a lot of reading. And BAM! Was bombarded on all sides with further confirmation of my original suspicion that my shift in focus from my audience to my-self was to blame for my lack of MoJo. Isn't it amazing that you see/hear/read exactly what you need to, at the exact time you need to see/hear/read it?

Okay, so now I'm focusing on my audience, which means...this blog is going from All About Me to All About You.

Have YOU lost your MoJo? Do you crawl reluctantly out of bed every morning...where you used to spring up, ready to face your day? Does your stomach sink when your cell phone rings...where before you used to leap to answer it? Do you dread listing appointments because you're tired of defending your commission and/or your pricing recommendations? Do you dread receiving offers on your listings because you know they're gonna suck? If you prospect FSBO's or Expireds, are you finding it harder to get started 'cause you're tired of the rejection or just the lack of any response?

Well, maybe my lesson learned can help you, too.

Real estate forums are littered with questions from rookies and experienced agents alike asking:

"How can I convince a FSBO that he needs a real estate agent (specifically me)?"

"What can I write to an Expired that will compel him to call me?"

"How can I convince my seller that he needs to reduce his price?"

"How do I tell my buyer that his wish-list is unreasonable in this market?"

"What can I write in my farm newsletter to inspire the reader to call me?"

In other words..."What Can I Do to Make My Life Better?" And that's fair. All of us want to make our own lives better, myself included. But maybe, just maybe...focusing on answering THAT question is what's drained your MoJo... and as a corollary, isn't working for you (or your clients).

How about asking instead:

"How can I help that FSBO sell his home for top dollar and the least amount of hassle?"

"What practical advice can I give to that Expired that will make the difference between a Sale...Or No Sale?" (and no, the right answer isn't "HIRE ME" unless you can actually ANSWER the question asked).

"What are the benefits to my seller of reducing his price? Are there any alternatives to a price reduction I could advise?"

"How can I help my buyer get as close as possible to his dream house within the price range we have to work with?"

"What might my farm area be interested in reading about?"

Try asking these sorts of questions every time you're stuck in Woe is Me-land and see if the answers start to come.

An Excuse to Contact Your Past Clients— for Old Fogies Only!

I'm doing my annual housecleaning...well, let me rephrase that lest you think much less of me than you did a few moments ago...I'm doing my annual FILE CABINET cleaning! Amazing how time flies, isn't it? I'm going through my real estate sales files from 2002 and 2003 and it seems like just yesterday...

My plan is to take the files to the shredder, but as I glance through the names on the files, I realize that ...DUH...most of these people are probably going to be thinking of moving soon! And, being the good little SOI'er that I am, I still have all their contact information stored in my handy-dandy contact management system and in my email address book. And of course, they HAVE heard from me once or twice (probably more like 5-10) times since they closed.

But anyway, do you think I'm going to call them all up and ask if they're thinking of buying or selling anytime soon? BAH! Not a chance.

What I'm doing is sending each a personal email wishing them a Happy Five Years in their home and asking if there's anything at all that might be in my file they want or need. I'm explaining that I'm getting ready to take my 2002 and early 2003 files to the shredder, but that Murphy's Law promises that the minute I do that, the calls will flood in with requests for pieces of irreplaceable paper that are now...well...shredded.

So far, so good. I sent out about 25 emails and almost immediately received responses. No one wants anything from the file, of course, but "it's nice to hear from you, how ya doing?" etc.

ANOTHER Excuse to Contact Past Clients— Use that Camera!

You just read a blog about a reasonably good excuse to contact your clients from years past.

One of the comments on the original blog suggested that I send clients a photo of the home they either bought or sold five years ago, just to add a little zing to my message. Great idea! Of course, that means that I'd actually have to HAVE a photo of the property from that time period, but, being the organization freak I am, I probably do. Gonna go digging through the archives today.

But that's not my point; it just reminded me of something I used to do with my buyers.

At some point during the buyer transaction, I'd "sneak" over to the house they were purchasing and take a bunch of photos. Bring 'em home, digitally file them away. Then, a year or two later, I'd create a slide show of the photos and zip it over to them. They were always, and I mean always, thrilled, usually because they'd made so many improvements and couldn't wait to show all their friends the beauty they'd created in their home.

Of course, this entails taking a long-term approach to your SOI business and certainly won't pay off for you anytime soon. But that's the beauty of a long-term SOI strategy—put the pieces in place today...and tomorrow...and next week...and in a few years, you'll be set.

Does Your Spouse Refer Business to You?

Does your spouse confidently and cheerfully refer you to everyone he knows who has a real estate need? Yes? Good for you! You can move onto the next blog on your list. You don't need me today!

But if you answered "no," do you know why he or she doesn't? Do you know the real reason?

Neither do I. But I'm going to throw something out there that you are free to accept or reject.

Do you come home every night complaining about your real estate career? Do you...um...whine about how awful the market is, or about how little training you're getting from your broker? Do you bemoan the fact that the last 10 FSBOs you contacted hung up on you before you could even begin your sales pitch?

Or, conversely, do you bounce in the door at night, bubbling with enthusiasm, ready to share your latest success story or lesson learned?

In my SOI writings, I urge agents to prove to their friends that they are an RCHB, which stands for a "Reasonably Competent Human Being." If your friends perceive you as an RCHB, they'll be happy to hire you, or to refer business your way. If they don't perceive you as such, they probably won't. Makes sense, doesn't it? I mean, referring business to a friend is a risky thing to do—no one wants to be responsible for a referral that goes badly, so we're all a little circumspect about who we have on our personal referral lists.

Here's the thing...the cold hard fact is that your spouse is no different. He has a social network that is important to him. She doesn't want to jeopardize her friendships and business relationships with a referral that goes sour. Neither does he want to be seen as "that pesky real estate agent's husband" to be avoided at parties!

So, what's the answer?

It's up to you to prove to your husband or wife that you are an RCHB who loves selling real estate and is darn good at it. And you don't "prove" this by telling him or her how great you are, you have to demonstrate it in your attitude and your enthusiasm.

Am I asking you to fake it? Well...not really, but...

Frankly, if you aren't an RCHB and you don't have a fair amount of enthusiasm about your career, you'll probably fail, with or without your spouse's referred business. The question really isn't "should I fake it?" but rather "how can I change my attitude?"

Now, if you don't need or want your spouse's support in your real estate career, then feel free to use him or her as your nightly sounding board to vent your frustrations on. It's okay, really! We all need someone to cry to. Just know that doing this puts your spouse in a difficult position when it comes to drumming up business for his beloved...

JANUARY 2008

Farewell, Alabama the Beautiful. I Will Miss You.

When you cross the border into Alabama, the state line sign welcomes you to Alabama the Beautiful. And for those whose only experience with the Deep South is connecting through Atlanta, that may surprise you. But, oh my, Alabama is, indeed, beautiful.

I've lived here in L.A. (Lower Alabama) for a little over two years. I transplanted from Denver in 2006, for love and weather, but am now heading back to the Rockies. It's bittersweet and I'm sure I will shed more than a few tears as I see that Welcome to Alabama the Beautiful sign fade from my rear-view mirror.

There's a lot to love about Alabama, especially my little piece of paradise down here in the southeast corner, just outside of Dothan, and I want to share what I've found precious about this wonderful place:

- WARM WATER! Just ½ mile from my house is a fantastic dog-walking creek that is great fun to splash around in for a few hours on a sunny afternoon (and most are). A few miles farther is the Choctawhatchee River where I've swam, row-boated, fished and laid out on a quiet white sand beach. Drifting down this river is my idea of heaven—it's sheer bliss and unbelievably beautiful. Oh, and of course, the blue waters of Destin and Panama City Beach are only 90 minutes away.

- AFFORDABLE REAL ESTATE! I thought I was dreaming when I first got here. I bought two rental homes on the south side of Dothan and, for those in more expensive markets—get this...The houses were brick, 2500sqft on ¾ acre lots in a beautiful GOLF COURSE neighborhood with windy streets and lots of trees...I paid $150,000 for one and $160,000 for the other. Yowsa! They've appreciated nicely over the last two years, but the market here is stable, so great prices still abound

- The TEN MONTH SUMMER! Okay, so this may not be a big selling point for everyone, but for me...heaven. It gets warm in April and stays nice til Christmas. Yeah, we have a few months of winter, but it never snows, ices or otherwise inconveniences you. I haven't found the heat or humidity to be oppressive, but I'm a human icicle, so it suits me. (I must say, however, that I absolutely HATE the frigid temperatures that the grocery stores set their a/c to—you literally have to take a coat inside with you in July!)

- The FRAGRANT FLOWERS EVERYWHERE! In my yard, I have gardenia, jasmine and wisteria growing naturally, all summer long. It's overwhelming sometimes (in a good way).

- LEARNING TO THROW DARTS! I've become quite a proficient Dart Thrower! (That's the proper term, not "dart-player".) It's a lot of fun and attracts a good, although interesting, crowd. Wonder if dart-throwing is big in Denver?

- SWEET HOME ALABAMA—WHERE THE SKIES ARE SO BLUE! Colorado with its 300 days of sunshine has nothing on Alabama. Yep, it rains here and rains hard, but most days are absolutely perfect.

Denver is...

Been gone from Denver a few years—two years and 6 weeks to be exact. Got back to town a week ago today. Love it, Love it.

So, to celebrate my first week back home, here's a little tribute to Denver...

Denver Is....

...Friendly
I've yet to leave the house for any sort of errand and not had a pleasant conversation with someone—a conversation that left me smiling on my way to the next pleasant conversation. Now, that may not sound like much to you, but I'm not at all a people-person and I tend to retreat into my own little world when I'm in public. People are so nice here! I'm inspired to hold up the tradition!

...Healthy
In my two years away, I'd forgotten how darn healthy this town is. 2 degrees outside? No problem! You still see people biking and jogging (not me). I've yet to see a cigarette and last night I couldn't find a parking space at the new organic grocery store in my neighborhood. When I tell someone I'm gluten-free (can't eat wheat), nine times out of ten they know what I'm talking about.

...Sunny

My first day here, last Sunday, was so darn sunny I could hardly stand it. Where else on the planet do you have Sun Glare reports in conjunction with the local traffic reports? Seriously, the sunshine is fabulous and can make an otherwise chilly day feel like spring. Maybe all the sunshine is why people are so friendly?

...Dry

Dry is good...except while you're adjusting. I have a pot of boiling water on my stove which needs replenishing every hour. Chapstick is never far from reach. When I put on my moisturizing lotion in the morning (at 40, I gotta think ahead, y'know), I have to add more 15 minutes later. But, once my body gets used to this, dry is great. There really IS such a thing as "dry" cold and "dry" heat, both of which make temperature extremes much more bearable.

...Easy to Navigate

On my way to Denver from Alabama, I stopped off in Kansas City to see family. Got lost, lost, lost and lost again. I grew up there, for gawd's sake! Denver? All grid. Straight lines that intersect at perfect right angles; even the highways are pretty much straight and uncomplicated. Oh, and most of the streets in Central Denver are alphabetical! How cool is that??? (e.g. Zenobia, Yates, Xavier, Wolff, Vrain, Utica, etc.).

...Home

It just feels right. It's good to be home.

What I've Missed About Denver

I left Denver in 2006, on a quest to become a Southern Belle. I've been living in L.A. (Lower Alabama) for the last two years and, alas, my dreams of channeling my inner Scarlett O'Hara didn't quite work out as planned. No complaints, no regrets...but two months ago I realized the truth...I don't belong here...I belong in Colorado.

Anyway, when I left Denver, I distinctly remember confidently saying "I won't miss Colorado at all!" Well, I was wrong. While there are things I'll miss terribly about Alabama, I'm thrilled to be home. In Denver.

For those who might be taking this wonderful city for granted (as I did), here are some things to remind you how darn special Denver really is:

• The BIKE PATHS! Denver is truly blessed to be crisscrossed with bike paths. You can strap on your rollerblades or saddle up the bike and cruise from one side of town to the other on fantastically smooth, comfortably wide pedestrian paths. Don't take this lightly; other cities don't have it! Where I lived in Alabama there was literally NO WHERE to rollerblade within 100 miles.

- The PARKS! Feel like taking the pups for a walk? There's probably a park within walking distance, especially if you live in Central Denver. Whether you're looking for some quiet, personal contemplative time for yourself or are in the mood to see and be seen...Denver's parks are truly a wonderful feature of the city.

- The HEALTH FOOD STORES! I couldn't wait to get back inside a Vita-min Cottage and am thrilled that there's a new Sunflower Market just SEVEN blocks from my house in Highlands!

- The HEALTHY Lifestyle! Until you're away from it, you don't realize how darned healthy people are in Colorado. Look around—everyone is walking, biking or heading for the slopes and...for the most part...not smoking.

- The DIVERSITY! I'm no political activist, but after living in the south, I have a much healthier respect for the live-and-let-live nature of Den-ver-ites. 'Nuff said.

- The DENVER GRID! Being a real estate agent, I absolutely LOVE the Denver Grid and the alphabetized streets. It's so easy to get around town (unless of course, you're dealing with downtown or that pesky I-25 curve that cuts through Wash Park/Platte Park. Messes with me every time).

- A TERRIFIC AIRPORT! Say what you will, but DIA is a great airport. From my house in Alabama, I had to drive 3.5 hours to Atlanta to go any-where.

p.s. Thought of one more thing. NO FLEAS. My poor Colorado dogs didn't know what hit them in Alabama. My beloved 15 year old Shandy couldn't handle the stress on her system and died shortly after we got there; I believe from her lack of immunity to the fleas. Lizzie—my dachshund—has practically chewed her tail off trying to relieve the itchies from an adverse reaction to the flea meds. She'll be glad to be home.

Should New Real Estate Agents Focus on Buyers or Listings? And Why?

I began my real estate career in August of 1996 in Denver, Colorado. Which was booming. A house I'd bought just two years earlier for $82,000 was already worth $150,000 and going up every day. Amateur investors were everywhere. Any real estate agent with a pulse could have 20 buyers lined up just from holding a few open houses and showing up for floor time.

Today's new agent is probably not inundated with active buyers the way we were, although listings are easier to come by. To compare, I didn't even interview for a listing until I'd been in the business for 14 months—buyers were plentiful; listings were not. And I think this experience served me well.

Working with a lot of buyers is quite different from working with a lot of sellers. I'll go out on a limb and say that working with buyers is a better business-building activity for new agents. Why? Several reasons:

- You typically develop closer relationships with your buyers, thus increasing the potential for referrals.

- When you work with buyers, you work harder. And that's good? Oh yeah, that's good. When you're new, you need to stay busy. An active buyer will keep you hopping. An active listing? Not so much.

- You learn more about the overall home-buying process when you work with buyers. You're intimately involved in almost every step of the transaction, from showings to offers to inspections to loan approval. This knowledge will serve you well when you act as a listing agent.

- When working with buyers, if you're observant, you'll see most (but certainly not all) of what a listing agent does. You'll learn a lot about both sides of the deal, where when you list you don't see much of what the buyer agent is doing.

- You will LEARN YOUR MARKET!!!

Newbies, Don't Be Intimidated...You Can Do It

I'm not a newbie, but I'm the new gal in my office after being away two years. I'm trying to hang out IN the office, which breaks a long-term tradition of working exclusively from home.

And, I'll admit: *"I'm Jennifer and I'm intimidated."* I see all the activity around me, all the hustle and bustle, people coming and going. The ink on my re-activated license is barely dry, so I don't have a lot of hustle and bustle on my own desk yet. I hear tidbits and snippets of conversations about situations that sound terribly complicated and even a little scary.

I'm a 12-year agent who has solved a gazillion difficult problems and sold lots and lots of properties, so why should I be feeling this way? I dunno.

I'm sure I'll get over it once I have my own complicated situations to resolve, but I just want to reassure our beloved rookies that it's not as hard as it sounds from those snippets you're overhearing. I promise you.

Once you're out there in the trenches yourself, you'll be intimately familiar with your own deals and you WILL be able to understand and solve the problems that attack your sanity on a daily basis. If you have made it this far in your life, you are obviously a competent human being. Trust that about yourself and dive in headfirst.

And enjoy! Solving problems is actually a lot of fun!

FEBRUARY 2008

You Won't Win 'Em All with Your SOI...and that's Okay

I'm pretty darn good at SOI'ing—that is—staying in touch with the people I know so that they remember who the heck I am and why they might want to think of my name when the topic of real estate comes up. My SOI enthusiastically supported me in my rookie year and throughout my real estate career... and I have no reason to doubt that they will continue to do so.

But, alas, even I'm not perfect. Sigh.

I just did an annual review of my mailing list to see if anyone hired someone other than me to sell their Denver home in the last year. The Denver MLS allows me to input an address and it tells me if there has been any activity on it in the last three years. It's always a bit of a rush when the address pulls up NO ACTIVITY, but then such a crashing disappointment when I see a SOLD ON date (or even worse, an ACTIVE SINCE date which means I JUST missed them!).

So, since I'm getting ready to launch a big SOI Reconnection campaign, it seemed like a good time to go through the list.

So, how'd I do?

Not bad, actually! Out of 156 contacts who own a home in Denver, only FOUR, yes FOUR of them hired someone else to sell their home! A few more did list elsewhere, but the homes never sold, so they're fair game.

The best news is that the people who "strayed" weren't people I'd made much effort with, so I can't feel too bad. In fact, none of them were anyone I'd actually had a conversation with since the closing—I'd just sent them stuff on a semi-regular basis.

And that's the thing about SOI. There's only so much you can do and you'll go crazy if you try to be perfect. If you could have a personal, non-salesy conversation with every single person you know twice a year, you'd probably bat 1000 with your SOI, but no one can do that! Well, maybe you can, but I can't.

So, I'll just quietly celebrate my 3% shrinkage and commit to making some new friends tonight at the neighborhood Super Bowl party!

My Dear Sphere of Influence,
"Thanks, But I Don't Want Your Loyalty!"

One of my readers asked the question "How do you build loyalty with your customers or potential customers?"

Interesting question.

I don't. I don't want anyone's "loyalty." Oh, sure I'll take it, but to me, the word "loyalty" is on the same playing field as "obligation," which I believe is a Dirty Word When You SOI. I don't want anyone to feel obligated to be loyal to me!

I want to earn my business, and keep earning it. I want my customers to use me, hire me and refer me...then use me, hire me and refer me again...and again...not because they're "loyal," but because they know I'm good at my job, they like me and they know I care deeply about their real estate transaction.

So, how do I make sure they know this?

By being a darn good real estate agent (which means I know my market, my systems and my contracts, among other things), by staying in touch with the people I know...and by never pestering them about being loyal!

I Was Cold-Called This Morning...and I Was Rude

I recently moved and apparently something about that activity has opened up the floodgates for cold-calls. One company calls me 6 times a day, at least according to my caller ID. I've had seven calls for security systems ("this is not a sales call—we're doing a promotion in your area!"), four for water purification systems and at least 20 trying to get me to subscribe to the newspaper.

Well, this morning (Saturday) at 8:15, I got a call from the Fireman/Policeman fund people. Okay, so do these guys really lay on the guilt trip, or what? But, sorry, I don't know this guy from Adam and just because he calls and tells me he's from so and so or such and such charity, I don't feel the need to happily open my checkbook. Especially when he calls early on Saturday morning.

Now, truth be told, I typically get up around 4am, so an 8am phone call isn't exactly jolting me out of bed, but still. It could have!

So, I politely told the caller that I was busy (which I was) and that this wasn't a good time. He kept pushing me. I said that I wasn't interested. He kept pushing. I said I didn't appreciate being cold-called at 8am on Saturday morning. HE KEPT PUSHING. I said, again, more loudly this time, that I DIDN'T APPRECI-ATE BEING COLD-CALLED ON SATURDAY MORNING! And hung up.

I'm sorry to all the cold-callers out there, but this is rude. I know we all have a job to do and if your job is to invade my home to sell me something, so be it. But when I say I'm not interested, let me go. PLEASE.

No Wonder Houses Aren't Selling...

Okay, rumor has it that the real estate market is in a slump. Is it true? S'pose so, everyone says it is.

I've been previewing my little heart out here in Charming Old Denver, catching back up on the market since my return to the trenches. I gotta tell ya, if YOUR market is anything like MY market, I can see why buyers aren't buying.

The inventory is CRAP! I've looked at 25-35 houses in the last two weeks and of those 25-35 homes, I found four that I would actually consider showing a buyer. The others? Well, they're way overpriced (like up to $100,000 in a $350k-$450k range), and/or they show poorly and/or they're HARD to show.

Now, these properties aren't listed by "discount" brokers or otherwise unpopular types—they're listed by some of the biggest names in the area.

I'm dismayed and frustrated. I actually HAVE buyers that would like to buy something, but I have nothing to show them. And I blame the listing agent community. It's our job to tell our sellers what they need to do to in order to sell their homes. I really want the listing agents in my area to do their job better so my buyers will fall in love!

Now I remember why working with buyers frustrated me. No, not because "buyers are liars" or because I hate being run all over town. I don't mind that. What I do mind, deeply, is the inability, even in a "buyer's market" to find enough decent listings to show my reasonably fussy buyers.

Okay, that's my rant for today.

MARCH 2008

Surviving the Inspection...I Love This Stuff

I just got through two tough inspections...Welcome BACK to Charming Old Denver real estate!

I've always worked in historic neighborhoods, so the ability to negotiate inspections has been a critical part of my success. And, yeah, I've gotten good at it. If you're interested, I'll share some of my secrets with you...

First, ATTEND YOUR INSPECTIONS! I can't believe how many agents don't and I think that's abysmal customer service. Yeah, I know the attorney-types tell you to avoid inspections like the plague, just in case you get sued as a result of being there, but to that, I say...baloney! I'd much rather take the chance of maybe getting sued (and in 12 years it's never happened to me) than risk losing the loyalty of my buyer client by not being there (and remember, he's the gatekeeper to all his potential home-buying friends).

Here's why I think it's important to attend:

- It's hard to negotiate repairs found during inspection that you didn't see firsthand.

- Your buyer expects you to be there and your credibility will take a hit if you don't attend.

- It's good customer service.

- When you're new, inspections are an excellent opportunity to further your real estate education.

- You need to be able to recommend good inspectors to your buyers and if you don't attend inspections, how can you judge?

Second...well, I'll save the rest for next time. Stay tuned!

More Tips to Survive the Inspection

In my twelve years of selling real estate in historic neighborhoods, I've gotten pretty darn good at holding my hard-fought deals together through the sometimes brutal inspection periods. When you work with 100+ year-old homes most of the time, it's rare to sail smoothly through the inspection process. So, you get good at it, or you fail. I once had a string of 25 sales get through inspection and to closing without falling apart, which must be some sort of record in this market!

So, here are some of my secrets to surviving inspections...

- ATTEND your inspections (see previous blog)

- Never, ever belittle your buyer's concerns. Never say "Well, it's an old house, you can't expect it to be perfect." Your buyer isn't an idiot, he knows that. The minute he thinks you're trying to talk him out of being concerned about an issue, he'll feel you're more interested in your paycheck than in his purchase. You'll lose his trust and, thus, his future referrals.

- Take your directory of contractors with you to the inspection. If issues arise, it's helpful to have phone numbers on hand to make phone calls on the spot for answers. For example, in one of my inspections last week, we came across an asbestos tile roof (in 12 years I've never heard of such a thing). The inspector expressed serious concern about it and my buyers were freaked out. I was able to call my roofer and get more information about asbestos roofs, which put everyone's mind at ease... and the inspection continued. I also had the phone number of my insurance agent with me, so we were able to call him to ensure that an asbestos roof is insurable (it is).

- If you don't have a handyman on call, make this your top priority. You MUST have a great handyman in your back pocket to be a great real estate agent. I often call my handyman during inspections with a question and he's been known to even drop everything and rush over to check it out...thus putting my buyer's mind at ease or at least making me look fantastic.

- If an inspection goes poorly, let your buyers sleep on it. Inspections can be exhausting, but after a good night's sleep your buyers may feel much better.

- When preparing an inspection notice for the seller, never, ever use inflammatory language. Just state your requests clearly and succinctly, without embellishment. For example, instead of saying "Seller shall repair the leak under the kitchen sink to avoid further mold and mildew damage to the cabinet, flooring and possibly the basement ceiling." Simply say, "Seller shall repair the leak under the kitchen sink."

- Keep your inspection requests to as few bullet points as possible. Group your requests into categories; for example, all plumbing issues go under one bullet, all electrical items under one bullet.

It can't be emphasized enough...always support your buyer, not your paycheck, no matter how badly you need that paycheck. Put yourself in your buyer's shoes and advise accordingly. The brownie points you win by truly being on his side will pay off big time for you; not only in this transaction, but for years to come when he tells everyone he knows what a great real estate agent you are.

Pay for Non-Performance? I Really Don't Wanna...

It's happened to all of us...we drive our buyers all over town, take them to lunch, return their Sunday evening phone calls...and then...BAM! They call us with the fantastic news that they found the PERFECT house! Unfortunately it's a FSBO and the seller isn't willing to pay an agent. Our buyer really appreciates all our effort and hopes there are no hard feelings...

Hard feelings...nah....

Your immediate reaction? I'm guessing most of us would sputter and stammer and feel betrayed and many would probably assert our "right" to a commission, especially if a Buyer Agency Agreement is involved. I'm not here to argue the rights or wrongs of that.

But...

I've been working with a lender for the last two months, trying to refinance my house. Being a self-employed writer-recently-returned-to-real-estate-sales, I'm a Stated/Stated kinda gal. Not a lot of loan programs out there for us, and they're dwindling by the minute. Every time my lender has found me a workable loan, it's vanished—POOF—and she has to start over.

So, a few days ago, I had lunch with another lender friend of mine and told him my woes and he said: "Wachovia has the perfect product for what you're looking for—here's the number of my contact there, give her a call!" I did, and she did (have the perfect product) and it's pretty much a slam dunk.

Here's my question. My first lender didn't get the job done. Her fault? Not really. But she didn't get the job done. Do I owe it to her to BRING HER IN ON THE DEAL and cough up a $2700 origination fee?

Yes? No?

"Advertising" to Your Sphere of Influence

I've never had much (any?) luck with mass-advertising (newspapers, bus benches, SEO), at least, not that I could tell. One year I took out over $20,000 worth of newspaper ads which resulted in, get this, ZERO phone calls. Enough of that nonsense.

However, I'm starting to think about the effectiveness of "advertising" to your SOI. Here's where my brain is going.

I live in a trendy, hip neighborhood that has barely noticed the recent doom & gloom of the real estate market. People still want to live here and decent homes sell quickly. I also happen to know a lot of people who live here in the 'hood with me—probably 20-30 members of my core SOI are neighbors. We're such a hip, trendy crowd...

So I'm thinking...would it be effective to advertise in the local neighborhood newspapers—not necessarily to attract the business of total strangers, but rather to reinforce my name recognition among the people who DO know me, or have at least heard of me?

I remember many years ago, there was an agent in town who advertised heavily on bus benches. I thought she must be a Top Dog because it seemed her name was all over the place. When we finally met (and became friends), I was shocked to discover that she was newer than I was and did significantly less business. But the perception I had of her was that she was very successful.

Here's my point...If I were a consumer, would all those bus benches have inspired me to call her up and hire her on the spot? Not a chance. BUT, if I'd met her, at an open house, at a party, wherever, would she have already had some credibility with me, due to her advertising efforts? Probably so, especially if she were professional and credible in person (which she was).

So...I'm wondering if the point of local advertising might be to put you in a position of credibility should you ever have the opportunity to meet those who have seen your advertising. Or, of course, to remind those who already know you of your existence, if they've forgotten...?

Is this a big DUH question?

Always Look for the Negative...Yeah, That Works (she says sarcastically)

I like to think of myself as an Outside the Box creative thinker. I love to look at a situation and come up with a different angle or solution to what traditional thought has come up with in the past.

But I'm finding, much to my frustration, that most people don't seem to approve of this approach.

Quite often when I share my latest idea or epiphany with other real estate agents, they immediately tell me all the reasons it won't work. It drives me crazy.

First, show me some respect that I've thought this through for more than 30 seconds (the length of time THEY'VE considered it before they criticize). Yeah, I already thought of THAT and I probably have an answer.

Second, open your mind to the possibilities of breaking tradition and trying something new. Maybe I'm onto something, maybe I'm not, but at least give it a chance to percolate in your mind before dismissing it. Might be life-changing!

Third, many in our industry are failing, yet they seem to be the ones most resistant to new ideas. I love it when someone who hasn't sold a house in six months tells me why my idea won't work...

Okay, rant over. Thanks for listening!

APRIL 2008

Sales Pitched at 24-Hour Fitness...
and I WON'T Be Joining!

Last night, I went to 24-Hour Fitness to meet a girlfriend of mine for Power Yoga. I don't belong to 24-Hour Fitness, but she assured me I could get a 24-day free membership. Cool.

Well, of course, in order to get my free membership card, I had to sit through a sales pitch. I HATED it and y'know what? I probably won't join just because I don't want to give that salesy little hardbody the satisfaction. I don't want him to think that he successfully SOLD me!

What really bugged me was that we were having a nice little time together— he showed me around the gym, we talked about food sensitivities—y'know, we're bonding, so I thought. Then, he whipped out his flip chart of why I should join the club. He made his case, but I politely declined to commit TODAY. Why? Because I hadn't even tried out the club yet, and I didn't feel comfortable committing to a year membership. I explained this to him, but he wouldn't give up. He had this baffled look on his face, followed by an annoyed look—implying that I'm 1) rude for wasting his time and 2) an idiot for not signing up. Gotta tell ya, implying that I'm a rude idiot does NOT win any brownie points with me. I was waiting for him to tell me he wouldn't give me my temporary membership card unless I committed to him on the spot.

Hmmmmm... let's re-write that paragraph and relate it to real estate.

What really bugged me was that we were having a nice little time together—he showed me around the neighborhood, we talked about the local restaurants—y'know, we're bonding, so I thought. Then, he whipped out his buyer agency agreement and told me why I should hire him. He made his case, but I politely declined to commit TODAY. Why? Because I didn't know yet if we were a good fit to work together. I explained this to him, but he wouldn't give up. He had this baffled look on his face, followed by an annoyed look—implying that I'm 1) rude for wasting his time and 2) an idiot for not signing up. Gotta tell ya, implying that I'm a rude idiot does NOT win any brownie points with me. I was waiting for him to tell me he wouldn't put me in his car unless I committed to him on the spot.

Anyway, I finally convinced the hard-body sales dude that I was not going to sign up, so he walked away for a minute to pick up the temporary card he'd printed for me. When he came back, he said he'd just remembered a special the club was offering! He told me about the special and then said "Do you STILL want just a temporary membership?" Oh, yes, even more so now, thank you.

Blech.

What's Your Angle? Do You Really Need One?

I was approached a few weeks ago by an agent asking my opinion on starting up a "green" real estate company—that is, a company that uses recycled products, provides information on environmentally friendly alternatives and knows where the Built Green properties are in his marketplace.

Hmmmmm. Okay, please forgive the upcoming cynicism.

While I don't doubt the guy's commitment and enthusiasm for the mission, he admitted that his primary intent was to attract a certain type of client (i.e., more "upscale") and to take advantage of the public's current interest in protecting the environment. Nothing wrong with that, exactly, but it just rubs me the wrong way.

Why?

Because I think that if we real estate agents want an "angle" to generate business, that angle really ought to include something about providing really good real estate service.

Any person on the planet can choose to protect the environment in their everyday actions and decisions. People who care will notice; people who don't, won't. Is the "green" angle compelling enough to attract consumers on its own?

Maybe I'm missing something.

Back and Forth, Back and Forth—
Just Make the Date Already!

Email can be veddy, veddy efficient. Yet...email can also be veddy, veddy inefficient.

I've been trying to get together with an old friend for two weeks now. We have a very close, loving email relationship—but we've rarely talked on the phone 'cause neither of us seems to be much good at it. We're both introverts and are much more comfy chatting thru our fingertips.

Problem is...we're trying to be oh-so-considerate with each other's time and schedule that we can't seem to get anything down on the calendar! You know what I mean...

Me: "So, are you busy next week? Wanna go get a drink? I'm free Tuesday, Wednesday and Friday."

My friend: "I'd love to see you—let me check my calendar and get back to you." (A few days go by.)

My friend: "Sorry it took me so long to get back to you. Tuesday or Friday work for me—how about you?"

Me: "Oops—my Tuesday and Friday are booked. How's your schedule the next week? I'm wide open."

My friend (two days later): "Me, too, just pick a day."

Me: "How about Thursday?"

My friend: "Thursday is good, what time?"

Me: "How about 5:30? Or later—around 6:30?"

My friend: "Either way. Where would you like to meet?"

Me: "Doesn't matter—want me to come your direction?"

My friend: "I don't mind driving your way—whatever works for you."

Me: "Let's meet in your neighborhood—I haven't been there in a while. What's a good place to get a drink?"

Blah blah blah blah blah...this can go on forever, can't it?

So...what I'm learning (yeah, I'm a little slow) is to offer up a date, time and place REAL early in the "conversation."

Instead of all the back and forth, how 'bout this?

Me: "Hey, are you busy next week? Wanna get a drink Tuesday or Wednesday?"

My friend: "Sounds great! Where should we meet?"

Me: "How about Finnegan's on Tuesday around 5:30?"

DONE.

Does Arguing with Your Clients Sound like a Good Idea?

We real estate agents like to argue with our clients. Oh, we don't call it arguing, we call it "advising," "persuading," "sharing our expertise" or even "taking control of the situation." But for the sake of this blog, let's call it what it is... arguing.

Say your buyer client changes her mind about where she wants to look for a home. She's dismayed by the prices in her preferred neighborhood and decides to look in a less desirable location so she can get more square footage. What do you do?

Or let's say that your seller wants to flat-out reject a low-ball offer on her home. What do you say?

How about the seller who accuses you of underpricing his home when it sells on Day One? Do you defend yourself?

What about the buyer who falls in love with a townhouse, even though you know a single family home would be a better investment?

To be continued...

Arguing Will Get You Nowhere! Try This Instead...

Our clients are intelligent human beings, capable of making their own decisions. Okay, so some might be more capable than others, but all deserve our respect that they have thought thru their situation (after all, they have more at stake than we do) and reached a decision they feel works for them. That's the first step—to SHOW our clients that we respect their intelligence and their right to make their own decisions. When you immediately "argue" with your client's point of view or decision, this sends the opposite message.

Now, I'm not saying that you shouldn't have an opinion or be allowed to voice one. BUT, if you don't want to be accused of being argumentative, you need to take a different approach from simply saying "Are you sure you want to do that?" or "I really don't advise that" or "I don't think that's a good idea." Say something like that to ME, after I've given MY personal situation some thought and y'know what? I'll dig in my heels and commit even stronger to my position.

You know what else? I think I'm a pretty smart cookie. I'll bet you do, too. In fact, I'll bet most of the people on the planet have a healthy respect for their own intelligence. Argue with me and guess what? I might think you aren't quite as smart as I thought you were—after all, you're arguing with ME and I think I'm right. What does that make you? Wrong...and kinda dumb. "Poor thing, you just don't get it," thinks me.

So, what's the solution? Ah, GLAD YOU ASKED. Because that's part of the solution. Wait for your client to ASK for your opinion or advice. Once they do, they'll actually listen to it. If they don't ask, they truly don't care and any advice you give that is counter to their opinion will be discounted anyway. They're the boss, after all, and if they want to kill their deal, it's their choice. And it IS their choice (not yours)!!!

If you show respect for your client's position and don't argue with it, they probably will, at some point, ask you for your thoughts. At that point, you can give it, respectfully, all the while KEEPING YOUR PAYCHECK out of the conversation or your thoughts.

So, let's take the scenarios presented in yesterday's blog and see how you can respond without arguing:

Scenario #1: Your buyer wants to look for a home in a less desirable neighborhood so she can get more square footage. This is a no-brainer. Show her the houses. Let her do her own soul-searching. YOU can't predict the future anyway, so who knows? Maybe it'll turn out to be a great financial decision, maybe not, but there is NO room for argument here. Last time I checked, adult human beings have the right to live where ever they want, without getting permission from their real estate agent.

Scenario #2: Your seller is offended by a low-ball offer and wants to reject it outright. Obviously, we want the seller to counter any offer he receives, but first, we need to show support and be offended right along with him. He's probably expecting you to argue with him and is steeled for it, so by not arguing right off the bat, he'll relax. Once he does (if he doesn't, you might need to let him sleep on it and re-group the next day), you could offer to draft up an equally ridiculous counterproposal (full price, 21-day close, whatever) and see if he's open to that. Then maybe you can encourage him to give a little bit so the buyer doesn't feel like a total putz. But again, if he wants your advice, he'll ask for it. If he doesn't ask, he doesn't want it, won't listen to it and will just be annoyed by it.

Scenario #3: Your seller accuses you of underpricing her home when it sells on Day One. Okay, let's imagine what's happening in her life. She's telling all her friends that her house sold in 24 hours and are they congratulating her? Nope. They're telling her that her idiot agent underpriced the home. Yipes. Do you defend yourself? This is a tough one because every bone in your body is screaming to. But be careful. Your seller is expecting you to be defensive, so don't be! Agree that the home might have been under market. Congratulate her for having such a nice property and working so hard to get it ready for market. Leave YOUR efforts out of it. If you schmooze her, she'll return the favor. Argue with her and she'll argue back. No fun.

Scenario #4: Your buyer decides to buy a townhouse, but you know that a single family home is a better investment. Another no-brainer. If she's concerned about investment, she'll let you know and you can share your thoughts. But show her the respect she deserves and let her make her own housing decision.

We are in a business where egos and emotions are involved in almost every decision. Acknowledge it, work with it, use it to your advantage. Everyone wins!

My New Buyer Calls at 7:30am on Sunday Morning... Do I Jump? You Betcha!

Want to build a raving fan base that will support your business for years to come? It's SO easy—way easier than cold-calling, door-knocking or farming and a heck of a lot cheaper. All you gotta do is look for opportunities to impress the heck out of those who have the potential to be your future past clients and stop worrying so much about whether you're wasting your time!

On Friday morning, I got a buyer referral from an agent in Breckenridge. The buyers live in the mountains, want to buy a home in Denver. This week? Nah, they have a house to sell first, so maybe sometime in the summer. That's cool—I like a full pipeline.

Around 2:00 on Friday afternoon, the buyer calls me and wants to know if I can show her and her husband houses on Saturday. Yep, with a little re-arranging, I can do that. So, we did. Went well. Nice, nice couple with two adorable little girls. Found a neighborhood they love, so I promised to keep them updated on the market activity in there. They headed back up the hill to their mountain home.

At 7:30 this Sunday morning, my cell phone rings. The buyers are so excited about what we saw yesterday that they want to make another road trip to Denver today to look at all the other houses for sale in the neighborhood, as well as the ones we saw yesterday. Well, I have an open house at 1pm, three offers to present at 4:30 and dinner plans tonight, so if I'm going to accommodate them, it will have to be this morning and I do have a lot of things to do between now and my 1pm Open House.

Did I rearrange my schedule for them? Oh, yeah. We're meeting at 11:00. Are they going to buy a house today? Not a chance. Are they pre-approved? I'm not sure, I think so, but I haven't asked.

So, why am I "wasting my time?"

1. My past clients are an enormous source of business for me. Because I put them on a five-year drip campaign and hound them for referrals? Uh, no. I think it has more to do with working my backside off for them and making their needs a priority over my paycheck. Even if (egads!) I'm inconvenienced.

2. The agent who referred them to me could also be a sweet source of future business for me—she works in a resort market just an hour away,

so if I impress her clients, in turn I impress her.

3. Here's the thing...meeting them as requested will take maybe two hours out of my day. Big deal. I think that's a very good use of two hours that I'd otherwise probably be surfing online or even whining to myself that I wish I had a few buyers. To me, taking advantage of the opportunity to impress someone who has the power to bless me with a $10,000+ paycheck is an excellent way to spend a Sunday morning.

MAY 2008

Hellooooooooo??? Are You out There, SOI?
Yes, Jennifer, We're Here!

For almost twelve years, I've run a nearly 100% SOI business—that is, most of my clients have come from the people I know, the people they know, or the people I meet. It's worked for me.

I have a somewhat organized, yet unconventional approach to keeping my name in front of my SOI. I don't bombard them with cheesy mailers; I don't pester them on a monthly basis for referrals; I don't sort them according to whether or not they will commit to sending business my way. Nah, I just stay in touch, as a real person who happens to sell real estate for a living. Oh, and I take great care of my clients...as my first priority—not as an afterthought once my prospecting activities are done (that's straight from my profile—kinda catchy, eh?).

And...business floods in. My phone rings (or email jangles), I answer it, and voila! I have a great new client.

But what has pleasantly surprised me since my recent return to real estate after two years away is how many of my past clients, some of whom I haven't spoken with in years, still consider me their Agent-of-Choice. Just in the last week, I've been contacted by four past clients—all of whom bought or sold over five years ago—wanting to talk real estate. Three out of four of the calls came from people I didn't think really liked me much since they'd never responded to my stay-in-touch efforts. I figured I'd done something to make them mad and even considered striking them from my database.

Nope. Not the case at all. They had lives to live and didn't need a real estate agent that day. But when they did...they knew who to call. (That would be ME.)

So, why do they remember me? I ask myself the same question. I really don't have a personal relationship with them, obviously, since we haven't actually spoken since the closing in many cases. Yes, I have included them in my postal mailings and emailings , but I'm sure they've met other agents through the years and probably get bombarded with Just Listed! and Just Sold! postcards on a regular basis. What's so special about me?

In the interest of research, I got up the nerve to ask a few of them. And the answers warmed my heart.

They called me because I did a good job for them and they knew how to reach me when the time came. Simple as that. Now, if I had done a lousy or even mediocre job for them, but stayed in touch, I doubt they would have kept my card around, but since they were happy with my service, they did. Oh, I'm sure that I've lost people thru the years who did happen to meet other real estate agents who befriended them more than I did, but overall, I have to say that I'm tickled with my retention rate.

Do a good job. Stay in touch. Pretty easy stuff, huh?

I'll Be Happy to Refer You as Long as It's My Idea... (that is, please don't ask me to)

I got a facial the other day. Some fancy schmantzy European Spa Facial with a massage. Yummy. It was really good. And, I swear, I look ten years younger.

So, I'm lying there trying to enjoy being cleansed, exfoliated, moisturized and massaged. Yet, I'm tense. I'm waiting for the facialist to ask me if I'd be willing to send her referrals. Maybe I just have referral fever on my mind 'cause I've written about it so much lately, but I was truly upset about it! Seriously, I could hardly relax preparing myself for the inevitable sales pitch.

I pondered this behind my moisturizing mask. Why was I so opposed to her asking me for referrals? Not because I wouldn't refer her—she was definitely refer-worthy, and I was actually kind of excited about handing out her business card to my friends.

But I wanted to refer her on my OWN terms, not because she asked me to! I wanted to surprise her with my referrals. I like thinking that this wonderful facialist doesn't desperately NEED my referrals; but she would certainly appreciate them, as one professional to another.

This story has a happy ending. She did not try to sell me anything—not an expensive cleanser or moisturizer or serum; nor did she beg me for my future business or referrals. And I grabbed a handful of her cards on the way out!

Gas Prices Too High to "Waste" My Time with Buyers? Oh, Puh-leeeaze!

I'm so sick of hearing how real estate agents can't afford to work with buyers anymore—UNLESS that buyer has signed a buyer agency agreement AND has an iron-clad loan commitment in hand—because of the high cost of gas. What a crock.

Let's do a little analysis.

Over the last several years, gas has hovered around the $3.00/gallon mark. Sometimes higher, sometimes lower, but I think that $3.00/gallon is a reasonable place to start.

In some parts of the country, gas is now around $4.00/gallon. That's $1.00 per gallon difference.

If your car gets 20 mpg, you're spending ONE EXTRA DOLLAR for every 20 miles you drive.

If you take a buyer out and drive sixty miles with him or her, that's three extra dollars you spent on him (over and above what you would have spent on him last year and the year before).

Are you really saying that you can't afford to spend an additional $3.00 in exchange for a shot at a $7,500 commission ($250,000 x 3%)?

Tell ya' what. I'll be happy to take your Denver buyers for a ride, whether they've signed a Buyer Agency Agreement or not. Whether they're pre-qualified or not. Because I know that being out in my market with a warm body in my car (and that warm body probably has lots of friends he can refer to me in the future) is a MUCH better use of my time than sitting back at the office congratulating myself on saving $3.00 in gas.

I'll even pay you a referral fee. So, on top of the THREE BUCKS you saved, you'll also get $1,875 just for giving me a call!

Please Tip in Cash (an alternative to Referral-Begging)

I learn a lot at nail shops. Weird, I know, but every time I get my toenails polished, I come away with a new revelation or epiphany. Must be some way to claim my mani/pedi's as a tax deduction.

So, yesterday, I had about 45 minutes to kill before my next appointment. I needed a manicure and saw a cute little nail shop, so I popped in for a quickie (manicure, that is).

As those of you who get regular manicures know, before your nails get polished, you have to go wash your hands to get off all the chemicals and lotions that the technician has been using on your fingers.

So, I obediently go to the wash sink and what do I see taped on the mirror? A tasteful sign that said, "We can't accept tips on your credit card, please consider using cash or check." Or something like that.

Was I annoyed at this gentle reminder to tip? Not really! They weren't asking for a tip, they were just assuming I would tip and were kindly letting me know how to do it.

Hmmmmm. My mind immediately started looking for a connection to real estate. Wasn't hard to come up with one.

I'm adamantly opposed to begging for referrals. (Begging = Asking, Bribing, Reminding, etc.). It's unprofessional, it's unnecessary and it makes the beggar look desperate. Many disagree with me and that's certainly their prerogative, but you won't talk me out of this opinion (and many have tried).

But anyway, what if... instead of begging...we ASSUME our friends and clients will refer to us and simply let them know the best way to do so, if they're so inclined? Maybe it's as simple as casually saying something like: "If you ever send any of your friends my way, tell them to use my direct line so they'll reach me quicker." Or "If you send any referrals my way, be sure to give them my website address so they can check me out ahead of time."

Compare that attitude to: "I {heart} Referrals!" or "By the Way, do you know anyone who needs a real estate agent?" or "I'm never too busy for your referrals!" or "Send me a referral and receive a $50 Starbucks gift card!"

Which sounds more confident...and professional?

"So, What Is a GOOD Real Estate Agent?"

Two nights ago, I did a presentation for a local real estate company on Prospecting Without a Sales Pitch. When I got to the part about why I think it's more important to be a good real estate agent than to be a good real estate prospector, a hand went up in the back of the room.

"What exactly do you mean by being a "good" real estate agent?"

Ahhhhhh…. I'm SO glad you asked.

Our industry celebrates production. Therefore, if you have lots of that (production), you are "good." Eh, I don't agree so much. I've known many a successful real estate agent who I would not in a million years accuse of being "good." Oh, sure, they get plenty of business, but what they do with it after the paperwork is signed? Not much.

So anyway, back to the question from my audience. "What makes a real estate agent GOOD?"

My mouth could barely keep up with my brain. What I said was something like this:

"You know your market, your systems and your contracts. You are a good negotiator. You put your clients' needs above your need for a paycheck. You know how to properly price a home. You know what your seller needs to do to get his home ready for market. You know how to build rapport with your seller so that he trusts you. You know how to take decent photos. You know how to write an appealing MLS description. You return phone calls promptly. You preview listings so you don't waste your buyer's time. You know how much it costs to replace a 50-year-old furnace. You have a handyman, a cleaning service and a good HVAC contractor. You're pleasant to other agents so they're happy to show your listings or accept your offers. You keep your brochure boxes full. Your lockboxes work…"

To me, THIS is a good real estate agent. Do you agree? Or do you think that being a Master Prospector is the key to "good"?

JUNE 2008

There's GOLD in Them Thar SOI!

"How can I prospect to first time buyers?"

"How can I meet newly married people?"

"How can I get my name in front of divorcing couples?"

"How can I market to renters?"

And even...

"How can I meet newly dead people (or more specifically, their heirs)?"

These are questions I read every day on real estate forums.

Responses are fairly predictable: "Hold buyer seminars, mail to apartment complexes, write to attorneys, attend bridal fairs, prospect to funeral directors and watch the obituaries."

Fair enough.

But here's the thing. The people you already KNOW, know first time buyers, married people, divorcing couples, renters and yes, even dead people's heirs. They also know couples with new babies, investors and relocating families.

So, it's your choice. You can bombard your target audience of strangers with your (expensive) marketing materials, hoping for a hit, or you can reconnect with the people who already know you and guarantee yourself one (or two or three or four or a dozen).

Our industry has made prospecting way too complicated and counterintuitive. It doesn't have to be. Back up, calm down and use the brains God gave you to find your next clients. They're all around you.

It's All About ME (a rant)!

I just got off the phone with the listing agent of a house my buyer has written an offer on. The seller countered and my buyer is waffling. She needs to talk to her parents and since interest rates bumped up this week, she's not sure she can still afford the house. Certainly that's her prerogative.

So, I called the listing agent and told her that my buyer is considering the counterproposal and that we'd get back to her as soon as we could. She throws a little tantrum that she's going out of town on Saturday and doesn't want to be putting this deal together at 8:00 Friday night.

Uh....and this is MY problem? My buyer's problem?

When she first said it, I laughed and said, "Yeah, isn't that how it always happens?" but she wouldn't let it go—she really wanted me to know how displeased she was with the situation.

Okay, so I'll call my buyer and pressure her into making a decision (which could very well be negative because she's not ready to do so) because the other agent has vacation plans...yeah, that's exactly what I'm going to do...

NOT.

My Four-Month Anniversary Back in Biz:
Eight Lessons from the Trenches

June 1st was my four month anniversary of re-activating my license after a two-year sabbatical.

It's funny, when you sell real estate for a living, you just do it, and you don't spend a ton of time analyzing it. But try taking two years off to write about selling real estate and you'll find yourself evaluating every move you've ever made and figuring what works and why and what doesn't work and why.

Which is what I've been doing for the last four months...analyzing and evaluating what works and what doesn't and why...for me anyway.

Thought I'd share...

1. Satisfied past clients are by far the best source of business for your future.

LESSON: Take good care of the business you have today before pursuing the business you hope to have tomorrow.

2. When you have a satisfied past client, all you have to do is stay in touch with them on a semi-regular basis so they know where to find you when they need you. You really don't need to try to be their best friend.

3. Knowing Your Market is a powerful way to attract business from both strangers and friends.

4. Advertising in the newspaper doesn't work.

5. Every action you take has the potential to bring you a $10,000 paycheck—you'll just never know ahead of time which action will be the magic one. So, always be doing something.

6. Don't delete someone from your database because you never hear from them and think they don't like you. They probably like you fine; they're just busy living their own lives.

7. Eye contact and a smile go a long way toward initiating rapport with strangers—and improving your mood. Get in the habit of smiling at Walmart.

8. A website is nice, but it probably isn't the magic bullet you're hoping for.

Asking for Referrals Versus NOT Asking for Referrals—Which Is More Risky?

I was interviewed Monday on Real Estate Radio USA and in the middle of the interview, I had an epiphany about Referral-Begging...(I love epiphanies, don't you? Although perhaps in the middle of a live national radio interview, the timing might not have been the best).

Anyway. Back to my epiphany. It's about whether or not to ask/beg/bribe your friends for referrals, which as you probably know, is a practice I'm adamantly against.

Yesterday, my seller client (whose house sold in TWO DAYS, yay!) sent me an email asking permission to give my name to two friends who are looking for a real estate agent. ASKING MY PERMISSION! As if I might be far too busy to handle even more clients.

I giggled to myself because that's exactly the impression I want to leave with my world. Of course, I told her I'd be thrilled if she gave my name out and thanked her profusely. Maybe too profusely, actually, but oh well.

But here was my epiphany. By not letting my client know that I <Heart> Referrals, I took the chance that she wouldn't know to send me any. I took the chance, that, egads, she might send her friends to someone else! Oh, the horror!!

However , I'd much rather take the chance of losing potential referrals out of innocent ignorance than to take the chance of annoying, pestering or otherwise damaging my credibility with my SOI by constantly reminding them to send referrals my way.

Besides, if I do a great job for my clients and treat them respectfully, they will think of me when the topic of real estate comes up in their social interactions. If they don't think of me, well, it has nothing to do with whether or not I pestered them lately about it...

Thanks for the Referral—Here's Your Toaster!

A few days ago, I posted a blog about how my seller client recently asked me if it "was okay" if she gave my name to a few of her friends. I shared the blog with her and she was astonished that it's common practice in our industry to actually pester our friends and clients for referrals.

Here's what she said:

"Referrals are kind of a no-brainer...I think that anyone who is happy with someone's service is actually THRILLED to recommend them to people, and does so naturally—they don't really need to be asked or reminded. I was so happy with Carrie our mortgage broker that I refer people to her right and left every chance I get—she's never once asked me to, it's just natural to tell people about someone you've enjoyed doing business with. And I agree, when people do ask for referrals, it does sometimes come off as slightly desperate or could just make people uncomfortable.

People's work should just speak for itself. If the clients are happy, you can be darn sure they'll want to tell the world about it :)"

Anyway, she followed up this comment with a story about how a few years ago her boss was "rewarded" with a toaster from an agent he referred to a friend of his. A toaster? Sheesh.

Sorry, but I think this is hilarious. Do a great job for your clients. Stay in touch with them afterwards. Truly, that's all it takes. If you really think you need a toaster to seal the deal...hmmmmm....

JULY 2008

My "Waste of Time" Listing Appointment This Holiday Weekend

Got a call today from a guy who found me from my blog. He asked me to come over this weekend and talk to him about selling his $600,000 house. Well... maybe that's not exactly what he said...in any event, he really doesn't want to sell the house; he just wants my opinion of market value so he can decide whether or not he should sell or buy out his ex-girlfriend. In other words, I'm pretty sure he's just looking for a free CMA.

Fair enough.

I have two choices. I can...

1) Politely (or not so) tell him that I can't afford to waste my time giving out free information, or

2) Show up on Saturday and cheerfully give him a CMA.

I choose #2.

Why? Because:

- I have nothing else pressing to do on Saturday morning

- He might decide to sell the house ($18,000 Ka-ching!) and if he's met me and likes me, there's a whole lot better chance I'll get the listing than if I tell him to kiss off, don'cha think?

- He might decide not to sell the house...this year...but might next year or the year after that (and I'll take an $18,000 paycheck pretty much any time of the year).

- He might think I'm really cool and refer me to all (or even one) of his friends.

- I haven't been hanging out in $600,000 houses lately, so it won't hurt me to catch up on the inventory and improve my market knowledge.

- I'm always game for the opportunity to fine-tune my listing presentation, even after 12 years on the job.

In short, I'll take the chance that I'm "wasting my time" with this guy. I think I can spare a few hours...

Wasting Time Again...Will I Ever Learn?

I love to Waste my Time in my real estate business; in fact, it's one of my most productive prospecting activities! Of course, there are other things I COULD be doing instead (dialing for dollars, cruising FSBOs, creating a new farming campaign, etc.), but I'd really rather just Waste My Time.

Here's my latest effort to Waste my Time.

I just got a buyer referral from a current client. Cool.

So, I talk to the guy and he's interested in a bank-owned house that is ridiculously underpriced—it's a dump for sure, but still—it's $89psf in a market where you rarely see anything under $200psf.

The house is showing up as active in the MLS, which surprises me, so I call the listing agent and am told they have multiple offers on the table, but the bank simply isn't responding. This has been going on for weeks.

My first response is to contact my new buyer and tell him it's a Wasted Cause and we should move onto other prospects. After all, I don't want to Waste My Time writing and presenting an offer that will in all likelihood be rejected or totally ignored.

Whooooooaaaaa. Slow down there, grasshopper.

I've never even met the guy and I'm already implying to him that I don't want to Waste My Time writing up an offer with him...for a house that's still technically available? That's kinda snotty. And besides, how much time are we talking about? An hour? Two? During which time we can build rapport, establish trust, get to know each other better? I don't know about YOUR world, but in mine it's not often a qualified buyer calls me up and says "Let's Buy THIS house."

Will we buy that house? Probably not. But I can certainly afford to spend an hour or two with someone talking about real estate and proving my competence and dedication.

Off I go to happily Waste My Time!

My Dear Home Seller: What's Your Plan B?

I recently had a listing expire after three months on the market. Nothing has sold in my client's neighborhood for almost a year, so it wasn't a big surprise. We gave it a shot and it didn't work out for us. No biggie. She was prepared for the possibility and has no hard feelings toward me.

But that's not an accident. I always prepare my sellers for the chance that their home won't sell, despite our best efforts (by "our," I mean mine and my seller's joint efforts to prepare and present a great product to market). I don't make a big deal about it and I certainly don't lecture them or otherwise insult their intelligence; I just ask a simple question:

"What will you do if the house doesn't sell?"

Then I shut up.

If the seller doesn't have to sell, then I've planted the seed that I/we don't control the market and if the house doesn't sell, it might be beyond our/my control. If the seller does need to sell, it forces her to think about the unthinkable—that she'll own a house she doesn't want and can't afford. The next thing you know, she's asking me what she needs to do to ensure that doesn't happen. Suddenly, I'M THE EXPERT and she'll listen to me!

It also works beautifully for sellers who want to test the market at their price. A similar approach—*"What if the house doesn't sell at that price? Will you be okay with that?"* often works wonders in getting the seller to really think about what he's doing.

I don't consider myself a salesperson; I consider myself an advisor. Therefore, I don't try to convince my sellers that I can "sell" their homes. With the above words, I am relieved of the personal responsibility of selling a house that, for whatever reason, may not be sellable today.

For the record, my listings are always priced well, always staged and always easy to show. That's my job—to help my seller prepare and present their home to market in the best possible light.

That's all I can do.

Y'think Your Current Clients Are Talking About Their Real Estate Agent? Uh, Yeah!

What's the best way to build a strong Sphere of Influence? Stay in touch with everyone you know? Nope. Send everyone in your SOI a $10 Starbucks Gift card? Give fabulous Christmas presents or closing gifts? Pay juicy bribes for referrals? Not even close.

No, the best way to build a strong sphere of influence is to be a fabulous real estate agent. It's simple; when you are blessed to have a buyer or a seller, TAKE CARE OF THEM! As your first priority...

Here's an email I got yesterday from my current seller/buyer who has, to date, referred six people to me during our less-than-two-months relationship.

"It's so easy—it just happens naturally every time someone hasn't seen me in a while and goes, 'Oh yeah—how's selling your house going?' Everyone is convinced the market is terrible, so as soon as they hear we sold our home in only 2 days, they are dumbfounded and of course want to ask a million questions as to how on earth we pulled that one off... sometimes I forget how many people are or may potentially be in the market for a home. I love having someone good to recommend."

Guys & gals, when we are actively working with a buyer or seller, remember that they are talking about their real estate experience with everyone who crosses their path! If their agent sucks, you can believe the world will hear about it. But if their agent is really special? IMAGINE the opportunities for good PR over the next month, two months, six months.

No fabulous closing gift or monthly newsletter even comes close.

The moral of the story...Taking Good Care of the Clients You Already Have blows away any other form of active or passive marketing. Set your daily priorities accordingly...and enjoy a full pipeline for years to come...

AUGUST 2008

When Scripts Suck

I have a friend who recently got her real estate license and dutifully went out looking for her Very First Broker. She found The One and excitedly signed on. She was promised all sorts of training and support and mentoring...yee haw!

Well...fast forward two weeks and my friend is ...shall we say...disillusioned. She's barely even seen her broker, much less received any semblance of training, support or mentoring. In fact, her broker actually said something like "Try not to bother me with too many questions." My friend is a self-starter and is comfy taking responsibility for her own success, but geez...

Finally my friend managed to locate her broker and sit her down for a talk. The broker reiterated her philosophy that real estate is an individual sport and that most of the agents in the office (herself included) were far too busy to help a newbie. She directed my friend to a Big Book of Scripts and advised her to study and memorize them. When my friend balked at the notion, the broker assured her that scripts work, because...well, SHE had used a script during the recruiting process and look how well it worked!!!!

Okay, so...if a script "works" to accomplish your goal (that is, getting a listing, securing a buyer or recruiting a new agent), but is pretty much a Big Fat Lie, does that make it a good script? Uh, no.

I've seen a lot of scripts and I even use scripts myself sometimes. To me, a "script" is simply a bunch of words strung together that you have somewhat memorized in the proper order. We all use scripts every day—"Hi, how are you?" "Thanks a lot, have a nice day." I use pretty much the same words every time I explain a purchase contract to a buyer or a listing agreement to a seller. BUT THEY'RE MY FLIPPIN' WORDS! I believe them, I mean them, I stand behind them!

Use scripts wisely. They aren't a tool to fool someone into believing your services are something they aren't, or to make you appear to be knowledgeable if you aren't. If you don't mean it, don't say it! No matter what results the Big Book of Scripts promises!

Can a New Agent Make It in Today's Market?

"Can a new agent make it in today's real estate market?"

Here are my thoughts...

I tend to be a Positive Attitude kinda gal—but not in the sense that all you need is one of those (a positive attitude) in order to succeed. I believe that it's simply one of the requirements to succeed, 'specially in our business where the vast majority fail. If you don't have a Positive Attitude, you will fail. So, while having a positive attitude is not a guarantee of success, a negative one is most certainly a guarantee of failure.

Neither am I a believer that daily meditations or repetitive mantras will give you this positive attitude. No, I think that you earn your positive attitude by being PREPARED for whatever life throws at you; thus you have the confidence and assurance that you CAN DO IT—whatever "IT" may be.

For rookie agent wannabe's...I suggest that you do not waste your time and your money and your emotions on this career if you are not prepared AHEAD OF TIME. To me, this means:

- You have bought or sold a house before and somewhat understand the process from a consumer's perspective

- You have the full support of your family (financial and emotional)

- You know your way around your town

- You know people in your town (100 or more)

- You have the financial means to attack your career with all your heart (and time)

Am I saying that you can't succeed if you don't meet the above criteria? Of course not, but I won't pussy-foot around the fact that the odds are stacked against you already, so the more pluses you have in the preparation column, the better chance you'll make it to your second year. Today, qualified buyers and motivated sellers are not lined up around the block waiting for you to hang your license on the door. Heck, there aren't even that many UNqualified buyers or UNqualified sellers! The ones that are out there are tougher to deal with than in years past (when plenty of newbies failed by the truckload, too).

So...don't jeopardize your family's future by pursuing a dream you aren't yet prepared to pursue. If you're new to town, spend the next year learning your way around and making lots of friends. If you don't have any money in the bank, take a second job and build up a nest-egg. Prove to your family that you ARE prepared to do this so that they'll have 100% faith in you.

Yes, you CAN DO IT!!! But not just 'cause you want to. Make like a Boy Scout and...y'know...

Pretending to Be a Democrat—That'll Teach Me!

DISCLAIMER: I was advised by those who love me NOT to post this blog due to the political undertones—y'know, one of those things you should never discuss in public? Well, I couldn't help myself, but please be advised that I will freely use the DELETE button for comments that are posted solely for the purpose of promoting one party or candidate over another (not because I endorse censorship, but because that would get boring fast). Anyway, this blog is not intended to promote any political viewpoint, simply to comment on a tactic that got on my nerves...

The Democratic National Convention is in Denver. Being the anti-politico/anti-news kinda gal I am, I've barely noticed, even though it's all taking place within easy biking distance from my house (and yep, I tried to rent out my house for $500/night, but no takers—sigh). And besides, I'm not a Democrat, although I do have lots of friends who are Democrats. ☺

One of these friends invited me to a DNC gathering on Tuesday night to listen to Hillary speak. The gathering was held at a sushi bar here in my neighbor-hood, so it seemed like a good idea to go (y'know, SOI-opportunity and all). I probably should have known better.

From the minute I arrived, I felt like a fraud and realized I should probably sneak out at the first opportunity. But alas, I was hungry and in the mood for sushi, so I stayed. As the party ramped up, I realized that the point of the party was to organize the supporters' efforts in canvassing the neighborhood with door-knocking and cold-calling campaigns. Oops.

I was approached half a dozen times by the organizers of the event asking me what I was willing to do to spread the word thru my neighborhood. I felt like the atheist at church camp asked for her testimony. Not only am I not a Democrat, there's no way on God's green earth I'm gonna knock on ANYONE's door or make ANYONE's phone ring to talk about ANYONE's political beliefs.

Why? Because I don't like to be bothered at home! Not by Democrats, not by Republicans, not by Girl Scouts! The only people I want ringing my doorbell are Fed-Ex, UPS and that dude with the gazillion dollar sweepstakes check.

Okay, so back to the party. I bravely expressed my viewpoint on the topic—that I don't like to be disrupted at home and therefore will not do it to others. Oops, again. That viewpoint was not welcomed in this crowd. I was lectured; even scolded for my "perspective" and I felt like a naughty little girl.

But here was the funny part. A few weeks ago, a guy knocked on my door, with an Obama pamphlet in his hand and asked me who I planned to vote for. Hmmmmm...last time I checked, this was a private matter between me and my ballot. I told this story to one of the women who was trying to get me to change my "perspective" on door-knocking—I said "a perfect stranger comes to my door and asks me who I'm voting for—I think that's obnoxious," and she said "Well, didn't he introduce himself first?" Uh, yeah, but since when does knowing someone's name obligate me to share my voting record with them?

She also asserted that because we were both Democrats (shhhhh, don't tell), I shouldn't have been annoyed at the disruption, or mind calling other Democrats myself and disrupting them. As if belonging to the same political party changes my very basic belief that people, in general, don't like to be bothered.

ARghghghghhghg....I guess I have some fun times to look forward to over the next two months—dodging the doorbell, screening the phone calls. Maybe I COULD volunteer to make the calls and if the person doesn't want to talk politics, I could always toss in a "Oh, by the way, do you know anyone who wants to buy or sell real estate?" (NOT)

SEPTEMBER 2008

Aspiring Real Estate Agents—Can't Go Full-Time Yet? Consider This...

Whether or not a new agent can succeed in this business starting out part time is a topic of much debate all over the world of real estate online forums. Rookies ask...Old Fogies answer...and the discussion usually deteriorates into a p*ssing contest between the two camps. I've written extensively on the topic and I have no problem declaring which side I fall on...I believe that this biz is tough enough to get started in without making it even harder by hitting it with only half (or less) of your time, energy and focus. So, in case that wasn't clear, I think a new agent oughta do it full-time, or not at all.

Oh, yes, I know the arguments...the main one is "But I can't AFFORD to give up my regular paycheck yet; I NEED to keep my job to pay my bills!" Others claim to know someone who managed to survive working only nights and weekends, or fitting in real estate around their "real" job.

Fair enough. My goal here is not to open that tired old can of worms yet again. You have your opinion; I have mine, she has hers and he has his.

But the fact remains that most rookies fail in their real estate venture. MOST. Even the ones who think they'll be the exception. Obviously, MOST won't be.

I hope it's a fair statement to say that if you want to succeed in a business, you'll have a better chance of doing so if you give it MORE effort rather than LESS effort—can we agree on that? Therefore, the ideal situation for new agents is to be able to go full-time, right from the start, right?

If we can agree on that, then how about this? If you're cool with the idea of working your backside off on two jobs (your "real" job + your new real estate career), why not keep your day job and go get a second job that actually PAYS you money instead of COSTS you money? For six months, a year, whatever it takes to save up a nice nest-egg that will enable you to pursue your dream of being a wildly successful (full-time) real estate agent. Tend bar, deliver pizza, clean houses, tutor, mow lawns...whatever you can do in your spare time to generate some spare cash to sock away.

I promise you, this business is a whole lot more fun when you're not freaked out about your next mortgage payment or exhausted from trying to start a new business after a long day's work. Those six months will fly by, and if you're lucky, maybe the real estate market will improve by then!

I Still Love My Guardian Angel
(she mutters thru clenched teeth)

In *Sell with Soul*, I spoke fondly of my Guardian Angel. I believe with all my heart that I have a Guardian Angel watching over me and my business, although very often, she disguises herself as an insurmountable challenge. Sometimes, it takes an enormous leap of faith to acknowledge and appreciate my Guardian Angel, especially when in the middle of one of her divine "protections." Over the weekend, I experienced such a protection from my Angel and as of this morning, I am able to admit that, yes, I am indeed grateful to her.

One of my own properties is on the market and has been getting tremendous activity—lots of showings and second showings and a few threats of offers. But nothing solid, which, frankly, surprises me a bit. It's priced very well, shows great and obviously is intriguing to the marketplace.

Well, sometime between Saturday evening and Sunday at noon, the basement flooded. I showed up at the house at 1pm ready for my open house, and when I walked into the basement to turn the lights on was dismayed to find the just-finished basement bedroom soaked. Brand new carpet ruined. Freshly-painted walls soaked. Well, crap.

Anyway, I'm still in the throes of getting everything cleaned up and fixed, but here's the good news. When the flood repair team pulled the paneling off the walls, they discovered a hole in the foundation that's been there forever. It was obvious that water has been coming through that hole for years, but for some reason, doesn't do it often, or at least, not that I'd ever noticed (maybe that's why there wasn't carpet in the basement when I bought it, hmmmm). But clearly, it needs to be fixed.

Okay, so I'm not thrilled about taking this on—I have to pull the house off the market, fix the problem and then re-carpet and re-drywall the room— but THANK GOD it happened to ME and not the buyer! Can you imagine the phone call a month from now when the new owner is all moved in and HER basement floods? Y'think she might come after me, perhaps with her lawyer along?

So, yeah, I'm reluctantly thanking my Angel this morning. Wish me luck as I meet with contractors this week to get this sucker fixed!

Can a Single Woman Expand Her Sphere of Influence Without Sending the Wrong Message?

I have a friend; let's call her Sarah. She is a new real estate agent and is committed to an SOI strategy to build her business. So far, it's going well—she's already experiencing some success and is optimistic that she will survive her first year without ever cold-calling, door-knocking, farming or advertising.

Here's the problem. Sarah has a new boyfriend. When said boyfriend realized that Sarah freely hands out her phone number (in the form of her business card) to anyone who asks (regardless of gender), he was horrified. Not that he doesn't understand she has a business to build, but he's convinced that when Sarah cheerfully offers her phone number/business card to those of the male gender, they are going to assume that she is interested in them romantically. "That's the way men think, honey."

Sarah dismissed his concerns, assuring him that she keeps her SOI efforts on a professional level and that there is no funny business going on—either real or imagined. She simply doesn't believe that the men she prospects to have any notion that she might be open to their advances. The boyfriend disagrees. It's causing some strain in their relationship.

Sarah asked me for my thoughts. Initially I agreed with her—that the BF needs to accept that his honey is in a business that requires her to socialize with male creatures.

But then I ran across a paragraph in a book I'm reading about the differences in brain chemistry between men and women and it made me rethink my position. The book said that "...men are very easily aroused and easily misconstrue the slightest hint of friendship as a sexual invitation." So I asked my own Significant Other for his thoughts, as well as a couple of other men I know. They all agreed with Sarah's boyfriend that if a woman shows friendly interest in a man, he's absolutely going to interpret that as romantic interest on her part. If she gives him her phone number? She might as well have invited him in for a late-night coffee...

Any thoughts? No gender-bashing or ridicule, please. I'd love to hear from the men in the crowd how you honestly feel about this, as well as from any women who have experienced the same thing with their men...

Is Walking Away the Financially Responsible Thing to Do?

Just in the last week, I've run into three people who are walking away from their houses. As in..."Mr. Bank, here are the keys. I'm really sorry."

All three are professionals in the real estate industry—two are mortgage brokers; one is a real estate agent. All three have the earning potential to carry the properties they're letting go, but at a steep cost.

Walk-awayer #1 owns a trendy loft in downtown Denver. He owes around $600,000 on it, with a monthly payment of $3900 + a $485 HOA fee. The last comparable sale in the building was at $430,000.

Walk-awayer #2 owns a beautiful home on a golf course. She owes $750,000 on it, and a comparable home down the street has been on the market for almost a year at $650,000. She can no longer afford to pay the mortgage, as her own mortgage business has taken a real beating.

Walk-awayer #3 owns a rental property that is worth about $45,000 less than she owes on it. Her adjustable loan is coming due for adjustment which will add about $275/month to the existing payment of $1500. The property rents for around $1250/month. It's located in a stable market; it's not likely to depreciate, but neither is it likely to appreciate much.

All three of these walk-awayers have analyzed the situation and reached the same conclusion. It simply isn't worth the brain damage to try to hold onto these properties and it's not the financially responsible thing to do for their families. Of course, being in the business, they are fully aware of the impact a foreclosure will have on their credit score, but have decided that the trade-off is worth it. Preserving the FICO score simply isn't enough justification to risk financial ruin.

Sure, it's a real drag for the bank who holds the mortgage and I won't jump on the bandwagon of those saying that the "Banks Deserve it!!!" But neither will I criticize the decisions of my three friends by dismissing them as "irresponsible borrowers." Both sides will suffer, but when it comes down to it, my friends need to protect themselves and their families first. At least, that's my opinion.

OCTOBER 2008

PUH-LEEEEEAZE Don't Use Your Office Email Account!!

What is so difficult about this concept? Why on earth would any real estate agent or mortgage broker EVER use their office email server (e.g., jennifer@ coldwelbanker.com or john@wellfargo.com—misspellings intentional) to communicate with their clients, prospects and sphere of influence?

Last year I collected almost 1000 business cards from agents at the NAR convention and when I was inputting them into my system I was stunned at how many of them (like 90%) used the office server.

Do you REALLY think you'll be at this office forever and ever? Or even more than a year or two? Chances are you won't, but even if you think you will, WHY TAKE CHANCES?

The reason for this simplistic rant this morning is I'm trying to reach a mortgage broker friend of mine who recently changed companies. But, oops, the only email address in my address book for him is the old one, which is no longer valid. Did he notify me of his move? Yes. Did he send me his new email address? Probably. But guess what? It apparently wasn't a priority that day to make a note of it in my address book and his announcement is long gone.

You know how many real estate agents or mortgage brokers are competing with you in your market? Like, a WHOLE BUNCH? Do you really want to risk losing the Perfect Buyer or Seller because you changed offices two years ago? Sending out a new business card or even an email announcement WILL NOT DO THE TRICK. Once your email address is recorded in someone's address book, it's there forever.

Take a look at your card. Is your email address YOURS or your company's? If it's not yours, relegate these cards to your car to use during showings and order yourself new cards TODAY!

Rant Over.

Is a Sphere of Influence Approach Enough in Today's Market?

First, allow me to apologize for using that tired phrase "Today's Market." Real estate is most certainly local, so "Today's Market" in Denver is much different from Today's Market in Detroit, Dallas or Des Moines. I get that. But, for the sake of argument (or discussion), let's just assume that in most US real estate markets, "Today's" is not as much fun as "a Few Years Ago's." Deal?

Anyway, I've been doing some thinking about SOI in "Today's Market" and have reached the conclusion that SOI alone is NOT enough to maintain the lifestyle I'd grown accustomed to. Now, before you (depending on your frame of mind) gloat and smugly say "I told ya so," or conversely, burst into tears with disappointment, allow me to continue.

In the good old days (prior to "Today's" Market), buyers and sellers were all over the place. Everyone knew someone who was trying to buy a house (and getting outbid) or who had just sold their house with multiple offers. People were amazed at the equity that had built up in their recently purchased properties. Anyone with a toolbox fancied him- or herself a real estate investor. In other words, real estate was a hot, POSITIVE topic of conversation. All you really had to do was get your cute little backside out there in the world and you could pretty easily drum up a prospect or two.

In my first year back in 1996-97, I implemented a go-to-lunch-with-a-friend campaign, which was wildly successful. I got a lead and usually a closing from every single lunch. Like I said...everyone knew someone who was thinking about "doing" some real estate. It was practically shooting fish in a barrel. Eat some sushi, sell some houses.

Today—eh, not so much. For various reasons we're all familiar with, people simply aren't buying and selling homes in the volumes of years past. Real estate is NOT the hot, positive topic it used to be and I'll bet many of you have faced that sympathetic look when you tell someone you sell real estate for a living.

So, what's a cold-call phobic to do? Just get over the fear of cold-calling or otherwise pestering people for business?

Nope.

Don't fret—those of you who favor a softer approach to building your business don't have to abandon that approach until Tomorrow's Market arrives!

You can continue to be who you are and experience the success you desire.

I'll tell you how next time!

Yes, a Sphere of Influence Approach IS Enough in Today's Market, if You...

As promised, here's the follow-up to my previous blog entitled "Is SOI Enough in Today's Market?"

Yes and No.

No, traditional "SOI" where you simply let all your friends know you sell real estate and then send them off into the world to be your marketing department is definitely not enough. Why? Because the volume of buyers and sellers is drastically reduced from days past when everyone and their uncle knew someone buying or selling. Now, it's not unrealistic that the people you know truly DON'T know anyone who needs your services today or tomorrow!

But yes, if you redefine what it means to "SOI."

If you expand the term "SOI" to include every warm body you come into contact with during your day-to-day travels, then yes, most certainly, SOI will work beautifully for you, even in today's market. Obviously, this means that you need to try to get your smiling face in front of as many warm bodies as you can, as often as you can. However, you can't just hit the streets (or the phones) with a smile on your face (although that helps A LOT) and hope that new clients will force themselves upon you.

In order to capture the attention of those warm bodies you run into, you need to have something they want. What might that be? Information—as in knowledge of your local market. Fact and figures, yes, but also a familiarity with specific listings, recent sales and even the overall vibe of your marketplace.

Sounds really simple, but apparently it's not because I'm wiping the floor with other agents' former clients who were dissatisfied with their previous agents' knowledge and familiarity with the market. Every single buyer I have right now belonged to someone else, but when they crossed my path for one reason or another, they were blown away by my ability to speak intelligently about their specific real estate wants & needs. They wanted ME! They asked ME to be their real estate agent! Gotta love it.

When you're out in public and can Talk the Talk confidently and casually, business will be almost magically drawn to you. You won't have to beg for it; you won't even have to ask for it. People will ask you if you have time for them.

So, how is this related to an SOI strategy? Well, you have to have an audience with whom to share your market knowledge and the best way to find a receptive one is to be in the company of people you enjoy. Your friends, sure, but also people who live in your neighborhood or attend the same parties or eat at the same restaurant or drink at the same bar or go to the same dog park or even shop at the same Walmart!

Being a nice-n-friendly guy or gal is great, and can even be enough to generate a minimal level of business in a strong market, but today, you need more. In order to effectively generate business from the people you know and the people you meet, you must have something they want. That something is information.

Master Your Market...and sell your share of it!

Dave Ramsey Sez: In a Tough Market, Work Twice as Hard. JA Sez...

I was listening to a Dave Ramsey podcast today and he was preaching about NOT whining—just get out there and get the job done—don't participate in the "bad economy," etc. etc. etc. Good stuff. I agree 100%.

Then he said something that really caught my attention—he said that if you're in sales and your market is tighter than it used to be, then you'll just have to work twice as hard. Simple as that.

My first reaction was, predictably (envision fist pumping in the air), *"Yeah! I've got what it takes! I'll just double my effort and I shall survive!"*

Then I said to myself..."Hmmmmm. *I don't really wanna work twice as hard. What if I work the same amount and cut my lifestyle for a while?"*

I like the sound of that, frankly. It'll do me good to learn a little restraint and discipline!

I think Dave would approve.

NOVEMBER 2008

Breaking up Is Hard to Do...
but It Doesn't Have to Be Ugly

Most relationships, whether they are business or personal, end. Your favorite inspector misses a Big Problem and gets you embroiled in a lawsuit. Your go-to mortgage guy blows a Big Deal for you and doesn't even apologize. Your business partner has a mid-life crisis and vanishes to the Caribbean without warning. Your romantic partner has a mid-life crisis and vanishes to the Caribbean without warning. Your $1M buyer dumps you for his sister-in-law who just got her license yesterday, after you've shuttled him around town for three months.

It happens. Relationships come, relationships go. Hopefully you learned something that you can take to the next one. Blah blah blah.

But when a relationship ends, it doesn't have to be nasty. In fact, a wise person might even strive to end his or her relationships with dignity, even on a positive note. After all, you have an investment in this relationship—your time, your money, your energy, your creativity, sometimes even your heart. Why blow that investment by being snippy, vindictive, confrontational or just plain mean? Ever heard the phrase "Don't Burn Bridges?"

I'm amazed how many people would rather burn bridges than find a way to part amicably. When I "break up" with someone I have a business relationship with, I really like to find a way to preserve a mutual respect between us, rather than just pissing on each other. After all, I have time and money invested in the relationship and I hate to see that time and money gone to waste because someone got their feelings hurt. Our business is based on creating mutually beneficial relationships, and he with the most relationships at the end of the game wins!

If a buyer dumps you, be gracious about it. You never know when your replacement will blow it and leave the buyer wishing he'd stayed with you. If you make it easy for him to come crawling back, he just might. If a seller chooses another agent to sell her home, wish her well and offer your assistance if she ever needs you. If your biggest client replaces you as his property manager, generously offer to assist him during the transition process.

Why? Well, it's just smart business. Never give anyone ammunition to blast your name!

Now, when romantic relationships end, you'll have to ask someone else for advice. I don't have a flippin' clue!

To Expand Your Sphere of Influence—Be in the Right Place at the Right Time...More Frequently!

A few months ago, I attended a Rick DeLuca seminar here in Denver. I got a lot out of it, which is surprising because I typically dislike events like that and want to leave within 15 minutes.

One of the concepts Mr. DeLuca brought up was the idea of, as he calls it, "Being in the right place at the right time...more frequently." My version? "Be out there in the world with your antenna up and a smile on your face."

Good real estate business comes in one lead at a time...not ten leads at a time. And with the size of our paychecks, one (good) lead at a time is plenty! I'd much rather have one great lead per week than 100 cold leads that I generated from any sort of mass-marketing effort.

So, the way I see it, we real estate-types have a choice. We can sit behind our desks and generate lots and lots of crap designed to bombard a target audience in hopes of getting a few hits...or we can go out there in the world in our sexy jeans, feeling sassy and confident, and share our enthusiasm and knowledge of real estate with the world...

I'm as guilty as any other introvert of prefering to sit behind my desk and make lists...respond to emails...blog...anything so that I don't have to shower and put myself out there. But, even with my not-the-friendliest-person-in-the-world personality, I know that I'm much more likely to Be in the Right Place at the Right Time when I'm OUT THERE than when I'm comfortably curled up at home.

Oh, don't get me wrong...I'd go nutso if I were OUT THERE all day, every day, so don't think for a minute I'm advising my fellow introverts to do the belly-to-belly thing (ugh, I hate that phrase) for hours at a time. Just an hour a day will likely change your career.

Give it some thought. How could YOU spend one hour, every day, Being in the

Right Place at the Right Time More Frequently?

DECEMBER 2008

Phooey on Prospecting...I Just Wanna Do My Job!

I hate to prospect, in any way, shape or form. By "prospect" I'm not really referring to any particular method, strategy or activity, I simply don't like drumming up business. I get no joy out of self-promotion, marketing or pursuing. I very much dislike the idea of spending any time at all worrying about where my next closing might come from.

But I LOVE LOVE LOVE selling real estate. Or, perhaps I should say that I love MANAGING the process of the exchange of real estate. I love pricing homes, I love solving problems, I love creating home brochures, I love negotiating contracts and inspections, I love previewing homes for my buyers, I love preparing for a tough appraisal, I love talking my buyer off the ledge when he's in panic mode.

The vast majority of my business through the years has, frankly, found me as a result of my sphere of influence (SOI) and my satisfied past clients (SPCs). I've rarely had to formally prospect and have been able to spend most of my time doing what I love—that is, managing the business I already have.

That's still where my business comes from—from my SOI and my SPC's, but I'm feeling a bit grumpy that it doesn't flow in nearly as painlessly as it did in years past. There are lots of reasons for this—some obvious, some not so, but the fact remains that I'd be happy as a clam if I could just BE a great real estate agent and let someone else worry about making rain...

But maybe this is, like, totally obvious, dude. Does everyone feel this way, or are there people out there who really enjoy the rainmaking part of our jobs?

All I Want for Christmas Is...

A couple of days ago I was asked by a friend what I really wanted for Christmas — if money were no object and the law weren't standing in my way.

Seemed easy enough. I'm not so old that I don't remember the thrill of putting together my Christmas list with every expectation that it would be fulfilled!

But, um, I had trouble with it. If someone were to drop a $10,000 or $50,000 or $100,000 check on my head, I couldn't think of anything I would want to run right out and buy. Weird, huh? No, not because I have every material thing I want, but because what I want more than anything right now is...

Peace.

Not necessarily world peace, although if I could buy that with my $50k, I'd certainly consider it. No, rather, I want some peace in my own little self-absorbed world. Financial peace, emotional peace, spiritual peace, professional peace. Some might even call it boredom! An absence of worry and fret.

What does this peace look like? Oh, it's little things, like figuring out what's wrong with my fancy printer, and teaching Baba not to jump on visitors. Bigger things like finally getting a squatter renter the hell out of my house without destroying it in the process, and getting the SWS bookstore back up and running. Really big things like not worrying about how the newly declared recession is going to affect my livelihood (and yours, my dear friends).

Don't get me wrong—I'm mature enough to know that today's stresses will be resolved...and then replaced with tomorrow's. But since it's Christmas... that's what I want.

The Realities of Today's Less-than-Vibrant Real Estate Market

I've been thinking (and writing) a lot lately about the realities of today's real estate market. While I'd love to be all Rah-Rah and Positive and Enthusiastic and Optimistic, I just don't think such emotions are necessarily warranted in many parts of the country. I'm lucky to work in a market (Denver) where real estate IS moving—there ARE buyers, there ARE sellers and there IS money to be made by the real estate community. In fact, I've even played in a few bidding war games the last several months.

But that doesn't mean I'm not worried or stressed, and so is everyone else I know whose livelihood depends on real estate closings. And I can't even imagine what it must be like to work in markets like Detroit, Tampa or Phoenix. Or, for that matter, to be a brand new green bean rookie agent.

Fact is, it's tough out there. Not impossible, but tough.

Don't get me wrong, I think this will pass and that there will be a tremendous backlog of business unleashed upon the agents who are still around. The Good Old Days will very likely return to some degree, hopefully sooner than later. But the challenge is to still BE around six months, a year, two years from now when those days are here again.

So, in my own self-interest, I've been examining some of my pet teachings to see if they still apply "as written" in this less-than-vibrant economy. I'm willing to make some changes to my business model in response to changing market conditions. But what changes exactly?

That'll be the theme of the next few blogs! Stay tuned!

Today's Market Realities, Part I: When to Venture out of Your Comfort Zone...and When to Stay in...

As promised, I'm writing a little series of blogs on how I'm coping with this... ahem...more challenging real estate market that may not be going away any time soon. Phooey on affirmations and positive thinking—let's get to WORK! (Okay, so there's nothing wrong with positive thinking—please continue to do it).

In the past, I've written about how it's just fine to stay in your comfort zone— especially if you're an introvert. My assertion has been that most of us are just fine the way we are—that we have plenty of skills and talents and wonderfulness about us that we can utilize in our business-building efforts, without doing something new and, well, scary.

Been thinking about this lately, especially with the dramatic decrease in the volume of business up for grabs in this less-than-vibrant real estate market.

When the pickin's are scarce, sometimes it's necessary to be a bit more aggressive to get your share of the available pie. Let's face it; in many markets there simply aren't that many buyers and sellers out there, so it's likely gonna take some extra effort to track down the ones who are.

For the Power Prospectors among us (which certainly doesn't include ME), this is no big deal. In fact, the PP's might actually enjoy the challenge. But what about us more Reluctant types? Those of us who shudder at the thought of chasing down our prey? Am I advising us to do it anyway? To ignore our fears, our hesitancies, perhaps even our conscience?

Probably, maybe and no.

Ignore your fears? Probably. Your hesitancies? Maybe. Your conscience? NO.

FEAR: Earlier this year I started speaking publicly, which terrified me at first, but I got over it and now I LOVE it. I conquered that FEAR by facing it and am a better person for it (and a bit wealthier since now people pay me to speak!).

HESITANCY: I have a HESITANCY of approaching FSBO's and Expired listings. I worry about making a fool of myself and dread the thought of being rejected, although I believe with all my heart and soul that I can help and might just be the best thing to ever happen to them. To date, my hesitancy to prospect to FSBO's and Expireds has kept me from doing it. I also HESITATE to spend any money on advertising, farming or web-lead purchase because I don't believe it's an effective use of my precious dollars. However, if you think it might work for you, there's certainly nothing wrong with such promotional activities.

CONSCIENCE: However, my CONSCIENCE will not allow me to do anything that resembles making a nuisance out of myself—that is, pestering my friends or pestering strangers with cold-calls, door-knocks or annoying pleas for referrals. No matter how desperate for business I might find myself, I will not subject other human beings on this planet to that desperation. That good old Golden Rule...don't do to someone else what you wouldn't want done to you...(and I tell ya, I despise telemarketers).

So, what's the punch line?

Well, that it may very well be necessary to step out of our comfort zones in order to survive this real estate market. However, that doesn't mean we have to abandon all our principles and throw ourselves on the altar of Old School sales philosophies.

When considering a new prospecting technique that you aren't terribly excited about...check with your gut. If your gut is just nervous because you haven't done it before, you might want to give that idea a shot. However, if your gut is telling you that it's wrong, then mark that particular idea off your list!

Seriously, Is It Time to Hit PAUSE on Your Real Estate Career?

While I don't advertise it, I do some one-on-one consulting for Very Special People. By Very Special People, I mean, people who buy into the Sell with Soul philosophy (yeah, I discriminate) and who are intelligent and self-aware enough to 1) be willing to play outside the box and forego traditional wisdom most of the time and 2) are willing, even eager to ask "How did I contribute to this problem" rather than simply whine about how everyone else on the planet sucks.

Anyway, wanna guess what the most common consultation I'm doing these days is? Seducing a Sphere of Influence? Nope. Writing a Non-Dorky Announcement or Reconnection letter? Nope. Getting a difficult listing sold? No again.

"I'm thinking of quitting. Can you help me decide?"

Sounds kind of grim, doesn't it? And, yeah, most agents who contact me with this question are, frankly, out of time. Either something has to happen RIGHT NOW or they're in deep doo-doo. Or, rather, deeper doo-doo.

What I'm about to say here may not be popular but the answer many of these consultees have gotten from me is: *"Yes, I suspect you need to quit, at least for now. Maybe not forever, but for now, it's probably the right thing."*

Are you asking yourself this question, or some version of it? You don't have to answer me out loud, but if you're at this point in your career, please don't be afraid to explore your options. There is NO SHAME in redirecting your career if that career is putting you and your family at risk of financial ruin. THIS IS A TOUGH BUSINESS! Yeah, we all know that, but sometimes we forget the reality of that statement. When something is "tough" that means a whole lot of people aren't going to make a go of it—maybe even you or me!

I'm not saying that giving up is the only option; of course it isn't. But it IS an option. Don't let your pride, ego or fantasies get in the way of making the right decision for you.

Christmas Card Lemons...to Lemonade

Am I the only idiot on the planet who can turn a simple Christmas Card mailing project into a full-time job? My plan...send out Christmas cards to my local Denver SOI (sphere of influence) and toss in my hot-off-the-press Referral Directory magnet as an extra-special holiday gift for my friends (hey, I sprung for the xtra large magnet at over $1 each!).

Simple enough...

Well, it's been anything but. One thing after another created delays in my sending-out-cards process—first, the cards I bought (and addressed & stamped) weren't big enough for the magnet (remember, I bought the xtra large one!), so I had to re-do all the envelopes. Then I realized that I needed extra postage for each envelope (that xtra large thing again), so I had to stand in line at the pre-Christmas shipping extravaganza at my local P.O. I finally got all the cards written, stuffed, addressed & stamped, so it was time to seal 'em up. I used cute little holiday-themed sticker-sealers I bought at Walmart so I wouldn't have to lick all those nasty envelopes.

Got the cards in the mail, marked that particular project off my list.

Couple of days later...empty cards started coming back. Apparently the cute little holiday-themed sticker-sealers weren't strong enough for the enclosed magnet (y'know, the xtra large one) and the magnets broke thru the seals and fell out.

SHEESH!!!!!

Anyway, where's the lemonade in this? Well, I sent out an email to my entire SOI telling them the story and asking them to let me know if their magnet didn't arrive. So far, I've gotten tons of responses back, wishing me well and letting me know their magnets made it (most of 'em anyway). In fact, this may turn out to be the best responded-to SOI email I've sent out in a long time!

To Present or Not to Present...I Have My Answer

You wanna know the top search term that brings new surfers to my website? Okay, there are two. The first is "New agent announcement letter." The second is "Sample listing presentation."

I offer a free sample listing presentation on my website if you join my VIP Lounge (that's free, too). Seems to be a popular item. I'm rather proud of my listing presentation—there's nothing boiler-plate or corporate about it—it's direct and to-the-point, conversational and informative. I've used it, or a similar version for years.

But over the last year or so I've been rethinking the idea of a formal listing presentation. I've been experimenting with not doing it and have walked away from my listing appointments much more pleased with myself. But I wasn't sure...for sure.

Well, this last week, I met with a real estate agent in Alabama to talk about selling one of my properties (the one where the squatter renter was FINALLY evicted!). She came to the house and asked me to show her around. She asked questions and actually listened to my (sometimes long-winded) answers. She took notes. As we toured, she casually mentioned other homes she'd seen or sold recently that were comparable to mine. Because she knew I was also in the business, she respectfully asked for my thoughts on a marketing strategy. And listened.

After I was done showing her the house and grounds, she said she wanted to go back to the office and do her homework, now that she'd seen the property. She'd be ready to present her findings the next day if that was okay with me. It was and she did and I hired her.

No presentation. No fancy graphs or charts. No bio, resume or testimonials. Just a subtly demonstrated knowledge of the marketplace, a sincere interest in my situation and a respectful acknowledgment of my intelligence and experience. Had she shown up with a 90-minute formal presentation of how wonderful she was, how awesome her company is and how dangerous it is to OVERPRICE, I'd have tuned her out within 5 minutes.

Do I know her marketing plan? Oops, no, not really. I suppose I could ask and maybe I should. But her non-salespitchy "presentation" made me trust her.

Now, truth be told, this sort of quiet confidence takes a while to develop. I certainly didn't have it my first year or even my second; maybe even my third. Well, heck, here I am in my 12th year just realizing that I don't need a fancy presentation!

I do believe that the process of creating a formal presentation is good for the soul—it helps you to figure out what you offer and why you're special, and for the times when a seller seems to want something in writing, you have it ready to go. I have much of my presentation available on my website, so sellers can check me out ahead of time or after they've met me.

But during that hour you're meeting with a seller for the first time, it's far more effective to just BE there with them...asking questions, listening to the answers and demonstrating your competence.

So...I have my answer. No More Listing Presentations for me!

Now THIS Is a Non-Dorky Business Card! (Well, it's dorky, but I love it!)

A couple of weeks ago, I had the privilege of having coffee with one of my readers. We talked about this and that...and that and this...and then he casually mentioned that he had created a "mock" business card that he "wished he could use in real life." When he showed it to me, I was floored—I think it's GREAT and that he should definitely use it in "real life"! He has the personality to pull it off and it definitely stands out from the crowd...

This picture *may* not be a true representation of the Agent. Most pictures don't look like the agents anyway. The agent listed below *may* even be better looking than the above picture.

KELLER WILLIAMS
NORTHWEST
CHANGING THE FACE OF COLORADO REAL ESTATE

Charlie Beninati

Broker Associate

Putting the fun back in the real estate experience!

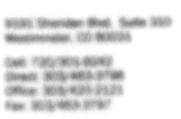

JANUARY 2009

Average "Days on Market"? Who CARES?

Why do we put such stock in the Average Days on Market (DOM) statistic in our MLS's? I suppose it might be meaningful if YOUR average DOM is much less than the overall DOM, but otherwise, I believe it's a totally meaningless number.

If I were to run a market analysis of all the 1920's Bungalows that have sold in my market (NW Denver) in the last three months...(okay, wait a sec, I'm going to do that right now...BRB).

Okay, I ran my analysis. The DOM of my subject search ranged from 2 days to 171 days. The average DOM was 53. However, out of 21 properties, seven sold in under a week (five of those in less than 3 days), eleven in less than three weeks, while five took more than 100 days to sell. Only three of the 21 properties had a DOM of anywhere close to 53.

So, when a seller asks me what the average Days on Market is in Northwest Denver, I tell them "*I don't know*" and explain why. I then explain why my goal is to sell their home in 30 days or less (obviously it's perfectly do-able in my market), and how I'm going to do that.

In Today's World...Sales Pitchee's Just Say No

I read somewhere (I believe it may have been in the book *Influence: The Psychology of Persuasion*) that human beings develop analytical short cuts in their brains in order to make judgments or decisions about new ideas or offerings that come their way. The example given was "You get what you pay for." Since we don't have the time or energy or even the desire to analyze every single product that is advertised to us, we make assumptions about the value or desirability of the product based on the price. Therefore, something that costs $9.99 (a too-good-to-be-true price) is not as good as a similar product that costs $99.95. While the $10 product may be every bit as effective as the $100 one, a vendor might actually sell more of his product if he increases the price, rather than put it on sale.

Interesting.

In 2009, we are overwhelmed by information and advertising. It comes at us from every direction and there's no way we can take it all in. Too many choices, too many options...to save our sanity we MUST develop an automatic evaluation method to avoid mental overload.

I'm realizing that if something comes at me as a sales pitch, I Just Say No. I'm paranoid enough, suspicious enough and been burned too many times by salespeople to give many the benefit of the doubt. I don't have time to check references or decipher trumped-up testimonials. If someone is trying to sell me something, my automatic evaluation system kicks in and I reject the sale.

I've found this to be true in my own world, with my own SWS "prospects." I get inquiries every day from people who want to interview me, who'd like a proposal for me to speak, who want to include my articles in their newsletter. They find me online or hear about me from others, and are intrigued. But I tell ya, the minute I approach someone and ask if they'd like to interview me, if they'd like a proposal for me to speak or would like me to submit articles for their newsletter, I almost ALWAYS get brushed off. Sometimes not even very politely! I approached a radio talk-show host once (he was just getting started, not some big shot) and he somewhat nastily accused me of just wanting to sell him something.

So, it appears that the way to sell something to someone is to let THEM find YOU. Create an attractive "product" and put it out there in the world for interested prospects to stumble onto.

I'm sure I didn't think this up all on my own, but I betcha' we'll see a massive paradigm shift AWAY from pursuit-oriented marketing TO attraction-based marketing. Might turn the sales-training world on its ear (which is a very good thing)!

Sales-y or Service-y?

If this blog goes where I think it's going, it might make me slightly less popular among the crowd...

A few months ago, I was interviewed about my views on the current state of the real estate industry. Blah Blah Blah, we covered all the generic, pithy topics and then moved onto some juicier ones. Yeah!

The interviewer asked me, *"What do you think it will take to turn the public's perception from thinking of us on the same level as used car salesmen and politicians, to thinking of us as trusted advisors?"*

Great question. I'd never been asked that before, so I took a moment to think. And the answer hit me like a load of used cars.

If we want to shift the public perception away from thinking of us as people who just want to sell someone something, with as little effort as possible, we need to attract a different kind of practitioner.

A career selling real estate is much like a career as a financial planner, an insurance salesperson or a mortgage broker. Most people enter these fields, not because they have a passion for property, mutual funds, long-term care insurance or good faith estimates, but because they are drawn to the idea of working on commission, hopefully significant commission. They are, basically, natural salespeople in search of a product to sell.

Nothing wrong with that. Selling for a living can be an honorable profession if it's done ethically.

But the perception of the real estate agent as a salesperson will forever lump us in with other people who sell, and will always be held in general suspicion. No way around that—when you're paid on commission, our clients and customers are always going to wonder if we have their best interests at heart.

Especially if they aren't nearly as blown away by our service as they were by our sales pitch.

So, if we want to change the public's perception of us, we need to change our approach, which possibly means a change in our compensation structure. Are we ready for this? I don't know, frankly. I like being paid on commission as much as the rest of you do, and I love the idea that working harder and smarter brings more money in the door. But is there a compromise? A way to satisfy our entrepreneurial needs for performance-based pay without sacrificing the perception that our integrity might be for sale?

Do we care? Or, are we okay with remaining in that bottom five of the infamous list of America's most UNtrusted professions?

FEBRUARY 2009

Following is a little series I did on the basics of a sphere of influence business model. Enjoy!

SOI 101—What Exactly Is an SOI (Sphere of Influence) Business Model?

A Sphere of Influence business model is a strategy that focuses on attracting business to you from the people you know and the people you meet socially, as opposed to pursuing business from strangers. It's possible to run a 100% SOI business and never have to make one cold-call, memorize a prospecting script or knock on a stranger's door!

There are three primary activities in an effective SOI business model.

Nurturing the personal relationships you already have within your social network (that is, your friends—I call this group my "Group One." Clever, eh?); and

Staying in touch with "everyone else" (that is, the people you know who aren't your friends—I call them my Group Two); and

Meeting new people.

Before you panic and say that you don't have the time, money or energy to do all this socializing, don't! Running an SOI business is much less time-consuming and less expensive than just about any other systematized prospecting method, and can be far more effective, more quickly. In fact, if you spend a few years creating your personal cheering section, you can pretty much coast through the rest of your real estate career. That's what I did and in my last five years I rarely worked more than 30 hours a week and my marketing budget was practically zero. My phone rang, I answered it, and whaddya' know? I had a new client.

Nurturing the personal relationships you already have
From a philosophical perspective, this means to ensure that the people in your social network (AKA Group One) know that you care about them. In a practical sense, it means that you strive to have a personal conversation with everyone in your social network as often as you can, at least once a quarter. A personal conversation can be a face to face lunch or coffee date, a phone call or even an email exchange. What it's not is a concerted effort to abuse your friends with

a sales pitch. Always approach your social network as a friend first, and a real estate agent second, or third, or fourth. Not the other way around.

Staying in touch with Everyone Else
Staying in touch with your "Everyone Else" group (AKA Group Two) just means that you keep your name in front of this crowd with periodic interesting, relevant, non-salesy written communications, delivered both through snail-mail and email. As long as your mailings are consistent and intelligent, you'll see a significant number of sales from even this minimal effort.

Meeting new people
An important part of an effective SOI model is to add to your Groups One and Two, especially in today's market where there is admittedly less business to go around. The more people you know, who know you, and think you're a generally cool person, the more that telephone will ring.

Running an effective SOI business model isn't nearly as complicated as some would have you believe. Yes, it takes some organization and commitment upfront, and an ongoing effort to stay in touch with the people you know and the people you meet, but once it's rolling and you're in the SOI habit, it won't feel like work at all! In fact, it might even feel suspiciously like FUN! And "the more fun you have selling real estate, the more real estate you will sell!"

SOI 102—The SECRET to a Successful Real Estate Sphere of Influence Business Model

The secret to running a successful SOI-based business is to be a great real estate agent who loves her job and knows her market and stays in touch with the people she knows, without ever pestering them for business or referrals.

That's it! That's the secret! To be a great real estate agent who loves her job and knows her market and stays in touch with the people she knows, without ever pestering them for business or referrals.

Let's take these items one by one.

You're a great real estate agent
This is huge. When I say that you need to be a great real estate agent, I don't mean that you need to be a great real estate prospector, even though that's what most of our training tends to imply. I mean that you take great care of your clients as your first priority, not as an afterthought when your prospecting

is done. Doing business this way helps you on so many levels. First, obviously, you'll have happy clients who will be delighted to refer you to everyone they know. Second and third, you'll be proud of the work you do and confident in the work you do, which will lead to the second requirement...

You love your job

When you're good at what you do and you know it, you'll probably absolutely love your job. And that excitement and enthusiasm is contagious to those around you.

When you're able to hold your head up high and announce that, *"I'm a Real Estate Agent and it's the Coolest Job in the World!"* people will be drawn to you—as one agent I know puts it, they want some of what you're smoking! When the topic of real estate comes up in a social setting and you're able to say those magic words "I'm a real estate agent and it's the coolest job in the world!" people will ask YOU for your business card. It's beautiful.

Which leads me to the third requirement:

You know your market

The best way I've found to build rapport with strangers is be master of your market. If you know your local real estate market, and you KNOW you know your local real estate market, you'll find opportunities to share that knowledge all over the place.

It's amazing how much confidence this gives you and it's pretty easy, to strike up a conversation with a total stranger about real estate...if you know what you're talking about. You'd be surprised how many people will ask YOU for your business card if you sound like an expert. I get a lot of my business this way—not from prospecting to strangers, but just from being confident about my competence—a big part of which is a good understanding of my market.

So, if an agent needs to build an SOI from scratch, he needs to spend some quality time learning his market and then putting himself in social situations where he can share his knowledge with people who are interested.

You stay in touch with the people you know

This, of course, is really important. If you know a whole bunch of people, but you never make any effort to have a personal interaction with any of them (above and beyond drip campaigns), your sphere of influence efforts will crash and burn. To be someone's favorite real estate agent, you either need to have done a fantastic job for them in the past (and stayed in touch) or make an effort to be in touch with them on a somewhat regular basis. Especially if someone hasn't used your services before, it's really easy for another agent to swoop in and take your place!

Just know that, yes, if you intend to generate business and referrals from the people you know, you will need to take time to talk to them.

You never pester anyone for business or referrals
The last requirement is that you never pester the people you know or the people you meet for business or referrals. This is a tough pill to swallow for many agents. We're trained to ask for business and to make sure that everyone we know and meet is aware that **we are desperate for business**. I know, that's not what we say—but it's how it comes across. When we constantly or even sporadically remind the people we know that We Love Referrals, we send a message that is counterproductive to our goal of actually generating referrals.

Sooooooo....Are you a great agent? Do you love your job? And know your market? And do you stay in touch with the people you know without ever pestering them for business or referrals? Yeah? Then get off the computer and go SOI!

SOI 103—"My Daughter's Best Friend's Parents Just Hired Another Real Estate Agent!"

"Dear Jennifer,

Got up this morning and saw that my daughter's best friend's parents listed with someone else! They've been on my mailing list and their daughter and my daughter have been best friends since grade school. I'm crushed. Should I continue to send them things or take them off my list?"

Jane"

I get these letters all the time—people who have embraced my Sphere of Influence (SOI) philosophy and then feel kicked in the teeth when someone in their SOI hires another real estate agent. They almost seem angry at me for leading them to believe that they could count on the loyalty of everyone in their contact database!

Well, first, I always give permission to my friends to feel really really bummed for an hour or two. If they're brand new in the business, they can even fret overnight about it. It's a natural reaction, and even I'm not immune to it. We tend to think that anyone we've ever breathed on is obligated to use us to sell their home, as long as we made sure they had our business card in their possession. Heck, just last week, I went out for drinks with a new friend and found out just that day she'd listed her house with someone else! The nerve! Yeah, I was a little flustered by that, I can admit.

But here's the thing...or things.

First, in the vast majority of time, when people make a business decision that adversely affects you, it has NOTHING TO DO with you at all. It's not personal—not one little bit. I'm rather thin-skinned, so I find myself hurt all the time by perceived slights, only to find out later that the "slight" was completely, utterly 100% reasonable.

When someone in your SOI chooses someone else to work with, it's almost a certainty that their decision made sense to them and had nothing whatsoever to do with their feelings for you. In fact, it's likely they didn't even think of you when making their decision—yes, the people in our world have their own lives to lead and aren't particularly concerned about ours.

However, if you truly believe that the hiring decision was personal, then you need to ask yourself why that might be so...and it's not likely that it's because the other guy is an idiot or a meanie. There's something about your relationship with them that led them to believe you were not the best (wo)man for the job. But if the extent of that relationship is a series of postcard mailings and an annual calendar, then it's quite possible another agent is higher on their friendship priority list than you are.

Should my friend continue to stay in touch with her daughter's best friend's parents? Sure! It's possible that they won't be happy with their choice in agent and might someday start fishing around for my friend's card when the listing expires. But they definitely won't do that if my friend acts at all miffed or unprofessional about it.

An SOI philosophy does work. 100% of the time? Uh, no. Not even close. But when it doesn't, yes, you have my permission to pout about it for a little while!

SOI 104: "I Think I've Blown It with My Sphere of Influence. Can I Recover Their Support?"

"Dear Jennifer,

I've been reading your blogs about SOI and my heart is sinking. I think I've blown it with my Sphere of Influence by constantly asking them for business and referrals. Is there a way I can redeem myself with my friends, or do I have to go make all new ones?

Bill"

I get this question a lot! Mostly from new or newer agents who have been brainwashed into believing that an SOI business model means that they're supposed to drive their friends nutso with constant reminders of their love for referrals. Most tell me that:

1) they felt it was wrong, but were convinced to do it anyway, and/or

2) they've felt their friends pull away and suspect they're avoiding the agent's calls.

Oops. Not at all good for business OR your social life!

Here's what I tell these distressed agents.

There are a couple of things they can do. If it suits their personality, they can address it head-on with an apology letter—very sincere, not too sappy, but friendly & apologetic, with a "let's move on" tone. I'm not convinced this is the best line of attack, but it might be effective if done well.

Of course, then the agent needs to follow it up with action: he needs to BE a non-referral-begging friend who happens to be a real estate agent. Coffee dates, casual emails, dinner parties—whatever socializing feels comfortable with the various members of his SOI. Oh, and he doesn't mention his real estate career unless it's appropriate, but strives to come across as a happy, enthusiastic, reliable, dependable, generally cool person who is probably a fabulous real estate agent, as well.

If the apology letter doesn't feel right, then he can just make a concerted effort to reconnect with his SOI, as above, and if the opportunity arises and it feels appropriate, give a little apology in person.

The other thing he can do is strive to build his SOI by meeting new people and NEVER breathing a hint of referral-begging with them. He can meet new people thru his existing SOI and by being out there in the world with his antenna up. I consider my SOI strategy to be more about meeting people THRU my SOI, not necessarily generating business directly from the people I know.

Of course, the best approach is to not annoy one's friends in the first place, so that there's no need for apologies or redeeming one's dignity after the fact!

MARCH 2009

I'm Sure She Didn't Mean It This Way...or Did She?

Trying to be a good little SOI'er, I contacted someone today who had been referred to me by a friend of hers to inquire about the service she provides. I called her up, introduced myself, reminding her that we'd met a few months ago at a party of our mutual friend, and indicated an interest in hiring her.

She clearly had her lecture spiel down pat. She proceeded to inform me that she works by appointment only, because she's awfully busy. She detailed the hoops I'd need to jump thru in order to be accepted as a client. She described the situations under which I would not be accepted as a client. And then she reiterated that because she's so busy, she really needed to get off the phone because someone (more important than I) was waiting for her.

No problem, lady. There are plenty of other people in Denver who do what you do. I'll just go annoy them with my business.

But, being the obsessive blogger that I am, I couldn't help but compare this experience to real estate. This kinda sounds like how many in our ranks treat their new prospects, doesn't it?

Introverts, Always Ask "What's in It For Me?" (and no, that's not a typo)

As much as I'd like to claim that I'm always looking out for the other guy, and always put my friends' and clients' needs ahead of my own...well...I just can't say that with a straight face. I can be awfully lazy at times (quite often, actually) and would much rather do exactly what I wanna do and the rest of my world be da*ned!

But...unfortunately, when you're self-employed, that's probably not the best approach to life. Because y'know what? In our industry, every warm body on the planet has the potential to bring you a $10,000 paycheck and there's no way of telling who that next $10k paycheck will come from. Blow someone off 'cause you're feeling lazy and you might just have blown that week's (or month's) opportunity for The Big One.

So, lately, when I'm asked for a favor, or even to go out socially (as an intro-vert, I'm not always in the mood) and I'm inclined to decline, I back off and ask myself, "What's in this for me?" And y'know what? I can almost always think of something "in it" for me, above and beyond the potential to have fun, eat some good food or drink good wine or even meet my next $10k client. I hesitate to give you any of my recent examples because they are SO DARN SELF-SERVING, I'm almost embarrassed.

But does it really matter what my motivation is, as long as I do the right thing?

So, give it a try. Next time you're tempted to decline an invitation or say NO to a favor asked of you, take a moment to be selfish and ask "what's in it for me if I do this?" If you truly can't think of anything, you have my permission to stay home! But I'll bet you'll find that more often than not...there IS something in it for you that makes it worth doing!

The Rookie Agent Learning Curve...Elongated?

We all talk about how tough a new agent's rookie year is, but once they've survived those 12 months, they're good to go. And in the old days, I would agree. I sold 25 houses in 1997, 35 in 1998 and close to 50 in 1999. So, by the end of my third year, I'd sold over 100 homes and most of my surviving rookie friends (the ones who started the same time as me and were still in the game) had similar track records. I think it's safe to say that once you've sold 100 houses, you probably have a pretty good idea what you're doing (although every day almost always STILL gives me a learning experience or two!)

But the rookies and first-year agents I've been talking to lately have a much different experience. Most sell fewer than 5 houses their first year and maybe double that in their second.

I met with a third-year agent the other day who has only sold 19 houses in his career and seems moderately happy with that. What struck me about this third-year agent was how inexperienced he came across—I was trying to help him negotiate multiple offers on his listing and was stunned at his level of (how else can I say it?), incompetence. He'd never heard of a back-up offer or understood the issues that might arise with an FHA loan on a fix-up property. He thought he was supposed to take down his For Sale sign and lockbox as soon as his listing went under contract. He hadn't yet selected a title company to work with. He didn't know that he had to change the status from "Active" to "Under Contract" in the MLS within 24 hours of accepting a contract.

I can see how a brand new agent wouldn't know any of these things and you don't call that incompetence—you call it inexperience (and hope she has good broker guidance). But all of these things were issues I learned about in my first year—and by my third year, heavens, this was kindergarten-level stuff! But it all seemed new to him.

First and second year agents—how comfy do you feel in your real estate agent skin and at what point did you start to feel that you could handle pretty much anything tossed your way? Or DO you feel that way yet? Old Fogies—is my experience unique? Or did our "generation" have a better opportunity to get up to speed faster?

New Real Estate Agents—Get Help if You Need It... Yes, Even if...

The new agent asks: *"Will it damage my credibility to have my broker involved in my first listing?"*

Yes, it might. Do it anyway.

There are variations on this theme—such as when a new agent objects to sharing his first few commissions with a mentor, or an experienced agent refuses to get help on his first short sale listing or commercial deal. After all, in today's market especially, we NEED every last penny of that commission!

But that's not really the point, is it?

We real estate agents charge a lot of money for what we do. Part of our fees includes a level of expertise that our clients have every right to expect from us. It's not their job to teach us our craft; no, that's OUR job—to learn it so we can be the experts our clients need us to be. Even if "learning it" takes money out of our pockets.

So, if you aren't yet the expert, it's simply the right thing to do to bring on someone who is. Yes, whether you've been selling real estate for weeks or decades. We owe it to our future adoring fans to take great care of them!

Real Estate Agents—A Better Approach to: "I Return Calls Between x and y..."

"Hi, this is John and you've reached my voicemail. Your call is important to me and I return my calls between 1:00 and 2:00 and 5:00 and 6:00. Please leave a message and I'll call you back during those hours."

The first time I heard this outgoing voicemail message I didn't realize it was a script from a program; I just knew I didn't like it. Why? I'm not sure, really—the closest I can come is that I almost felt scolded, as if I called at an inopportune time and should have known better. Or like it was a power play or something.

Okay, yeah, I'm a bit sensitive.

Anyway, I suddenly started hearing this outgoing message all over the place and figured out that it was part of a program that apparently lots of people had signed up for.

Fair enough. Whatever works.

I never warmed up to it. Oh, I know what the point is—it gives your callers an expectation of when you'll call back, provides structure for your day and demonstrates that you're a busy person. All good things, I suppose.

But what if you stated your "I return phone calls" message and then strived to return your calls earlier, thus making your callers feel special! One of my lenders does this and it actually does the trick—instead of feeling relegated to the to-do-at-4pm pile, I feel as if MY phone call was actually important to him!

IMO, it's a terrible business strategy to intentionally do something that might make your clients or prospects feel anything less than your Number One priority. Are they? Of course not, but every person on the planet longs to feel special, longs to feel important and if you can make that happen for them, there might be a future referral in it for ya (and you won't even have to beg for it)!

APRIL 2009

The Rookie Series—Ten Secrets to Looking as if You've Done This Before!

A little disclaimer...despite the catchy title of the series; I'm not going to tell rookies how to trick their clients or prospects into believing that they're a competent real estate agent, capable of handling someone's real estate needs, so that they'll allow the rookie to practice on them and learn what he's doing. Nope. What I am going to cover is how to BE a competent real estate agent who IS capable of handling someone's real estate needs, so that the rookie will have the confidence to sell himself to prospects and, yes, get the experience he needs.

But I will never, ever ever advise anyone to "Fake it til you Make it" as a business philosophy. Will it happen? Oh yeah, it'll happen every day, this year, next year and for years after that. I've been selling real estate for a dozen years now and I still have to bluff my way through situations on a regular basis. But that's actually one of the topics covered—HOW to do that, without jeopardizing your credibility or your license.

Here are the Ten Secrets According to JA:

1. Know Your Systems

2. Practice with Your Printer (sounds silly, I know)

3. Preview, Preview, Preview

4. Drive Your Route Ahead of Time

5. Cheerfully Waste Your Time

6. Find Your Handyman

7. Let Your Seller Prospect Do Most of the Talking

8. Get Comfy with Your Commission

9. Admit that You're New

10. Know what to say when you don't know the answer

Stay tuned...

The Confident Rookie Series—SECRET ONE: Master Your Systems BEFORE You Need Them!

How comfy are you with your systems? Specifically, your MLS and your contract software? For me, if I'm not proficient with the tools of my trade, it's easy for me to shy away from using them. Well, in OUR trade, shying away from using the MLS or your contract software is pretty much fatal to your chances of bringing in a paycheck.

Last year, after two years away from the trenches, I re-activated my real estate license. The RE/MAX office I re-joined had a new fancy-schmantzy contract software program I'd never used before. Well, the heavens smiled on me and I got a buyer off my blog literally the first day back. We went out looking at houses and they found one they liked and wanted to make an offer.

YIPES! I had no idea how to even fire up the program, much less navigate through it, so...get this...I put them off with some stupid excuse until two days later so I could get a crash course on the software. But even with the crash course, I was a bit of a basket-case writing up the offer, from a technology perspective.

For a new agent, I imagine this would be doubly or triply unnerving! At least I'd actually gone through a purchase contract with a buyer a couple hundred times, so I wasn't nervous about that...but the actual technology of it just about shut me down.

So, the first step is admitting you have a problem. When you run an MLS search for a buyer, do you trust your results? When you're looking for comparables to price a home for a prospective seller, are you sure you found them all? No? Then practice practice practice. And get some training, either from the local MLS provider/board or from another agent in the office. Do 5 practice market analyses on 5 office listings. Do a CMA on your own house. Search for homes Just Like Yours and go preview them.

If you use contract software (as opposed to handwriting your contracts), GET SOME TRAINING. These systems are not intuitive and you'll be a basket-case like I was if you're sitting down with a buyer to write an offer and can't figure out how to print it out. Or how to auto-populate the fields from contract to contract. These programs are typically pretty powerful and can do a lot of things for you...LEARN THEM.

Yeah, yeah, I know that Learning your Systems isn't nearly as sexy as learning how to prospect, but unless you're a master fake-it-til-you-make-it-er, those prospects you bring in won't be worth much to you without a decent knowledge of your systems.

The Confident Rookie Series—SECRET TWO: Practice with Your Printer!

Picking up from the previous blog about how important it for rookies to Master Their Systems before they need them; today I'll add just a little bit more to that project.

Practice with Your Printer. This may sound silly, but when you're writing an offer for a buyer, it's nerve-wracking if you can't get the printer to work. Seriously.

I wrote my very first offer back in 1996 at 6:00pm on a Friday night in my new real estate office. I called my broker away from Happy Hour to help me (yep, he was a bit looped). I'd had training on the contract software and was pretty comfy with it, but had never actually printed a contract.

Using my own brand new contract software (registered under my name & all!), I created the contract with my broker's help, and then went to print it out. Oops. Great big DRAFT watermark across every page. Hmmmmmm. Tried again. Same thing. My buyer was sitting in the conference room waiting for me, but neither I nor my broker could figure out what was wrong. And, being Friday night, there wasn't much chance of finding any customer service at the software company.

I was a mess and felt like an idiot. I ended up re-writing the entire contract on pre-printed forms and life went on. Turns out that I needed some activation code to remove the DRAFT watermark.

But there are all sorts of things that can go wrong when printing from new software, aren't there? Especially if you're in a networked real estate office.

So, as you're practicing with your contract software, be sure to also practice printing out the contracts. Please don't hesitate to waste paper. If your software requires legal paper, be sure you know where it is and how to load it. If you have the option of either legal or letter, be sure you know how to select the one you want. Know how to "insert" or "remove" n/a's and such.

And...always have a back-up plan. Here's mine:

Plan A: Business as usual—use the regular office printer

Plan B: If that fails, try the other printer at the office (we have two)

Plan C: If both of those fail, email the contract to the receptionist to print out

Plan D: If I'm really crashing & burning, know where the pre-printed contracts are and write it up manually.

Again, I know this sounds trivial and even silly, but just wait until YOUR buyer is sitting in the conference room waiting to sign his offer and you can't produce anything for him to sign!

The Confident Rookie Series—SECRET THREE: Don't Wing It with Your New Buyer!

Before you go out with a buyer for the first time, preview every single house you're considering showing him or her. I promise you, you'll rule out more than half of them and will be relieved that you did. If you show a typical buyer a house that shows poorly, smells funny or has a crazy floorplan, he'll figure you don't know what you're doing, because buyers think we know every house in town.

Even with interior photos and google earth and virtual tours, you cannot properly evaluate a house without going to see it. I mean, think about it—if a house has a major flaw, do you think the listing agent is going to spell it out for you in the MLS description? Or make sure that it's highlighted in the photos? Uh, no.

As a new agent, making a habit to preview-before-showing will give you tremendous confidence as you work with your new buyers. You'll look far more experienced and self-assured, and won't be caught off-guard by a mis-advertised or fatally flawed property.

Oh, and you'll also ensure that you don't get lost with your buyer in the car! More on that next.

The Confident Rookie Series—SECRET FOUR:
Drive Your Route Ahead of Time

Today's Confident Rookie Secret is to ALWAYS drive your route before meeting with a buyer. It's mortifying to get lost with a buyer in the car and even worse if they're following behind you. Unless you're showing in a neighborhood you know intimately, always always always drive the route ahead of time, even if that's at 6am before you meet your buyer at 9am.

Driving Your Route is not the same as Previewing. When you preview, you're ruling out properties—you might start with a list of 12 or 15 homes and narrow it down to the best 7 or so. Therefore, your previewing route will not be the same as your showing route.

A GPS is not the answer. You need to be able to get from house to house smoothly and effortlessly, as if you know every thoroughfare and side street in town...without that nice Garmin lady interrupting your conversation every 30 seconds. Of course, a printout of Mapquest Directions is even worse! Being able to talk with your buyers as you navigate from house to house will do wonders for your air of professionalism. And of course, becoming increasingly frazzled as you make u-turns and wrong turns will have the opposite effect!

Sometimes you don't have much time between making the appointment and the appointment itself, so you might be tempted to rationalize that you simply don't have the opportunity to Drive Your Route. But I promise you— you'll wish you'd made the time. I've gotten up at 4am and hit the streets at 5am to ensure I didn't make a fool of myself (and I've been doing this almost 13 years!). The good news is that there's much less traffic at 5am!

Remember, the goal of these Ten Secrets is to give the rookie real estate agent the tools to look and feel confident and knowledgeable in situations he or she may not have been in before. We can't prepare you for every single contingency, but the more you are prepared for the aspects you can control, the less stress you'll put on your antiperspirant!

The Confident Rookie Series—SECRET FIVE: Cheerfully Waste Your Time

Regular readers of my blog know how I feel about wasting time. I'm all for it! Especially for rookies. This is one of the main reasons I'm opposed to rookies jumping into the business only half-way (that is, part time). When you have to carefully guard your time, you can't risk wasting any of it...and that's a shame.

Even as an almost-thirteen-year agent, I still cheerfully "waste my time" every chance I get.

Huh?

I mean that you should take every opportunity to be out there in the world talking about or looking at or learning more about real estate. If you are doing something that accomplishes one of these items, that's time well-spent, even if the activity is not leading you directly to a paycheck. Not only are you learning more about being a real estate agent, you're also putting yourself in front of people who could end up being your biggest fans.

When you're new, take every opportunity to learn something, even if it takes time, even if it takes gas. Think about it—would you rather practice on someone who may NOT buy or sell right away, or someone who will? Sure, on the surface, you'd rather work with someone who is leading you to a paycheck, but there's certainly a strong argument for perfecting your technique on non-clients first!

So, what might be some "time-wasters" to embrace?

- ☐ Showing an office listing to an already-represented buyer who calls off the sign?

- ☐ Helping a friend protest her tax assessment by providing sold data?

- ☐ Helping a friend protest a low appraisal for a refinance?

- ☐ Meeting with a potential seller when you know full well he isn't going to hire you?

- ☐ Showing homes to a buyer who can't yet qualify to buy a home, but thinks he can in six months?

- ☐ Helping a relocating renter identify the right neighborhood for him or her?

All of these activities teach you more about your market and give you practice communicating market data to potential clients. They also give you an opportunity to impress someone who might end up being your biggest client and/or referral source. Sounds like a good use of time to me...

The Confident Rookie Series—SECRET SIX: Find Your Handyman

One of the very first things I advise rookie agents to do—well, at least in their first few months—is to find a handyman. A good handyman will save your backside and your commission over and over again and make you look good. I don't know how any real estate agent functions without a handyman on call. Find him, give him work, make sure he's paid promptly. Bob is my handyman and he's saved more of my deals than I can count.

How can a handyman help you look more experienced? Well, just the knowledge that you have someone on your team who can take care of home repairs for your buyer or seller gives you a Can-Do attitude. For example, when I work with buyers who are nervous about all the little maintenance items their inspector points out, I sweetly tell them, "We'll just put that on the Bob-List" so they know they won't have to go to the yellow pages. When your sellers get a laundry list of repairs after the inspection, I comfort them by explaining that we'll have Bob come over and give us an estimate (today). When I'm helping a seller get ready for market, I look like the hero when I bring Bob in to get done in a day what would take the seller a month to do...and usually for under $1000 (less than a mortgage payment!)

How do you find a handyman? Put up your antenna! Ask other agents in the office. Send out an email to your Sphere of Influence. Call some property management companies. If you know anyone in construction, ask them. Ask at Home Depot. When you get a few names, give 'em a test drive in your own home.

FIND YOUR BOB.

The Confident Rookie Series—SECRET SEVEN:
Let Your Seller Prospect Talk!

New agents are always nervous before their first listing appointment. Probably before their second, third, tenth & twelfth, too. It does get easier, I promise, but here are some tips for getting through those nerve-wracking firsts...

My absolute best advice to first-time listing appointment-ers is to LET THE SELLER DO MOST OF THE TALKING! Seriously!

Two reasons for this.

First, this seller has probably already endured two or three sales-pitches from other real estate agents who barely took a breath to let him talk. They very likely didn't express much of an interest in him and his situation—they just directed his focus to their fancy-schmantzy listing presentation. Have you ever sat through one of those? BORING. I'd tune it out in about five minutes if I were a seller.

Second, you need to know as much as you can about the seller's situation and motivation before you can properly advise him. Heck, you need to know this stuff before you can decide if you even want the listing! So, besides the fact that the seller will love you if you let him talk more than you do, it also gives you the opportunity to better understand if, and how you can best help.

So, here's what to do when you get to the house. Have the seller show you around, ask questions, take notes, and really listen to the seller's answers. If this is the first time you've seen the inside of the seller's house, you can't really be expected to tell him what it's worth—you have to go home and do your homework. Nothing wrong with that. But the more you listen and show interest, the more that seller will be impressed with you! LISTEN, and the seller will trust you. Leave your sales pitch in the car.

That said, you do need to be prepared with a marketing plan in case the seller asks for one. You might be surprised how often they won't, but if they do, it's probably a good idea to have an answer. This is where the process of putting together a formal listing presentation is helpful. It forces you to figure out what the heck you ARE going to do to get that house sold and what services you'll offer.

The Confident Rookie Series—SECRET EIGHT: Get Comfy with Your Commission

Most new agents are terrified about the prospect of discussing their commission with a potential seller. If this is the case for you, you're going to need to be 100% comfortable with the commission fee you're going to propose. If you aren't, you're dead meat. If you have concerns that you're overcharging for your value, it will be crystal clear to the seller prospect. In my first year, almost all of my listings were taken at a very low percentage because that's all I thought I was worth, due to my inexperience. As my experience and expertise grew, I became more comfortable proposing (and sticking to) a higher fee.

I'm not being real helpful yet, am I? On one hand, I'm shooting down your confidence, yet, on the other, I'm telling you that you must HAVE confidence to negotiate effectively! Well, that's the cold hard truth. But I won't leave you hanging...here's what to do.

You need to convince yourself that you're worth it before you can ever convince a seller.

On your first few listings, commit to yourself that you will go way above and beyond what is typically expected of a listing agent in your area. Commit to yourself that you WILL earn your fee, if not with your experience, with your enthusiasm and effort. Spend your own money marketing your listing if you have a great idea that you think might work. Spend as much time as you need to properly price the house. Do open houses all weekend long. Pay for a home-stager to consult with your seller. Include a home warranty. Be willing to bring in help if you'll need it—even if you have to pay for it.

In short, take this opportunity not only to blow the sox off your seller, but to actually experiment with various listing techniques to see what actually works. If, at the end of the day, you spend your whole paycheck on your experiments, that's really okay! The lessons you learned and the impression you made on that seller will serve you well in your future...and pay you back many times over.

The Confident Rookie Series—SECRET NINE: Admit that You're New

A lot of new agents worry about being taken advantage of by experienced agents, if the experienced agent were to find out that they're new. So the obvious solution is to pretend that they aren't new, right?

Unfortunately, no. The thing is—if you're new, it will almost certainly be obvious to the agent on the other side of the table, whether you own up to it or not. And the more you try to fake experience, the more obvious it will be. When I'm on the other side of a transaction from a rookie agent who is trying to pretend she knows what she's doing, she almost always embarrasses herself. However, if the rookie agent tells me upfront that she's in her first year and to bear with her if she goes overboard crossing her t's and dotting i's...I'm a lot more willing to make the experience pleasant for her.

And I think you'll find more agents with this mindset than not. Yes, there are some amazingly jerky people in our business and if you happen to run into one of them early in your career, they may very well make that transaction miserable for you...but the good news is that—think about it—you'll only have a handful of "first deals" so chances are good you'll have a decent agent on the other side. Just be upfront with them about your lack of experience, confidently, and they may even go out of their way to help you. The same goes for inspectors, appraisers, attorneys, closers and lenders.

However, what if you do run into a jerk on your first or second sale? I did—my third sale actually—and 12 years later I still remember him vividly. He was abusive and condescending and said some pretty nasty things to me—you can read about him in Chapter Eleven of *Sell with Soul*. And he did intimidate me to the point of embarrassing myself in front of my client. Turned out that he later checked into a mental facility for "anger issues."

An abusive agent is going to abuse everyone he comes in contact with—it's not just you and it's not personal. He'd abuse me, he'd abuse Johnny and he probably abuses his mortgage brokers and title reps on a regular basis. Keep your cool, follow your instincts and you'll get thru it.

But this doesn't mean that your inexperience as a new agent won't be used against you, even by a nice-guy opposing agent. That other agent has a duty to represent his client's best interests, so don't believe for a second he's going to help you negotiate against him or his client. If you don't know how to help your buyer determine if a listing is overpriced, if you don't know how to get your buyer what he wants at the inspection, if you don't know how to appeal a low appraisal, the other agent will definitely take advantage of you. It's his job.

So if something sounds fishy to you—AT ALL—ask for help from someone in your office. Even if it doesn't sound fishy, have someone review what you've done...or better yet, what you're getting ready to do before you do it!

The Confident Rookie Series—SECRET TEN: What to Say When You Don't Know the Answer

A few weeks ago, a newer agent came into my office all flustered. He'd been out with his buyers over the weekend and felt that he'd made a fool of himself by not being able to intelligently answer his buyers' questions. It almost sounded as if he was ready to throw in the towel—at least until he knew more about what he was doing!

Calm down, I told him. First, trust that it will happen to you thru-out your career. Don't panic. Don't make stuff up, but don't panic.

I asked him what the questions were that he couldn't answer. And guess what? Most of the questions were really good ones—that is—chances are that even a more experienced agent wouldn't have known the answers either! But the problem with being new is that you don't know what you SHOULD know and so you figure you should know it all.

This is where not panicking comes in.

Take a deep breath and really think about the question. Is this something you should or could know?

For example, let's say you're showing lofts downtown and the buyer asks: "*What are the pet restrictions in this building?*" Well, unless you live in the building yourself or unless you make a habit of memorizing condo rules & regulations, you couldn't possibly know the answer. Or how about if a buyer asks you where the property lines are on a rural property? If you aren't the listing agent, this is probably not something you can accurately answer.

This doesn't mean it's not your job to get the answer—it is. But if you don't know the answer off the top of your head, it's okay!

So, how do you respond?

First, DO NOT use those tired old words *"I don't know the answer, but I can certainly find out for you!"* in that prissy, almost defensive voice. You know what I'm talking about, don't you? That cheerful, oh-so-helpful voice that clearly tells your client that you don't have a clue, but wish you did?

Instead, try this. Relax, and VERY casually say, *"Hmmmm, I don't know. Lemme find out."* Write it down, and move on.

Or, how about this? *"Wow—I've never gotten that question before. I'm looking forward to finding out the answer!"* Write it down, and move on.

Or, in the above scenarios when you're working with a buyer and he has questions about the property you're looking at, take control and call the listing agent immediately. That will make a great impression on the buyer.

Of course, sometimes you'll be asked a question you should know the answer to and you don't. This is happening to me more often lately as I venture deeper into the world of foreclosures & short sales. My stock answer has become *"Y'know, I should know the answer to that, but I don't. I'll find out for you."* This somewhat self-deprecating approach seems to be working—at least no one's fired me yet for saying it!

Getting Busy? Seize This Opportunity to Care for Your Clients!

A lot of agents I'm talking to are seeing a glimmer of hope—that is—they're busy! The phone is ringing! The email's jangling! Listing contracts are being signed and buyers are getting approved! Woo hoo!

I always say that when you're busy and feeling like hot stuff, go look for more. You have momentum, you have MoJo and that's apparent to everyone you meet. Even if you're feeling overwhelmed, do more of whatever it is you've been doing to generate business, with a smile on your face and gratitude in your heart.

BUT

Don't lose sight of the fact that since you actually have clients, this is a wonderful opportunity to knock their sox off with your service. The very very very best source of future business is your Satisfied Past Clients, so even before you run off to do "more of what you're doing that's working," make sure all these current clients are tickled pink with you. Stay in touch, keep that brochure box full, hold an extra open house. Return phone calls quicker than you have to. Aggressively pursue and deliver feedback.

There's no better prospecting strategy than taking exceptional care of your current clients! If you're busy right now, don't miss this opportunity!

"How Can I Compete with a Minimum Service Real Estate Company?"

I got a good question the other day from Melissa. Melissa finds herself competing against companies who provide minimal service for a minimal fee. Nothing wrong with that, mind you, it's a business model that has its place. But it can make it hard on those who offer full service for a higher fee, especially when the seller says those magic words "*I need every penny out of my house to break even!*" How do you persuade a seller that your services cost more because they're worth more?

I could probably write a book, or at least a chapter of a book on this topic (oh, yeah, I've done that!), but for our purposes today, let me share a response I came up with in the shower this morning.

When the seller says something along the lines of: "*I'm sure you're worth your fee, but I simply can't afford you,*" how can you respond?

Well, I don't believe you should argue with him. Arguing makes you look insecure and somewhat desperate. And it doesn't work. So don't do that. Neither should you put down your competition—that will only subtly criticize the seller's judgment; after all, he chose to consider going the minimum service route. But what if you say something like this:

"*I hear ya and I understand. You have a tough decision to make. On one hand, you can pay this other company a much lower fee upfront and hopefully retain more of your equity. On the other hand, you can hire a full-service agent, whether it's me or someone else, and due to the increased exposure and marketing expertise, you might end up with even more of your equity. Either way, there's no guarantee that your house will sell for what you need it to. I'm sure you'll make the right decision. Do you have any questions for me that might help you in making that decision?*"

The fact that you're sitting there in the seller's home means that he hasn't ruled out paying a full-service company. In fact, he probably wants full-service; he's just not convinced of its value. But if you first show him that you care about his situation and you trust his judgment, he'll probably give you the opportunity to persuade him. Just wait til he's ready...

MAY 2009

Where the Heck Do You Live (and Work)?

I get emails from agents all around the country (which I love, keep 'em coming!). Sometimes I'm so impressed with someone that I want to remember where they work in case I ever need a referral resource there.

Many of these agents have fancy-schmantzy signatures on their emails, so that's the first place I look. And you know what? Very rarely is the agent's market area mentioned. Oh, I understand why, it doesn't seem like it would be all that important especially since most of your email communication is with people you know who obviously know where you live. But just in case...

Anyway, if I'm really impressed with someone and have a few minutes to spare, I'll click on their website link, if provided, to learn more about them. And I tell ya'—an awful lot of you do not make it clear on your homepage where the heck you sell real estate! Oh, there might be a picture of a skyline (which likely isn't much help) and I've even seen sites with a physical address that DOESN'T INCLUDE THE CITY AND STATE! Phone numbers—yes—and if I'm familiar with the area code, it might mean something to me, but don't count on it.

If you communicate via email with people outside your market area, you might consider including your city & state in your email signature. And definitely take a look at your website to ensure that it's awfully darn clear where you sell real estate!

Lecture Over.

UNSUBSCRIBED! Some Utterly Random Thoughts on the Matter...

If you have a mailing list with that handy-dandy UNSUBSCRIBE option, you probably know how painful it is when someone does...that is, UNSUBSCRIBE!

Of course, I'm mildly devastated (is that an oxymoron? Yes, I believe it is) when I get my little report of unsubscribes after I've sent out a newsletter—either to my readers or my real estate Sphere of Influence. After doing it a few years now, my skin has toughened a little bit, but still...it's not something that's ever gonna feel good, right?

But here are some random thoughts on the matter of unsubscription.

- Sometimes people unsubscribe because they accidently signed up twice and are unsubscribing one of their email addresses. I've even had my readers write to me explaining this so that I wouldn't get my feelings hurt. I love you guys.

- I got unsubscribed-to last week by someone who sends me HER crap almost every day—sometimes more than one a day! I don't get that—it seems kinda rude. If you're going to send me your stuff, you should reciprocate and accept mine.

- Doesn't it suck when someone in your Sphere of Influence unsub-scribes you? Especially someone you thought really liked you? WhatdidIdo?

- Several months ago, a guy unsubscribed to one of my free newsletters and felt the need to write a long letter of explanation as to how my ideas and philosophies were "whack" and utterly worthless in today's world. Note—the guy had been a licensed real estate agent for three months, so I guess he knew what he was talking about. Anyway, it was heartwarming to know that my whack philosophies affected him so deeply that he was inspired to spend that much time telling me about it.

- I rarely unsubscribe from a newsletter I volunteered for (however, I don't hesitate to do so when I'm spammed). I figure I'd rather just hit DELETE when the messages come in if I'm not interested, rather than risk hurting someone's feelings (who is a real person, most of the time). They'll never know if I DELETE, but they'll definitely know if I unsubscribe them. Why create that little bit of sadness in the world if I don't have to?

I will say (with thinly disguised arrogance) that my SWS-reader unsubscribe rate is extremely low—like maybe one a week. Why? I dunno. I have some thoughts on the matter which I'll probably share in a future blog, but for now, if you're one of my readers who hasn't unsubscribed me—THANKS!!!!! The absence of your email address on my unsubscribe report is noted and appre-ciated!

Do You Take Control? Please Do!

You know those twilight zone moments? When you have what you think is a very simple question, but then can't find a suitable answer anywhere? When you ask the question, you either get a long, complicated answer or a blank look, as if your question is absurd?

This was my experience lately with a video project I wanted to do. It was very simple (I thought)—I wanted to create a demo/promo video for my speaking services. I had three hours of material from which to harvest five-to-ten minutes from, so my plan was to go through the three hours and cut out snippets that made me look cute & fun & knowledgeable (and of course, skinny).

I thought I had it figured out, but then ran into a technical roadblock. And another. Something to do with converting the video file I had to something editable. Frankly, I don't get any joy out of figuring out technical issues, so I called up a video editor I know to ask his advice. I got an earful of techno-jargon, along with all the reasons my (simple?) request was way more complicated than I thought it was. He then offered me several suggestions (none of which made any sense to me) to resolve my dilemma.

(Okay, what am I missing here??? Everyone I know has a video camera and knows how to YouTube; surely they aren't all way more technie than I am???)

I got off the phone frustrated and confused and...frustrated and confused. Now, don't get me wrong, I wasn't trying to sponge off the guy—I was perfectly willing to pay for his assistance once I realized I was probably incapable of handling it myself.

What would have been really cool was if he had said something like *"Jennifer, why don't you just bring me the raw material and I'll put it in a format you can rough-edit. It'll cost you $30 (or $50 or $100)—I'm a little backed up right now, so it might have to wait til the end of the month, but let me take care of it for you."*

I might have fainted with relief. So maybe it's good he didn't say that—I had a lot to do that day.

Anyway, we as real estate agents (and mortgage brokers and home stagers and insurance agents) have the ability to make our clients and prospects faint with relief, too. We know SO MUCH more than they do about what's happening and truly—much of the time, they don't want to/need to know the ins & outs of the process. Often they don't even need to know their options—they just want "it" taken care of without having to learn something new. This is why they hire us. To take control and take care of them.

So, let's take control and help. No drawn-out excuses or explanations, no lectures on the state of the economy (uh, like it's a secret?), no long-winded diatribe on the horrors of buying short sales or REOs...there's plenty of time for those conversations later, at the proper time. But if you want to make a great first impression on your potential new client—just show 'em your Can-Do attitude—because...you CAN DO!

"Mismatched" Spouses—Introverts & Extroverts

Got a great question from a reader yesterday!

NH writes:

"Dear Jennifer,

What do you do when your spouse doesn't get the SWS concept? My husband is a born salesman if you know what I mean. He has no problem striking up a conversation with anyone, in fact I get some leads from him because he isn't ashamed to brag about me and refer me. I feel blessed to have someone who believes in me so much and supports my career. But we have now had two heated discussions because I was explaining the SWS concept and why I thought it was the perfect thing for my personality (which is the total opposite from his) and he started "coaching" me on how to get out there and to face things that scare me; cold-calling, door knocking, etc. He said, 'Everything can't be all fun and there are things in every one's job that they don't like. You can't always take the easy route' (when it comes to lead generation).

You probably know how I was feeling. I'm not sure what to say anymore because every time we discuss it, someone ends up getting hurt. Has anyone else had this problem, if not with someone close to them, maybe a team leader, broker or fellow agent?

NH"

Oh, yeah, NH, I SO feel your pain! I've dealt with this all my life, although not as much anymore because I can throw the "I wrote a book about it!" card around. The thing is, extroverts often really don't understand us—they just think we're wussing out when we refuse to do things that make us uncomfortable. I've had my share of knock-down, drag-out fights myself over my more reserved personality and, like yours, they always end badly.

I believe that a large percentage of the real estate failures (that is, agents who enter the business and then quit) are due to the cookie-cutter training that insists there's only one path to success, regardless of one's personality. That simply ain't true. Once a salesperson (regardless of his or her product) acknowledges, accepts and even celebrates his natural God-given talents and interests, he can blossom doing things HIS way.

But force him to do it THEIR way and he'll almost certainly fail. It's not a matter of being stubborn or stupid or lazy or wussy. We introverts just have a different perspective on the world and the people in it. It's not better, it's not inferior; it's just different.

Always Be Closing...?

I'm sure you've heard the infamous ABC's of sales from the scene in the movie *Glengarry Glen Ross*—when Alec Baldwin is slamming the sales force with a string of memorable quotes starting with *"Put down that coffee—coffee is for closers,"* followed by *"Get them to sign on the line which is dotted!"*

He then points to the chalkboard where he's written "ABC—A= Always; B= Be; C= Closing.

Always

Be

Closing.

Whatever.

Can you imagine how delightful it would be to be around someone who is Always Closing? Or, to BE that person who is? I suppose it comes naturally to some; but to those to whom it does not, BLECH!

But it occurs to me that the Always Be Closing mantra is a beautiful sentiment if applied in the proper situation.

In our business, a real estate **closing** is the goal of what we do. Not only because it's when WE get paid, but it's also payday for the mortgage broker, the title company, our own broker, the home warranty company, the county tax assessor...all sorts of people and businesses benefit from a real estate closing! Not to mention (duh), the buyers who realize their dreams of home ownership, the investor who will soon be hiring contractors and home stagers and property managers and someday, maybe YOU to sell the home again, and the sellers who can breathe a sigh of relief that they can move on with their lives.

Yes, a closing is a beautiful thing.

So, I propose that we real estate agents Always Be Closing. No, not sales-pitching everyone to death, but rather, getting our buyers and sellers to the closing table!

What if My Seller Asks for a 'Listing Exclusion'?

For those who haven't encountered a "listing exclusion" yet, it's simply a request from a seller that if a certain person or persons buy the home after it goes on the market, your listing commission won't apply. For example, perhaps the seller knows a guy at work who says he'd be interested in purchasing the house, but he's still thinking about it. Your seller doesn't want to wait for him to make up his mind to go on the market, but neither does he want to pay you if the guy actually ponies up. So, the seller asks you to "exclude" this particular person from your listing agreement.

Should you do it?

My advice? Sure. Don't argue, don't explain, and don't make a big deal out of it. Write in the exclusion and get on with putting the house on the market. The chances that this guy is actually going to purchase the house are slim, but if he does, the seller will probably need your assistance to get the contract written and to closing. For which you most certainly may charge a reasonable fee.

No reason to go to battle over this. Save your energy for bigger things!

June 2009

Does Your Friend Owe You a Courtesy Call when She Hires Someone Else?

Question: *"I understand that I won't always get my friends' business, but when I don't, is it reasonable to expect a courtesy call explaining why they hired someone else?"*

It's tough when someone you know entrusts their real estate business to another agent, isn't it? When you're new, the disappointment can take days to get over, but even for Old Fogies like me, it'll still sting for an hour or two.

I believe that it's best to give your friend the benefit of the doubt and assume that she had a perfectly good reason for her decision not to bring you in on her real estate transaction. Trust in that, swallow your hurt and move on. Don't risk the friendship (or future business!) by demanding an explanation, complaining to mutual friends or sulking the next time you see her.

It might help you to behave properly if you look at the situation from a purely mercenary perspective. Your friend might become disillusioned with her chosen real estate agent—either during the transaction or afterwards. If it happens "during" and you've been pleasantly professional (as opposed to accusingly indignant), you might just find your friend back on your doorstep begging for your help. But even if this doesn't happen, the agent she chose might have been a major disappointment and you can actually cement your position as your friend's go-to guy or gal for her future referrals. But I guarantee neither will happen if you pout, whine or fuss about her decision.

I don't think the general public realizes how hurtful it is when our friends hire someone else—I doubt they even give it much thought. In most cases, it's not AT ALL personal, so they don't even think to feel bad about it, or feel they owe you any explanation.

So, does your friend owe you a courtesy call? No. If you get one, dandy (and please don't make her regret her decision to do so). But if you don't, please don't fret. More than an hour, anyway.

"Dear Real Estate Professional, I'd Like to See a House, Please"

A few months ago, I posted a Help Wanted ad for a graphic designer on www.Guru.com. If you've never used Guru—it's a wonderful resource! Basically, it's an online database of freelancers who are looking for work.

Anyway, within 24 hours of posting my ad, I got at least 30 responses. Complete with resumes, pricing estimates and requests for further information about my project. All 30 responders seemed to sincerely want my business and not a one of them lectured, belittled or condescended to me.

Well, duh, you say, they're after your business, why on earth would they be anything but delightful in their first encounter with you?

My thoughts exactly.

Well, last night, one of my SWS readers sent me a link to a thread on Trulia. I'm not familiar with the Trulia forums, but it appears that it's a place where regular people post questions to the real estate community, hoping to get answers (again, duh).

On this particular thread, the buyer was simply asking for information about a listing she found online. I was stunned at the level of lecturing, belittling and condescension expressed by the responding real estate "professionals." More than half of the responders sternly advised her to speak with a mortgage broker before "bothering" (okay, that's my word, but the message was clear) a real estate agent. Another instructed her to better educate herself on the process before looking at homes, and provided links. Only two agents actually offered to show her the home, but even they seemed disinterested in becoming her favorite real estate agent.

I gotta ask...WHY are these agents wasting their precious time on the Trulia forum if all they're going to do is alienate the prospects they're supposedly there to find?

Are graphics designers on guru.com more desperate than real estate agents (HA!) and therefore only grudgingly concede to being polite, enthusiastic and responsive? Whereas we in the real estate industry are so buried under a pile of qualified buyers and motivated sellers to the point where we simply don't have a minute to spare to be polite, enthusiastic and responsive?

ROFLMAO. I crack myself up.

High School Dating Versus Real World Dating... and Yes, It Relates to Real Estate

Had a conversation with my Significant Other's 17-year old daughter about dating. She's going into her senior year of high school and is involved in her first serious relationship. Two months already! I, being a way-out-of-touch-42-year-old, asked her if teenagers still "go together" officially or if they date casually—as in—more than one person at a time.

She looked at me as if I were a loon and explained that yes, they "go together" and it's unheard of for a teenager to date more than one person—that would be called "cheating" or worse.

Fair enough—that's how it was in my high school days; probably in yours, too. After all, high school is a micro-culture and it would be pretty tough to have two boyfriends without causing a ruckus in English class or at the football game.

But as we get older and begin to look for a lifetime mate, we realize the wisdom of shopping around. Of not committing to someone after a date or two. Of not pledging "loyalty" to a virtual stranger. Heck, in the real world, you could date someone different every night of the week and two on Sundays without ever hurting a feeling. And perhaps you should. After all, you're on the hunt to find just the right person for you and the only way to do that is to explore your options.

During our collective searches for The One, someone's gonna get hurt. Someone's gonna get dumped. Someone's gonna feel misled. It's happened to all of us and we've done it to others, probably more than once. It's part of the process of finding The Right One for each of us.

And if I date five men and reject four of them in favor of the one I like most, have I done something wrong?

No, I haven't, not even if those other four men are disappointed. Not even if I went out with some of them more than once. Not even if I shared personal information with them and they shared some with me. (Of course, this assumes I haven't made promises to anyone I didn't intend to keep.)

It's the same in our business. Our prospects are out there in the world searching for just The Right One to do business with. They're visiting open houses, asking for references from friends, and dropping in at real estate offices in hopes of finding someone they can see themselves working with for an extended period of time. During their investigation period, they will share personal information; they'll allow the agent to provide free advice and they might even indicate an interest in seeing the agent again. It's part of the process and they should be allowed, even encouraged, to do so. The fact that they're "dating around" should not be construed to mean that they are "disloyal" people who are not to be trusted.

And yes, when they do select one agent over the others, the others may be hurt. They might even rant about the experience in a blog or around the coffee machine. They might proclaim the need for an earlier discussion of Buyer Agency and a commitment to enforce tighter "rules" in the future. They may even complain about the lack of loyalty among the general public.

My friends, no one owes us loyalty unless they've overtly promised it to us. We earn loyalty and we continue to earn it throughout the course of a relationship. If you get dumped (or better said, "selected against") by a prospect, trust that the prospect found someone they were more compatible with and be happy for them. Move on, continue to trust the process, and don't lose hope that the Right One (actually, several "ones") is/are out there looking for you. Because they are. Put on your happy face and jump right back in!

Lessons from The Bachelorette

As a follow-up to the previous blog about high school dating, loyalty and the wonderful world of real estate...

A few weeks ago, I was watching The Bachelorette (yeah, I know, spare me the eye-rolls) and there was a scene where the Bachelorette had a one-on-one date with one of the hopeful bachelors. The rules of the game say that if the Bachelorette does not give the guy a rose during the one-on-one date, he has to go home—in other words, he's been eliminated.

As the bachelor was preparing for his date he said something like, *"I'm a little nervous about this date; what if there's no chemistry and she sends me home?"*

HUH?

Last time I checked, it's not much fun dating someone with whom you have no chemistry. In fact, it's pretty darned awful. Even if a guy or gal is the most gorgeous creature on the planet, if there's no connection, what's the point?

Dating is a two-way street; in the real world, anyway, we evaluate each other during the process and either party is entitled to make the decision to move forward or not. If the answer is "not," we thank the other person for their time, move on and are grateful we have the freedom to do so!

It's similar in our business, although when there's money involved, we can probably put up with a bit more relationship angst! But I often see agents pushing for a listing or a buyer agency agreement—even when they aren't necessarily the right (wo)man for the job, or they recognize that the buyer or seller is clearly going to be difficult.

I'm sure a lot of it is ego...we want to win that lover or client, even if we suspect it's a relationship headed for nowhere. And that's fine—I'm as competitive as anyone and sometimes I just want to WIN, even if the prize isn't something I actually want.

But when you don't win—when the other person selects against you, trust that they made the right decision for them. Support that decision and you may end up with a lifelong friend—which is nothing to sneeze at!

Any Idiot Can Give Their House Away...
If Price Is All that Matters, What Do They Need Us for?

Real estate agents are quite fond of the philosophy that "Price conquers all," meaning that if you price a listing low enough, it will sell regardless of the challenges the property presents.

Fair enough.

But I must ask. So what? Is that our job as real estate professionals to simply recommend a price low enough that any piece of junk will sell?

Or, rather, is it to help our sellers get the highest possible price in the shortest possible time, whatever a realistic price and time may be? If our job is to simply sell it fast, at any price, well, shoot, just about any idiot can give their property away! Isn't that why homesellers hire us in the first place, to do a better job for them than they can do for themselves?

Real estate agents are always bragging about their listing expertise and defending their commissions by claiming they MORE THAN EARN THEIR FEE. Uh, well, I have to disagree if the only solution we offer our sellers is to price aggressively. There ARE other things a seller can do to maximize his sales price, and it's our job to 1) know what those things are, and 2) be willing to share those secrets with a seller and 3) help the seller accomplish those things.

What if you went to your doctor with a pain in your leg and the only solution he offered was to cut the offending appendage off? Yes, that would cure the pain in your leg, but maybe there's a better way that involves a little more effort on his part (and yours). Or if your plumber simply removed the toilet that wasn't flushing instead of figuring out how to repair it?

Of course, if I request that the doctor amputate my leg, or that the plumber tear out my toilet, or that my real estate agent simply gives my house away, well, then, they have my blessing. But in most cases, c'mon, our clients deserve a little more effort and expertise than that, don't they?

I'm not sayin' that price isn't important—of course it is. But if we keep preaching that "Price is the ANSWER!" to the exclusion of any other effort on our part, we may end up preaching ourselves out of a job...deservedly so, I might add.

July 2009

Okay, Miss Smarty-Pants, HOW Do You Get Your Sellers on Board to Get Their Home Ready for Market?

I've publicly made the claim that at least 90% of my sellers hire my stager and my handyman and almost all spend at least $1000 (of their own money!) prior to going on the market.

Am I just lucky to have intelligent and motivated sellers? Maybe. But I'll give myself more credit than that, although I have to say that every single seller prospect I've spoken with in the last 18 months has brought up the topic of *"What do I need to do to the house to get top dollar?"* They bring it up first! I spoke with a potential seller just yesterday who doesn't want to sell til next spring, but wants to get started now on home improvement projects! Maybe I am lucky—is this NOT typical of sellers in other markets?

That said, here are a few ways to help a seller see the light, and then do something about it.

First, go in with the assumption that the seller wants to know what it's going to take to get top dollar. Don't pussy-foot around the topic, although it's best if you're polite about it, of course! Like I said, ALL my sellers ask me first, so maybe there's some vibe I send out that inspires them to do so, I don't know. But I will say that if a seller didn't seem interested in preparing his home for market, I probably wouldn't be interested in listing his home. I don't say that to be snotty or arrogant—it's just a fact. I don't want a listing I'm not proud of.

By far the best way to get your sellers to clean up, fix-up and decorate-up is to help them do it. No, you don't have to do it yourself, although I've certainly rolled up my sleeves once or twice or a dozen times. By "help" I mean that you have the human resources on call to Get the Jobs Done. Contractors you know and trust...who know, trust and love you. How anyone sells real estate without a good handyman, stager and cleaning person on board is a mystery to me. When you can walk into a seller's home and confidently say, "Yes, that needs to be fixed—we'll put it on the Bob-List," or "Yep, let's get Bob over here to give us an estimate on that," or "No big deal, Bob can fix that," you're golden. Not only are you the hero, but you'll also get yourself a sellable listing.

What I see most agents doing (if they do anything at all) is to give the seller a list of things that need to be done, smile sweetly and leave them to it. Well, that's a recipe for failure. Our sellers are busy people and probably don't know a good handyman, painter, stager or cleaning crew. They'll open up the yellow pages, make a few calls and throw up their hands in despair. I'd do the same thing; in fact, I have when I was selling an out-of-state property and didn't know who to call myself. My agent didn't help; I didn't get the work done...and guess what? The house didn't sell. Bummer for us both.

Here's how I handle it.

Seller: *"Tell me what I need to do to get ready for market."*

Smarty Pants JA: *"I see a lot of maintenance and repair issues that really should be dealt with before we go on the market. Let's get Bob over here to give us an estimate. Are you around this Saturday?"*

I use the same approach when discussing home staging. Frankly, I suck at decorating and furniture arrangement, but I know bad décor and awkward rooms when I see them. So, I just say *"I'm a terrible decorator, but my stager, Geri, is the most wonderful woman you'll ever meet. Give her a call and set up a time to meet. I think she charges $250 for a 3-hour consultation. I promise you—it'll be the best $250 you ever spent."*

And I believe that. With all my heart. And that's another part of the story— YOU must believe that the first impression and condition and décor matter... and you must trust your resources. If you don't, you'll never be able to sell the concept. I can "sell" staging all day long because I have a great stager and I know it works. I can whole-heartedly bring Bob into my clients' lives because I know, beyond a shadow of a doubt, that he'll make me proud.

If you don't have a Bob or a Geri, make it among your top priorities to find them. Finding contractor resources is a topic for a different day, but for this day, just know how important it is to your business. I credit Bob and Geri for at least half of my paychecks thru the years. Seriously.

Persistence Pays Off...? Eh, Maybe There's a Better Way

Everyone has heard how you have to be in someone's face at least 7 times before they'll buy from you. Or something like that. The other day I read a story in a business magazine about an advertising salesperson who contacted a prospect 34 times before clinching the sale on call 35. The salesperson gleefully described how the prospect became more and more irritated with her as the calls continued, eventually asking her (that's putting it mildly) to leave her alone and never call again. Undeterred, the ad sales babe made that 35th call...and got the sale.

A sign of a good salesperson? Maybe. But maybe not.

Why on earth is it necessary to badger someone 34 times (or even 7) in order to spark interest in a service or product? Could it be that the product or service isn't all that compelling, or egads, the sales pitch sucks? If I call someone once, pitch 'em and they turn me away...and I call them again, pitch 'em and get turned away again and then do it again...and again...with the same (although increasingly hostile) result...might that not mean that I'm doing something WRONG? Why on earth would I continue to something that clearly isn't working?

Let's compound the insult. I do this all day long to my entire database of prospects. Day after day. Rejection after rejection. Every once in awhile I score a YES, which supposedly makes all those rejections worth the effort. But, but, but...has no one ever considered the possibility that all these rejections might be trying to tell me something?

Doing something that doesn't work very well enough times that someone finally succumbs to the pitch doesn't sound professional (or very efficient) to me. Maybe it's time to toss th old marketing clichés out the window and come up with a new paradigm! If something ain't good enough to work the first time, maybe it's just not good enough!

So, is there something you're doing over and over and over...without much result, but assuming that your persistence will eventually be rewarded? Maybe it's time to rethink that approach...

Making New Friends to Sell Real Estate to—a Guide for Introverts & Other Reluctant Networkers

I don't know what it is lately, but I'm getting slammed with emails from readers (that sounds negative, I don't mean it to be—I love hearing from y'all!) about how to meet people to add to their Spheres of Influence. Since a lot of my readers lean toward the introverted side of the personality teeter-totter, they bemoan the fact that they "just aren't that friendly" or "don't enjoy networking events." ME, TOO, and ME, NEITHER!

So, how does a not-that-friendly, networking-phobic real estate agent make new friends?

First, let's clarify why we might want to have more friends as a real estate agent. Agents who follow the Sell with Soul philosophy aren't interested in pestering people for a living—that is, they aren't going to cold-call, door-knock or otherwise impose self-promotion techniques that they would not enjoy being used on them. They'd much rather attract business to them organically, rather than risk annoying people with an aggressive pursuit.

So, that's the mindset we're talking about here. In a very basic sense—inspiring people to ask for your business card instead of your asking if you can give it to them.

A little history about me—before I became a real estate agent, I didn't have a lot of friends...by choice, I liked to believe. I didn't willingly attend parties or other social events because I dreaded those polite conversations where I struggled to find something to say to fill the silence and often that "something" was eye-rolling ridiculous.

So, I avoided social situations when I could, and when I couldn't, I'd hide in the corner with a glass of wine, a plate of cheese and a deer-in-headlights look on my face. I rarely invited anyone to dinner or out for coffee, and when I received such invitations, my automatic response was to find an excuse to say no.

And I was happy enough. Didn't bother me; I like my own company and don't mind being alone. I was successful at my job as an account manager for an insurance company; I had a cool boyfriend and a nice house. What did I need friends for?

Well, going into real estate changed all that, forever. Call me mercenary, but once I was a real estate agent, I suddenly saw the value in having a social network. Hey, the more people I know...the more chances I have of selling some real estate! And I did. Sell a lot of real estate, that is. To and for the people I knew.

And you know what? I'll admit that my initial friend-finding mission was purely self-serving. Believe me, I was and still am an introvert and have no problem hanging out by myself for days on end. I still have no interest in small talk or polite conversation and would rather eat cottage cheese (ick!) than attend a networking event.

BUT...guess what? Having friends is WONDERFUL! And I'm not talking about "wonderful" from a business perspective; I'm talking wonderful as in—it's fun! For many of you, this is a big DUH, but for us introverts, it's not quite so obvious.

Reluctant Networkers—Your Next Biggest Client May Be at Walmart!

Picking up from my previous blog about how introverts (and other Reluctant Networkers) can and should make more friends to sell houses to, here are some thoughts on how to go about doing that. And trust me, you'll find no nonsense here about accosting every stranger with a business card or elevator speech, or reminding everyone you know how much you LUUUUUUV Referrals!

It's actually much simpler and lower-stress than you might think, especially if you are an introvert. You're not trying to find your new best friend or partner for life, you're just trying meet a few (or a lot) more people who think you're generally a decent person who probably can handle the intricacies of a real estate deal. Some may become good friends, but most won't, and that's fine. While I toss the word "friend" around, I'm referring mainly to "people who know you," not all of whom are friends. Most aren't, actually.

So, when someone tells me they have a small Sphere of Influence (SOI), I find out they're almost always thinking that they SOI is their "friends and family." And that's not right. Your SOI is "everyone who knows you and knows that you sell real estate." That's important to keep in mind.

Most advice for expanding an SOI centers on joining groups, networking, volunteering & such. Terrific! If that's up your alley, see ya at the Chamber. But it's not everyone's cup of merlot. (And actually, no, you won't see me at any Chamber).

I prefer a much more subtle approach. And it works, promise.

Every time you leave the house (which you should do on a regular basis), practice making eye contact with strangers. If you're an extrovert, this may come naturally to you, but if you're like me—more reticent about such things, it probably doesn't. Usually when I go out in public, let's say to Walmart, I avoid eye contact. I look at the floor, the ceiling, the apples, or my shopping cart... anything but the other people in the store.

However, I notice a big difference in my shopping experience when I make a concerted effort to LOOK at the other people I'm shopping with. Wow—it's fun! When I smile, they smile back! What a concept.

One day I went to a big box liquor store and using my make-eye-contact-with-strangers campaign, I struck up conversations with eight different people! Okay, so I didn't sell a house to any of them, but you never know.

So, do I think you'll build a huge SOI by hanging out at Walmart or the booze-store? Maybe, maybe not. But it's a great practice ground to get in the habit of bringing the outside world into your world instead of studiously shutting it out. Even for introverts, it's not hard to smile pleasantly at people who cross your path, especially if you're NOT in a networking situation where there's that subtle added pressure of effectively promoting yourself.

BUT...think about this...what if you smiled pleasantly and made eye contact with ten strangers a day...and struck up a conversation with just one of the ten? Just one? Every day? For a year? Y'think you might have a sweeeet SOI 365 days from now?

"Good for You, Let Me Know if You Need Anything."

That's the response my first-month real estate agent friend got from her Big Name broker when she emailed to say she had a $1.5M buyer lead. *"Good for you, let me know if you need anything."*

Are you kidding me?

My friend, smart as she is ;-] can barely spell MLS. She doesn't know what radon is, she doesn't know any inspectors, she doesn't yet have a relationship with a lender. She doesn't know how to select the best homes to show her new buyer.

But of course, she's been thoroughly trained on scripts, farming and other prospecting strategies as part of her Big Name training package.

We've all been there, and it's a scary place. An exciting place to be, for sure, especially when a $1.5M buyer comes to call (hmmmmm...yeah, I can do that math). And yes, being new implies a level of scariness when presented with one's first customers. But Puh-leeeeaze! To tell a brand spanking new agent to *"let me know if you need anything"* is criminal, in my opinion. Okay, that's melodramatic, so if not criminal, let's say irresponsible. Heck, how about downright STUPID? My friend is on a 60/40% split, so the broker's take on this deal is...how much? A LOT. And the chances of my friend closing this deal without help are slim-to-none. Oh, and the guy is qualified up to $3.5M but claims that he's "cheap," so he asked my friend to try to stay around $1.5M.

My friend calls me for help. Of course, I don't know her market or her contracts or her MLS or her local customs, but so far, I've been a hell of a lot more help to her than her on-site, stands-to-make-$20k-on-the-deal broker.

I won't name names, but this is a national company that recruits rookie agents and promises them world-class training. I'm underwhelmed, to say the least.

Thanks for listening.

JA Thru the Years...in Pictures

Yesterday, I found a folder deep in one of my dusty file boxes of all my real estate agent photos thru the years. Remember, Old Fogies, how when you used to have to get physical copies of your photos to send in with your business card orders? Anyway, I found a bunch of them.

Call me narcissistic, but I thought they were fascinating. I didn't think I'd changed all that much over the last 13 years, but my stash of photos sez otherwise.

Here they are, in all their glory.

My very first professional
photo from 1996; age 29.

Circa 1998; I always thought I
was a natural blond...guess not.

Circa 2000; my, I was fluffy.

Circa 2002; to date, this was my favorite
photo. Loved the little hair flip.

Circa 2002; Same session—couldn't
decide which one I liked better.

2004—My attempt at
creative photo editing

2008—The latest

My one & only Glamour Shot—
God only knows when (or why)
I took this...and no, I didn't use it
in my marketing!

Do You Use an Autoresponder?
Please Be Careful with It!

Okay, so you're not in any in any danger if you use an autoresponder...at least, not (to quote Jack Nicholson) *"grave danger, is there any other kind?"* But you definitely run the risk of running off perfectly good clients, prospects and referring agents.

I send out newsletters every week or so to several thousand real estate agents around the world. Every time one goes out, I'm slammed with autoresponders. And, my friends, I love y'all, but most of them are awful. I don't mind the ones that tell me you're on vacation (have a wonderful time!) or that you've experienced a family crisis (hugs) or are at a convention, but many are so bluntly written that I feel an initial shock when reading it. Call me hypersensitive, but when I receive an autoresponded message back that informs me you're busy and will return my email at such and such a time, I feel a little miffed. Oh, sure, intellectually, I realize it has nothing to do with my importance in your life, but like I said, I always feel a little twinge when I read it. And I tell ya—thousands of my readers don't have autoresponders, and I'm never emotionally offended by NOT getting an auto-response!

I got one yesterday from someone I'd sent a "real" email to (not a newsletter). It was apparently generated by the person's SPAM filter and sternly advised me to resend my message so that it would get thru this time. Uh, you're kidding, right? I'm going to fish through my SENT folder to find the message and resend it? Well, maybe if I have time later, and remember to do it (I haven't yet).

But the worst one I've ever seen came today. Again, from a SPAM filter program:

Hello Jennifer Allan,

This message serves as notification that you will not receive any more courtesy notices from our members for two days. Messages you have sent will remain in a lower priority queue for our member to review at their leisure.

Future messages will be more likely to be viewed if you are on our member's priority Guest List.

Thank you,

(signed by the guy who received my newsletter)

About this Notice

This courtesy notice is part of a free service to make email more reliable and useful. Boxbe (www.boxbe.com) uses your existing social network and that of your friends to keep your inbox clean and make sure you receive email from people who matter to you.

Ouch!!!!!

If you use an autoresponder, why not send yourself an email today and see what it says. If it's anything other than warm and inviting, change it, or get rid of it. In all likelihood, it's really not necessary to have at all...

Should You Price to Ward off Appraisal Problems?

Sellers want more for their homes than the market is likely to pay. That's a fact; it's been a fact forever, during boom times and busts, and will continue to be a fact long after the Recession of 2009 is behind us.

Nothing wrong with it; it's human nature and we're all guilty of putting a higher value on our own precious stuff than anyone else is going to. But part of our job as listing agents is to gently persuade our seller clients that we need to price properly in order to get their home sold.

But should that "proper price" take into account what the house might appraise for?

In my opinion, no.

WHAT???? Jennifer, are you out of your mind?? What if you overprice the house and it sells at that price and the appraisal comes in low?? What then?

Indeed.

I take great care in pricing my listings—I want to get my seller the highest possible price in the shortest amount of time, assuming that's his goal, too. And I've been doing this long enough to understand that pricing it RIGHT is best way to get the highest price, as opposed to pricing it high and hoping a bigger idiot comes along and pays that price. So, before I continue, let me assure you that I know how to price a house to sell quickly, without giving away my seller's money.

If I feel a house will sell for more than the market data indicates, I'll not hesitate to price it accordingly. If a particular house shows so well and feels so good that it blows away the similar competition and recent sales...even if "on paper" it's not "worth" more, I'll put that higher price on it. My seller deserves the opportunity to see her hard work or design-sense or whatever pay off for her.

(Again, remember, I'm not stupid and I'm not inexperienced. I know what I'm doing.)

So, back to the original question. "What if it sells at full price and then doesn't appraise?"

Frankly, I'll deal with that when and if the problem arises. If I get my seller "too much money" for his house, and the appraiser or underwriter doesn't agree with me and the buyer, then we'll go to Plan B. Which, yes, may include the seller coming down on his price to meet the appraisal. Or getting a second appraisal. Or whatever other solutions we can come up with.

And, yeah, it might suck and everyone might get mad. But I'll deal with that at the time!

I'd much rather take the chance of getting top dollar for my seller and then scrambling to justify it, than to pro-actively risk leaving my seller's money on the table when we could have gotten more. In other words, I don't believe in underpricing a home in order to avoid appraisal issues, and I don't believe it's a good tactic to use when discussing price with a seller prospect.

August 2009

Is Shaking Hands Too 20th Century in Today's Germophobic World?

Last year (or the year before? Egads), I wrote a blog called "Always Extend Your Hand First" which encouraged the more introverted among us to always initiate the handshake instead of waiting for the other person to do it. Why? Because if the other person doesn't do it, and no handshake ensues, the relationship starts off awkwardly.

I got an email yesterday from someone who didn't agree with me (and that's always cool). She said that she's finding more and more people avoiding hand-contact upon introduction due to concerns about germs & flu's & such. So, she's decided never to initiate a handshake and let the other person decide the matter.

Hmmmmm. I'm a bit skeptical. While I'm no hand-shaking expert, I can't say that I've noticed any trend toward avoiding introductory contact. And I wonder if this reaction has more to do with the non-initiator's attitude toward touch than a concern over the other person's preference.

Don't get me wrong—I'm not disagreeing with or belittling my reader's opinion! Maybe she's onto something I've been too socially isolated lately to notice.

However, I believe I shall continue to initiate handshakes—I'd much rather take the risk of being rebuffed by my introductee, than of alienating a potential new friend or client.

What You Can Do TODAY to Ensure a Sweeeet Tomorrow

I, like you, am really into immediate gratification. I like to see a payoff for my efforts, like, five minutes from now, or else I get discouraged and don't wanna play anymore. Faxes are too slow. The microwave takes too long. I want it NOW (whatever "it" is that I want...right now).

When it comes to wanting cash...as in, a paycheck, I'm definitely into "sooner rather than later." While I'm aware that I'll have bills to pay in January, February and March, I'm not nearly as concerned about them as I am about the ones due in September, October and November. And, frankly, there are just so many hours in the day, so it's only logical that I should focus on activities that pay off sooner rather than later, right?

Sure, there's some logic to that and it's how most of us run our businesses, throughout our entire careers. We have a cycle we repeat over and over... prospect hard, then deal with the business our prospecting brings in, then notice our pipeline's about empty, panic, then prospect hard again. And the cycle repeats. Some agents, in trying to break this cycle, implement sophisticated systems that are designed to generate a steady stream of leads that they can tap into when they see a break in their business looming. I've never had much luck with such systems—they just don't fit into my business model, so I can't speak to whether or not they do what they promise to do. Somehow I doubt it. And besides, they cost a lot of money!

But if you've ever experienced the euphoria of having a relatively consistent pipeline, I'll bet you'll agree that it's worth the effort you have to put into it upfront. As in, today. And tomorrow. And next week. For business that may not come to fruition until six months from now or longer. But here's the cool thing. Once your longer-term efforts start paying off, two things will have happened. One—you'll be in the habit of doing these things to the point where they'll seem like a natural part of your day and, two—you'll have generated the momentum within your business to keep that ball rolling.

And you know what else? Most of the things you can do today to ensure business in six months don't cost you a thing. They'll just take a little of your time, your creativity and your commitment to showing up every day.

Just What a Rookie Agent Needs—CHARM SCHOOL!

Okay, I've heard it all.

I have a friend who just started selling real estate. She hired on with a Big Name company that promises lotsa training. So far, my friend is underwhelmed, but the other night she called me almost hysterical.

My friend can't get anyone to help her role-play writing an offer, yet she was encouraged to attend "Charm School." Charm School? Yes, Charm school. As part of her training.

What, you ask, is charm school?

Well, as far as I can tell, it was a corporate-sponsored training class where agents were instructed on the niceties of life. Such as, "Get a good haircut." "Make sure to wash your car before taking buyers out." "Don't swear in front of customers." "Dress appropriately." And my favorite: "Make sure your fingernails are clean."

Are you kidding me? Seriously, someone in power thought it was a good idea to ask grown-up professional men and women to attend a class on fingernail maintenance?

To make it even more comical, my friend's office is in a rather ritzy part of town—one where I doubt it's necessary to encourage the local adult human beings to spend money on personal grooming. This is an area where the cheapest car in the lot is a Lexus, and $600 handbags on sale for $399 are considered a steal.

I can't imagine that this presentation didn't offend every real estate agent without shouting distance.

The training offered to newbies in our industry never fails to entertain me.

Call Me Mercenary...But a Personal Crisis Can Be Good for Business

I've struggled for several days on how to write this blog without coming across as mercenary, crass or just plain tacky. And forgive me if I fail in that effort. But I can see a financial silver lining in just about any situation.

A real estate agent friend of mine recently tried to adopt a child. It was a painful process, and unfortunately, the adoption failed. My friend has a fanatically loyal circle of friends with whom she'd been communicating the details of the process, asking for their prayers and keeping them updated via an e-newsletter.

My friend announced the failure of the adoption via the newsletter. In that newsletter, she included the following:

There's a part of me that feels a little foolish for dragging all of you through this—kinda like a woman who tells people too early that she's pregnant, and then miscarries. But there's a much bigger part of me that is overwhelmed with gratitude at the incredible outpouring of love and support that I've received from you over the past month, and particularly during the past week.

I'll let you know if any further developments emerge. And in the meantime, remember that September 20th date I asked you to save? [This was to be a party for the little girl.] Go ahead and keep it saved. It's time for my annual Clients and Friends Appreciation Picnic, and who better to appreciate than all of you? Details will emerge soon, but the date will be September 20th.

I'm also going to have a lot of unexpected time on my hands in the coming weeks, and a much-too-quiet house. So I plan to catch up on all of the lunches, dinners, coffees and cocktails with my friends that I've missed over the past month. So if you live here in town, expect a call from me . . .

Thank you all, so much. I can't believe how blessed I am to have such amazing friends. Know that all of you and your intentions remain in my daily prayers.

Now, I know with 100% certainty that my friend was not looking for a Sphere of Influence marketing opportunity within the context of her disappointment. But she created one, nonetheless.

Is my point that you should exploit the sadness in your life for personal gain? Uh, no. Even I'm not that opportunistic! But do know that your friends care about your challenges and, if handled deftly, you can create a little lemonade out of an otherwise bitter situation. And, truth be told, there's nothing like a little extra business to take your mind off your troubles!

Can You "SOI" in a Resort Community (that is, can you depend on your sphere of influence for business)?

So, you work in a resort community where most of the buyers and sellers live somewhere else. It's not likely you'll run into them at the grocery store or local coffee shop, and they probably won't be having a housewarming party you can finagle an invitation to (or even offer to host!). And unless their friends all decide they want to keep up with the Joneses and buy a vacation home, too, your past clients probably won't be a good source of referrals, no matter how deliriously happy they are with you.

CAN you rely on your Sphere of Influence (the people you know) to keep you in business?

Yes!

First, obviously, there are people who do live in the community, who know you and know that you sell real estate. You should definitely apply the principles of SOI to them. Remember that they are the gatekeepers to everyone they know, which may very well include some out-of-town homeowners or future homeowners.

Second, you will likely need to do some marketing to strangers, both directly to absentee owners as well as local advertising to attract buyers. I'm not an expert on that sort of marketing at all, but see what other successful agents are doing...and do it more creatively (that shouldn't be hard).

From my experience working briefly in a resort market, I saw that the top producers prospected heavily to expired listings, and there were plenty of those. Perhaps you can create a better, more creative expired listing campaign and incorporate it into your prospecting plan (again, the bar is set pretty low).

Obviously, a local blog is a must. People buying second homes will almost certainly begin their search online. BE THERE.

If you decide to reach out to strangers, I believe you can still apply the principles of SOI to your efforts. For example, make your advertising interesting, relevant and non-salesy. Create a website that reflects YOUR personality, not just a boilerplate REeee-la-tor site. Use your blog to demonstrate your familiarity with your area as well as to showcase your sparkling personality.

Consider doing a postcard mass-mailing to absentee owners with a fun blurb about your blog (and definitely make sure your local sphere knows about it). If you advertise in local real estate magazines, don't just showcase listings—create a fun, attractive ad for your blog. Create an online referral directory for out-of-town homeowners.

Return phone calls and online leads promptly—and when you get online leads, pick up the phone instead of simply replying via email.

Spend time learning even more about your market so that when A Stranger Calls, you are able to speak intelligently and confidently about the market. Be particularly conversant about the more desirable properties—be familiar with and KNOW how much it costs to live on the beach, the slopes or the river. But also know how much you can save by buying a block or two away.

When you're out and about, have your antenna up and a smile on your face, but keep your business cards to yourself unless asked. Don't risk being that annoying real estate agent who always seems desperate for business.

September 2009

WHY Don't We Care About Training for Rookie Real Estate Agents? Seriously, I'm Asking!

From time to time I post a blog about the abysmal state of rookie real estate training in America.

Do I have an agenda? Eh, maybe. Yeah, I sell books about real estate training and I even have a boot-camp type program specifically for rookies, but that alone doesn't inspire the contempt, yes, contempt I have for the real estate training industry.

I'm disgusted by the "fake it til you make it" attitude. I'm annoyed by the focus on prospecting competence over, well, COMPETENCE competence. I'm frustrated by the stories I hear of promises made during the recruiting process that are broken as soon as the rookie shows up to work. I could go on and on.

But today, I'm asking. WHY? Why is it this way? It occurs to me that if 80-95% of our new agents fail within the first year, then something isn't working and maybe we ought to try something different. Like...training? REAL training, not some fluffed up, time-wasting, sales-pitch-disguised-as-education to promote some product or another?

Here are the reasons I've heard for NOT training our new licensees.

1. Not a good use of resources. Since the majority of new agents will fail, it's a waste of money and time to implement a decent training program.

2. Not a good use of resources, Part II. Since the agents who do not fail will likely leave their first broker in search of a better deal elsewhere, why would Broker 1 spend time and money training the rookie to be his future competition?

3. That's the way it IS. This is a sink or swim business. If you don't have the drive to learn the business yourself, you shouldn't be here at all.

4. That's the way it IS, Part II. "We" didn't have our hands held and we somehow survived.

5. Real estate agents are competitive; therefore, there's no real

motivation to help someone who will become your competition.

It's easy for us Old Fogies to brush off the need for training—after all, we don't particularly want any more competition. And besides, "we" didn't get formal training and we came out okay. But then in the next breath, we complain loudly about "the guy (or gal) on the other end of the sale who doesn't know what he's doing and is screwing up my deal."

Maybe it's just that we've forgotten how much there is to learn in your first year and how complex the process really is. I talk to rookies every day, so I'm reminded of their pain and confusion...and their utter frustration with the lack of support they receive from the broker or trainer.

So I'm sincerely asking—WHY do we seem to care so little about quality training in our industry?

Ten Tips to Being a Good Refer-ree (that is—one who receives referrals from other real estate agents)

I've been doing a lot of referring these days. Both of my own leads to other Denver-area agents, and also coordinating agent-to-agent referrals around the country.

I'm seeing some distinct differences in how my referrals are handled by the refer-*ree*, and I tell ya, the ones who handle them better are far more likely to see more from me than those who don't!

When you are on the receiving end of a referral, remember that the referring agent probably has some concerns about you. He's worried that you'll forget you owe him a referral fee. That you'll make him look bad by treating the client poorly. That you'll drop the ball with the client and cost the refer-*rer* his referral fee. That you'll resent paying the referral fee when all is said and done. Stuff like that. Reasonable? Maybe not, but I promise you, it's going thru his head.

So, if you'd like to ensure that your first referral from an agent isn't your last— here are some tips...

1. Be appreciative! I mean, sincerely, enthusiastically, over-the-top appreciative. As if this referral is the most generous thing anyone's ever done for you.

2. On the other hand, if you aren't the right (wo)man for the job, disclose that upfront, and offer the name of someone who is. Your helpfulness will be remembered.

3. Contact the client right away—duh!

4. LET THE REFER-ER KNOW YOU CONTACTED THE CLIENT (right away) and share all the juicy details of the conversation (within proper privacy limits, of course).

5. Tell the refer-er how much you enjoyed talking with the client and thank him or her again for the referral.

6. Keep the refer-er updated on your activities with the client. Let him know when your listing appointment is scheduled or your first showing takes place. As you make progress toward the closing table, let the refer-er know. Be sure to contact the refer-er as soon as the transaction closes.

7. DO NOT complain about the client or imply in any way that you're working harder than you usually do for her (which might be interpreted as the beginnings of referral-fee-resentment).

8. If it turns out the the client isn't ready to buy or sell right now, don't fuss about wasting your time and stay in touch with her, and the refer-ee.

9. Sign and return the referral agreement immediately. No excuses.

10. And of course, knock yourself out impressing the sox off this referred client. Not only will this bring you future business and referrals from the client, but also from the refer-er.

Attracting Real Estate Business by Being a Master of Your Market

What does it mean to be a Master of Your Market? To me it means that if someone tells me where they live, I get a mental image of their neighborhood or subdivision or condo building. I don't necessarily know how big their house is or what year it was built, but I can probably guess within a decade or two, and I have a general sense of the overall ambience, what amenities are nearby and even a personal anecdote or two about the area I can toss out.

What being a Master of your Market doesn't mean is that you're a walking encyclopedia of facts, figures and statistics. No amount of research sitting behind your desk will give you the level of intimacy and familiarity with your market that you'll need to be a master of it. Again, a good definition of a market master is the ability to visualize a neighborhood when given an address—and there's no way you'll get that from MLS research.

How does being a Market Master help you attract business?

Well, as a real estate agent out there in the world with your antenna up, what do you have to offer the Average Joe who strikes up a conversation with you? Does he care how many listings you have? Does he care how gorgeous your home brochures are? Does he really want to hear about your 32-step marketing plan for selling houses? Probably not. But if he's at all interested in what $300,000 buys you in his neighborhood (and you know), or how much it costs these days to get into South Park Hill (and you know), your ability to make intelligent conversation about the market will get him, if he's gettable.

But if the best you can come up with is something like: *"I'm not sure about that, but I'd be happy to find out for you;"* well, it doesn't have quite the same effect.

The same thing applies when you're sitting on floor time or at an open house. If the best you can do is hand a visitor a list of other homes in the neighborhood, but can't really make conversation about them, the possibility of watching that stranger walk back out your door just went way up. But if you can chatter about nearby listings or comparable neighborhoods, you just dramatically increased the chances that your visitor will ask for your business card.

When you're on floor time, or take a sign call, again, if you can speak intelligently about the market either surrounding your listing, or that your office specializes in, you'll easily capture those leads.

So, what should you be doing right now to ensure that you're a Market Master? I'll answer that next!

Becoming a Market Master—Here's How...

Previously I promised to share some ideas to become a Master of Your Market so you can capture more of that business that crosses your path in your day-to-day wanderings!

First, if it's customary to "preview" in your market, do that. A lot. (If previewing IS customary in your market, you might be surprised to hear that it's frowned on or flat out not allowed in some! If that's the case in your market, you might want to move;-])

I advise all new agents to spend some serious quality time previewing in their first few months. By "serious," I mean every other day if they can. The best way to effectively preview is to practice what I call "Opinionated Previewing" or "Previewing with a Purpose." That means to look at somewhat similar homes and compare them to each other or against your "subject" property. You would practice both when you preview in preparation for an open house, or preview for a new buyer. If you don't have a new buyer or an upcoming open house, go preview all the houses in a certain price range or architectural style. Being able to compare homes to each other helps you internalize the data you're gathering (so you can spit it out intelligently if the opportunity arises).

A great side benefit of pro-active previewing is that karma always seems to provide you with an audience to share your newly found expertise with. What I mean is that if you go out and preview all the Bungalows between $250,000 and $350,000, within a week or two, you'll almost certainly meet someone with one of those to sell, or who knows someone who'd like to buy one! It's previewing magic!

Another way to Master Your Market is to always have your antenna up for opportunities to show properties to buyers. Even buyers who probably won't ever lead you to a paycheck. It's one thing for you to go out alone and preview, but quite another to have someone else with you to provide feedback on what you're seeing. And if you make conversation with this person, you'll get to hear their impressions of neighborhoods and styles and features, which will help you better understand what's important to the consumer. So, drive across town for a sign call. Take a buyer out to look at properties even if she says she won't buy til next spring.

If you've chosen to master a particular geographic market, you'll want to learn about the flow and amenities of the area as well as the housing stock.

Drive the area using a variety of access points. Visit the grocery stores and the neighborhood parks. If you have friends who live there, ask them what they like and dislike about their neighborhoods. Read local neighborhood newspapers and subscribe to other agents' newsletters who specialize in your new favorite neighborhood.

Do open houses in that neighborhood as often as you can, even if you have to do them for an agent in a different office.

The job of "becoming" a market master is never really done. Markets change (duh) and in order to truly be a master, you have to keep up with the changes. Don't go overboard—you do have other things to do besides preview (I hope!), but try to keep Market Mastery on your to-do list. You'll feel awfully smart the next time you capture a great new client at a party because you knew how much that Victorian down the street sold for!

Nurturing Your Relationships TODAY for Business Tomorrow

So, what can you do with your Sphere of Influence TODAY to fill your pipeline for 2010?

Well, just about anything, really. Except begging, bribing or pestering. If, today, you begin making a concerted effort to reconnect with the people you know, by the end of the year, you'll have made a real impression on a lot of people. And I'll bet you'll have met a lot MORE people to include in your sphere to make a real impression on.

What do I mean by reconnect? Well, it depends on how formal you want to get with it. If you've been hankering to change up your business model away from traditional prospecting and into something a little more fun, then you might want to explore the various programs available to walk you thru doing just that (and, yeah, I have one or two of those).

Or, just set some easy goals to have a couple lunch dates every week, to pick up the phone and call a friend if you have a bona-fide reason to. Accept invitations to parties you might normally decline. Have your own casual dinner party or afternoon BBQ. Organize a girls night or boys night out. Go through your email inbox and look for old conversations you can pick back up. Oh, heavens, there are a gazillion things you can do to get back in touch with the people you know and increase the likelihood of making new friends.

Just promise me you won't beg, bribe or pester anyone for business during your reconnection efforts. Or, ever. If you do, your friends and acquaintances won't appreciate being reconnected with and not only will your Sphere of Influence business model fail, you'll likely lose some friendships over it.

And that's bad.

AVOID BURNOUT! Stop Taking Responsibility for Stuff that's Not Your Responsibility to Take!

The other day I had a three-way conversation with two agents who are in the middle of career crises. Both are trying to decide whether to stay or go, interestingly, for opposite reasons. AgentFriend1 has too much business and is burning out and AgentFriend2, well, doesn't. Have too much business, that is. And she's burning out, too.

We talked about burnout and both agents confessed that they become deeply involved in their clients' personal situations and get sucked into the emotional drama of it all. Which isn't uncommon in our business; after all, we ARE deeply involved in the whole mess—if our seller doesn't have enough equity to properly price; if our buyer's loan changes and they have to come up with an additional 5% down; if our listing doesn't appraise and the deal crashes... yes, these events DO affect us both financially and emotionally. And frankly, if they didn't affect us, we probably wouldn't be effective at our jobs.

But you can draw a line and preserve your sanity. Terry Watson (www.TerryWatson.com) calls it "the Monkey." He describes how we wrongly let others put their monkeys on our backs—even though we have our own monkeys to deal with, thank you very much! We real estate agents are really good at accepting our clients' monkeys as our own.

And you know what? Our clients are HAPPY to give us their monkeys and then blame us when things go wrong. Further, we accept that blame—which puts us in a position where we have to apologize for our inability to solve a problem that ISN'T OURS TO SOLVE.

Here's an example. The seller owes $415,000 on his home. The market value is no more than $395,000 and that's pushing it. In order to break even, the seller needs to sell at $430,000 at least. The seller "doesn't want to do a short sale," so he looks to his agent for another solution. What solution does the agent come up with?

1. Price at $439,900 and hope for a miracle

2. Reduce her commission to nothing and price at $420,000 (and hope for a miracle)

Of course, there are other solutions, but we monkey-acceptors want to please, so these are the ones we propose. (And then we're miserable because we have an unsellable product, but that's another story.)

Here's another example. You interview for a tenant-occupied listing. The seller doesn't want to inconvenience the tenant, so he asks for a 24-hour showing requirement; for day-time showings only; that you attend all showings, and a 60-day possession. You want to please the seller, so you agree, knowing what he's asking will make the property unmarketable...and you miserable.

Do too many of these deals and I think burnout IS an inevitability.

Of course, it's easy to advise, "Well, just thank the %$SOB^# very much for the opportunity and walk away!" I hear that advice all the time, and sure, that's an option. But there's a better way...a way to respectfully decline the monkey and move forward without alienating someone who could be a wonderful client and future referral source.

Stay tuned...

Declining the Monkey Without Being Snotty About It—Part II

The first trick to respectfully declining your clients' monkeys is to know which monkeys are appropriate to decline. And which are rightfully yours to carry. Yes, when our clients hire us, they have a right to expect us to take on some of the burden of their real estate transaction. Entering into a real estate agent/client relationship creates responsibilities on each side. The clearer you are on whose responsibilities are whose, the easier it will be to assign them to the appropriate party.

Put another way, what factors of the transaction are within your control, which are within your client's control and which are out of either of your control?

You control:

- the services you are willing to provide

- the marketing you are willing and able to do

- the price at which you are willing to take a listing

- whether or not you will take a short-sale listing

- the expertise you have in advising a seller how to prepare for market

- the resources you have in place to help a seller prepare for market

- the times you are available to your buyer

- your willingness to show short sales, foreclosures, FSBO's or new construction

- how often you will communicate with your client

- how much you charge for your services

Your client controls:

- the price he is willing to list and sell for

- how much he is willing to "come to the table with" if he's upside down in his mortgage

- whether or not he's willing to short-sell

- the amount of work he is willing to do and the funds he has available to prepare for market

- what marketing services he will require from his agent

- whether or not to allow unrestricted showings

- the times he is available to look at houses

- how much he is willing to offer on a home

- whether or not he wants to pursue short sales, foreclosures, FSBOs or new construction

- whether or not he is happy with the inventory in his price range

- how much he is willing to pay for real estate services

Neither of you controls:

- changing lending requirements

- overall market activity

- the cost of home maintenance and repair

- interest rates

- closing costs

- the underwriter

- the agent on the other side of the deal

- the buyer or seller on the other side of the deal

So, how are these "control" issues relevant to getting the various monkeys assigned properly? Any thoughts?

I'll share mine next time...

How to Decline the Monkey, Part III

Previously, I wrote about CONTROL. Specifically, which issues of a real estate transaction (i.e., Monkeys) YOU control; which ones your CLIENT controls and which ones neither of you has any say over. My point in spelling it all out wasn't to give anyone permission to be snotty with a buyer or seller when he tries to hand off his Monkey; no, I just wanted to clarify which Monkeys are appropriate to decline. ("Declining the Monkey" means to refuse to accept responsibility for problems that are not yours to solve.)

Believe it or not, politely declining to take on your clients' monkeys has a lot to do with respect. Respecting your CLIENT'S intelligence, abilities and willingness to do his part. Acknowledging that your client has a brain and a checkbook, and that he can probably find some free time. A lot of us don't seem to give our clients the benefit of the doubt that they are willing or able to do their part, so we either offer to do it for them or walk away frustrated.

Sure, an upside-down seller will be more than happy to dump his upside-down monkey on you, if you agree to take it. A frustrated buyer would be tickled to let YOU figure out where that extra 5% down is going to come from when the terms of his loan change. But you CAN gracefully hand that monkey back to the buyer or seller without his ever noticing the hand-off!

Let's use the example from my initial blog of the seller who owes $415,000 on a house that might be worth $395,000. To come out whole, he really needs to sell around $430,000. Oh, and he doesn't want to come to the table with money or short-sell the house.

What do you do?

Of course, you can refuse to take the listing, and indeed, that's what you might end up doing. Or you might agree to take the listing at a too-high price, and regret it every day for the next six months. But are those the only two options?

NO!

There is another solution to this problem. One that may result in a sellable listing. What IS this magic solution?

I dunno.

It's your seller's solution to discover. And if you let him keep his monkey, he may very well come up with the solution on his own. Maybe he'll decide to kiss up to Aunt Lulu and ask her for a short-term loan to cover the spread. Maybe he'll decide a short sale isn't out of the question. Maybe he'll agree to make the improvements you recommend to give him a better shot at a higher price.

Or maybe he'll come up with something brilliant none of us thought of.

But...but...but...how DO you show your prospect or client the respect of letting him keep his own monkeys? What do you say? Or not say?

You know the drill...stay tuned...

What to SAY (or not say, as the case may be) to Respectfully Decline the Monkey!

It's really easy for Old Fogie types (like me) to confidently proclaim that WE don't accept Monkeys that aren't ours to mess with, and WE (said in a deep, gravelly voice) just tell our clients the way it is and if they don't agree; NEXT!

But it's not that easy, especially for newer agents who really aren't sure what their responsibilities are, and are not in the mood to NEXT anyone. So, here are some tips.

- Don't be an objection-buster (aka Silence is Golden). When a client throws out objections, concerns or stumbling blocks, think before you speak. Often these objections, concerns or stumbling blocks will be HIS Monkeys, not yours. Just smile, nod and make an "I hear ya" noise, and let the client continue. If he wants your input, he'll ask for it directly, but until he does, just listen without offering solutions.

  If, after your moment of golden silence, you realize that this IS your Monkey, go ahead and offer a response or solution. If you aren't sure, just write it down or commit it to memory to ponder later. You can always accept a Monkey after the fact, but it's much tougher to return a Monkey after you've accepted it prematurely.

- Ask "What's Your Plan B?" as if you are not guaranteeing the desired outcome...which you aren't. I use this strategy with sellers who are being a little stubborn about pricing, accessibility or condition. I sweetly ask them what they will do if their home doesn't sell for the price they "need," or at all. This subtly lets them know that while I'll do my best, I need their cooperation to get their home sold and without it, I won't take full responsibility for their home selling—that's not a Monkey I'll accept.

- A la Jackie Leavenworth, the Real Estate Whisperer (www.coachjackie. com)—if a buyer or seller looks to you to solve a problem that isn't rea-sonably yours to solve (e.g., you give up some of your commission to put or hold a deal together), you can gently say something like, *"I've found that when a real estate agent wants to make a deal more than the other parties involved, it's not the right deal to make."*

So, what's the punch line?

If you know which Monkeys are yours to carry...and which are not...and you respect the other party enough to let him keep his own Monkeys, you'll be a much happier, healthier and RESTED real estate agent!

A Perfect Example of Keeping the Monkey... Agents Bickering over Commission to Keep the Buyer and Seller in the Deal

Considering my recent ramblings on Declining the Monkey, I had a timely conversation yesterday with an agent friend of mine. He has a house listed for a friend (at $449,000) and agreed to a very low commission 'cause the friend was close to being upside down and "didn't want to short sell."

Fine. As a self-employed independent contractor who works at a 100% company, he can charge whatever percentage he sees fit. As it should be.

So, along comes Ms. Buyer Agent with an offer of $405,000. The seller counters the offer at $430,000. The buyer counters the counter at $410,000. Mr. Listing Agent tells Ms. Buyer Agent that if she can get the price to $425,000 AND kick in 1% of her commission, they have a deal ('cause, remember, the seller "doesn't want" to short sell).

Ms. Buyer Agent (who is pretty new), balks, but doesn't outright refuse. An argument between the agents ensues. Mr. Listing Agent says that he can't kick in any more because he's already at his I-don't-get-up-in-the-morning-for-less-than fee. Ms. Buyer Agent says that after her split (which would be based off the "full" commission advertised in the MLS), she would walk away with less than $3,000 on what should be a payday of over $8,000. Mr. Listing Agent shrugs and says "Well, that's what it's going to take to get this deal done," and dismisses her as short-sighted ("Wouldn't you rather have 3,000 dollars than zero dollars?").

Ms. Buyer Agent sulks off, but apparently decides that, indeed, $3,000 is better than $0, returns to the table and agrees to the terms. Between the two of them, the commissions shared on this $425,000 sale will be around $5,000. Not EACH. Total.

So, what we have here are two agents who want the deal more than either the buyer or seller wants the deal. Besides the fact that this deal has very little chance of ever closing (we all know how these marginally motivated "successful" negotiations come out), this is a prime example of Accepting a Monkey the agent has no reason to accept.

The seller (presumably) wants to sell his house. The buyer (presumably) likes this house more than any other she's seen. If either or both of these statements are true, the BUYER AND SELLER need to (and probably will) reach agreement with each other. If neither of these statements is true, then the deal has no business being struck. It is NOT the agents' problem to solve, financially anyway, that the seller doesn't want to come to the table with money and/or the buyer doesn't want to pay the seller's price.

+

And that, finally, is the end of the Monkey series. I hope you enjoyed it!

Even if They Don't Complain...Sellers Notice

If the brochure box is empty...they notice

If their brochures still show the original price after two reductions...they notice

If their agent hasn't done an Open House in six months (or ever)...they notice

If no feedback cometh after showings...they notice

If there haven't been any showings in a month...they notice

If their Craigslist ad hasn't been refreshed...they notice

If their agent hasn't updated them on market activity...they notice

If their online photos are from two seasons ago...they notice

If the only time they hear from their agent is when he calls to ask for a price reduction...they notice

Just because a seller doesn't complain doesn't mean he's happy. And just because he's not complaining to his agent doesn't mean he's keeping quiet elsewhere. Trust me on this. If his agent doesn't seem to care about selling his home...the seller notices.

Sixteen Ways to Keep Your Seller Happy with You

What's the Number One Thing "they" say that homesellers complain about?

All together now...

Communication (or lack thereof) from their agent. And, having been on the other side of the For Sale sign a time or two, I can certainly second that emotion. But "communication" isn't just about calling every week to say "Hi, how're doin'?" No, it's also about keeping the seller informed on local market activity. On providing feedback from showings. On notifying him of new competing listings and recently closed sales. And, frankly, on making sure the seller knows exactly what his agent's been up to to promote his home!

If the only time a listing agent contacts a seller is to ask for a price reduction or a listing extension, well, I can pretty much guarantee that seller is less than tickled with his agent. And that agent deserves every bit of his seller's discontent! Oh, the seller may not complain to his agent, but I'll bet he's not keeping quiet around the coffee machine!

The good news is that keeping a seller happy isn't that hard. They just wanna know what's going on and that their agent cares. Is that too much to ask?

Here are sixteen things you can do to keep your seller happy with you. And a happy-with-you seller just might be a great source of future business!

1. Notify him as soon as the listing hits the MLS and send him a copy of the listing.

2. Send him links to all your online advertising (Realtor.com, Craigslist, Postlets, Active Rain, your own blog, etc.).

3. Send him a copy of the home brochure before it goes to print and ask for feedback.

4. Make sure he knows when home brochures will be delivered.

5. Schedule an open house right away (yes, you should do an open house).

6. Call after the first showing(s) to see if he has any questions about the process.

7. Pursue and deliver feedback, especially in the first month

8. If you do any print advertising, send the seller copies (including Just Listed cards).

9. Send him a "state of the market" report showing all the competing listings. Update this report every two or three weeks.

10. Call periodically to find out if he's running low on brochures (if it's impractical to keep the box full, just remove it).

11. Be sure to provide feedback after open houses (...if someone else does your open houses for you, be sure to follow up with them afterwards).

12. Schedule an appointment to review the latest market activity.

13. Preview any new competition and provide feedback to your seller.

14. Refresh your Craigslist ads and send the seller a link.

15. Ensure that your photos are in season.

16. Ask for feedback on how you're doing.

How many of these items do you already do? If you do at least 50% of them, you're blowing away your competition. Sad, isn't it? The last few times I've had my own properties listed, my agents did ZERO of these activities. ZERO... Zero.

A happy seller is a cooperative seller. An unhappy seller is not, and will likely become more and more uncooperative as time goes by. You pick!

October 2009

Why Did My Friend Hire Someone Else?
Oh, Let Me Count the Reasons...

Ooooooh...it hurts. It hurts a lot. When someone you know hires someone other than wonderful YOU to represent them in the purchase or sale of a home.

It's painful—I know it is. I've been there and, especially in my first few years, was devastated every time it happened. So I get it. I understand why it can ruin your day. Especially if that paycheck would have reeeeeeally come in handy right about now.

But you know what? When it happens, it's almost never personal. Seriously. No, I'm not saying that "business is business—get over it." I'm saying that the person who hired someone else probably had no idea it would bother you. They didn't select AGAINST you, they picked someone else! There's a big difference!!!!

Of course, sometimes it might be personal. Perhaps you WERE selected against. When that's the case, you have two choices. You can either be mad at the person for "betraying" their "obligation" to you or you can ask yourself why they felt someone else was a better choice. I vote for Option B. Look in the mirror, take the blame. Strive to improve.

It's also possible that the person is just a jerk and hired someone else to hurt you. I really doubt it. That's a pretty self-absorbed viewpoint, as if this other person's world revolves around you. But if that's the case, well, then that's a friend you really don't need to worry much about, right?

So, what are some reasons a friend or acquaintance might either:

1. Pick someone else, or

2. NOT pick you?

Reasons a friend or acquaintance might pick someone else to be their real estate agent:

•   They forgot you sell real estate.

- Their best friend just got her real estate license.

- They met a real estate agent at an open house and really liked him.

- They called on a For Sale sign and really hit it off with the listing agent.

- They're buying in a specific neighborhood and want to work with the neighborhood expert.

- The agent they hired promised them a commission rebate.

- The husband's boss's wife is a real estate agent, and he wants to kiss up.

Reasons a friend or acquaintance might not pick YOU:

- They don't want to share their financial information with someone they know.

- They thought you specialized in a different part of town.

- They had a bad experience with another agent in your company.

- They worked with another agent in your company in the past and would feel bad hiring you instead of them.

- They know too much about your personal life and doubt your stability (ouch).

- They think you work in higher price ranges and wouldn't be interested in their piddly little deal.

- They know several real estate agents and don't want to hurt anyone's feelings, so they hired a stranger.

Ten Ways to Show Your Seller You Don't Care

Now that the listing agreement is signed and your FOR SALE sign is in the yard, you're done, right? Onto the next ~~victim~~ prospect to WOW with your fancy listing presentation and 132-point marketing plan! Of course, most of those 132 points are pretty much fluff & nonsense, but by the time you've overwhelmed the seller with your promises of Exceptional Service and Total Commitment, he probably won't notice.

No, he probably WON'T notice at the time, but he'll certainly notice later. The good news is that by then it's too late! He's committed to ~~stuck with~~ you! And you'll be damned if you'll let him out of your listing agreement after you've spent ALL THAT MONEY and ALL THAT TIME on his listing! Besides, he probably won't have the guts to even ask (whew!).

Want to Show Your Seller How Much You (Don't) Care?

It's easy! Just follow these simple steps...

1. Don't send your seller a copy of the MLS listing entry to get his feedback.

2. Don't let him know when his house officially goes "on the market."

3. Don't offer to do an open house, and be sure to argue with him if he asks you to.

4. Don't call the seller after your open house with feedback.

5. Don't call the seller after you show his house with feedback.

6. Don't call after the first few showings just to check in.

7. Don't monitor showings, but the next time you talk, ask, "Have you had any showings lately?"

8. Put up a brochure box, but never fill it (or let it stay empty after the first batch is gone).

9. Don't send the seller copies of your advertising.

10. Don't contact the seller at all until it's time to ask for price reduction or to extend the listing.

If you follow these simple instructions for each and every one of your listings, you will be assured a long, glorious career of prospecting, prospecting, prospecting to keep that pipeline filled! You'll never have to worry about repeat or referral business distracting you from your all-important prospecting schedule...

"Jennifer, What Do You Think of Client Appreciation Parties?"

Earlier this week, I spoke on the subject of Selling to Your Sphere of Influence—No Sales Pitch Required! at the Colorado REALTOR® Convention.

As I usually do, I did my best to debunk many of the sacred cows of the SOI- business model training industry, such as how important it is to ask for referrals, why it's a great idea to categorize your friends based on their history of referring to you—stuff like that.

The crowd seemed to accept my protestations that this behavior is not only obnoxious, but that it's not terribly effective. Cool.

I closed my presentation by encouraging the audience to evaluate from their gut every prospecting strategy that crosses their path...to ask themselves if the strategy they're considering is one they're excited about and proud of; to be honest with themselves as to how they would respond to the strategy if used on them and whether or not it would annoy them, if used on them. And to trust what their guts have to say on the matter.

A woman in the back of the room raised her hand and asked if I "approved" of Client Appreciation parties. I asked her if she would enjoy holding such an event and she said she would. I responded with "then absolutely—have that party" with the explanation that if you enjoy doing something, it's probably a good prospecting activity for you. Me? Nah, I'd be too afraid no one would show up and it wouldn't be worth the pre-party stress!

But later I gave this some more thought and wish I had just another 45 seconds in that room to share the rest of the story...

Which is...I just can't get excited about the phrase "client appreciation party." Oh, it's not the worst thing in the world, but to me, it sounds like an event specifically held to make me feel obligated to the host with my future real estate business as opposed to a party where I'll have a great time. I dunno—there's just something about that title that gives the introvert in me the heebie-jeebies—even more so than a run-of-the-mill party invitation might evoke.

Am I saying not to have the party? Heavens no! Party on, my friend! But call it something else! Have your party in conjunction with an event of general appeal—Oktoberfest, Halloween, your or your spouse's birthday, the World Series or Super Bowl, your housewarming celebration (even if you moved over a year ago!), or just your "first annual wine and cheese tasting" party.

Don't approach your precious Sphere of Influence as a real estate agent first and foremost, as if that's all you are to them. Be a friend or pleasant acquaintance who throws a good party and, oh, yeah, also happens to sell real estate.

Adventures in Pricing—Historic Homes in Urban Neighborhoods

A few months ago (sheesh, almost six months already!) I stopped actively selling real estate. Oh, not to worry, I still keep my fingers in the pie and my toes in the water of the Denver real estate market, but I don't actually list or sell properties in my own name. However, being the control freak that I am, anyone who gets a referral from me can count on lots of—ahem—help from me, especially if they're working with someone from my precious Sphere of Influence. I'm sure my—ahem—help is very much appreciated.

Anyway, I recently referred a sweeeeet Charming Old Denver listing to a fellow SWS'er—Mary Beth Bonacci. It's in one of Denver's many historic neighborhoods and was built in 1908. If you're fortunate enough to work in charming old neighborhoods, you know how challenging it can be to accurately price these homes. After 100 years (give or take a dozen) of renovations—not only of the subject property, but also of the surrounding neighbors, the influx of infill development, changes to perceived trendiness "boundaries," the comings and goings of neighborhood amenities, not to mention school district nuances and zoning codes...you can pretty much bet that there ain't another house just like the one you're trying to price.

Oh, sure, on paper, there are probably dozens. After all, builders weren't much more creative back then than they are today. Drive down a street in Denver's Washington Park and you'll see Bungalow after Bungalow built in 1927—the tract homes of the 20's. On the next block, you might see Tudor after Tudor built in 1935—the tract home of the 30's. Similar square footages, similar lot sizes, the same existence of or lack of a basement...

And of course, all the MLS descriptions of your comparables proclaim the homes to be Renovated with Pottery Barn Flair! Or to have a Gourmet Custom Kitchen with Stainless Appliances & Granite Counters! Oh, and in a Perfect Location, too.

But I digress.

I decided Mary Beth needed my help pricing the sweeeet listing I referred to her. And she graciously agreed to let me—ahem—help.

Actually, we had a great time. 'Specially me—since I'd been out of the loop a few months, it was a bit of a novelty to get out there in the trenches and exercise my pricing expertise again.

But, as it usually does, it amazed me that many agents price simply from what the seller tells them about their home and what the MLS data tells them about the market. In other words, they have a telephone conversation with the seller, spend an hour in front of the computer and voila! They create a "professional" CMA and proudly present it to their seller prospect as gospel.

And proceed to the market with an improperly priced home...

Perhaps this strategy works just fine in a newer tract home development. But in a historic neighborhood? No way.

Stay tuned for some hints & tips on pricing urban homes in historic neighborhoods....I love this stuff...

Pricing Historic Homes in Urban Markets—Step One: Make like a Boy Scout...

Pricing historic homes in urban markets is a bit (a lot?) more time-consuming than pricing newer homes in planned developments. But, at least to my way of thinking, it's a whole lot more fun! Hope you think so, too...

Step One is to Drive by the Home. Never, ever, ever begin the pricing process until you've at least driven by the subject property. You need to have an accurate mental picture of the home and its general location on the planet in order to take the next step. When you drive by, be sure to look for any locational challenges such as nearby railroad tracks, overhead high-tension power lines, undesirable neighbors (either commercial or residential) or obvious parking issues. If the home has an alley, drive through it to see what the back of the house overlooks.

Very few older urban homes are in a perfect location; almost all have some locational challenge that buyers will object to. You need to be aware of any such objections upfront. On the other hand, if the subject property IS in a perfect location, that's something you need to know as well, because most of the comparables you'll be using won't be.

While we're on the topic, it's far better if you can get inside the house before you prepare your CMA. I usually handle this by doing a 2-step listing presentation—the first being an information-gathering/rapport-building meeting and the second focusing on the current market—i.e., pricing. (Actually, I do a three-step listing presentation, but I'll talk about that later.)

That said, whether you do a one-step, two-step or even three-step listing presentation, never meet face2face with a seller without first, driving by the house and, second, perusing the relevant market data online. You need to be at least conversational about the local market, even if you haven't done your detailed research yet. Remember, the general public thinks all we do all day is drive around and look at houses, so if you stutter, stammer and hedge when the seller asks you about his neighborhood's market activity during your first meeting, he'll certainly doubt your professionalism and expertise. Being able to casually toss out a few neighborhood statistics or hyper-local market factoids will do wonders for your confidence and credibility.

If there are any homes for sale or any that have recently sold within one block of the seller's home, know the details of the listings or sales, even if they aren't comparable. Your seller knows all about them and he'll expect you to as well.

Homeowners in urban markets tend to be pretty enamored with their neighborhood and will expect their real estate agent to be, too. So, be as prepared as you can, as early as you can.

Next Time—Step Two—Gentlemen (and ladies), Start Your Research!

November 2009

Pricing Historic Homes in Urban Markets—Step Two: Preview, Preview, Preview!

In the last installment, I recommended that you always, always, always drive by your subject property before doing anything else. If you can get inside, so much the better...

So after you have a good visual of your subject property, it's time to go check out the competition—otherwise known as "previewing."

When I interview to list a property, I often find myself bonding with the home, to the point where it's almost as hard for me to be objective about it as it is for the sellers. I really have to fight the temptation to be overly critical of "my" listing's competition, while excusing "my" listing's challenges and flaws. Sometimes I'll take another agent with me on my previewing tour to help keep me objective.

Selecting the Homes to Preview

Which homes should you preview? In a word (okay, a phrase)—as many as you can. Even if they aren't exactly comparable. With every house you tour, you gain a little better grasp on the up-to-the-minute marketplace, which makes it much easier to pinpoint the proper price range to recommend. It just happens naturally. As you look at the competition, you'll start to get a feeling for where your listing falls in the scheme of things, and the more you look at, the more confident you'll be in that feeling.

I try to preview at least 10 houses when I'm pricing a home. Sometimes I'll get lazy and only hit five—and I always regret it. It seems that it's right around the sixth or seventh house that I start to trust my gut about pricing. And that gut feeling is further confirmed on the eighth, ninth and tenth.

Depending on my price range, I'll preview all comparable houses within $50,000 (on each side) of where I think my listing will fall. By "comparable," I mean homes that offer similar square footage for the money. I probably won't preview a 1,000sqft Bungalow if I'm listing a 2,000sqft Victorian; they just won't attract the same buyer, even though they may very well be priced similarly. I always preview any homes within one block of my seller's property, even if they aren't comparable at all. It's just good practice in case the seller asks you about it.

Always preview the low outliers. A "low outlier" is a house that looks good on paper, but seems to be a screaming deal. You need to know why it's priced so well...but hasn't sold. There probably is a good reason. If there isn't, then this is the listing to beat. But we'll talk about that later.

How about the high outliers? The houses that are priced way above the rest, which are probably getting your seller all excited? Look at those, too. Chances are that they're just grossly overpriced (and the more houses you look at, the more sure you'll be of this). If they aren't overpriced, there's something really fabulous about them, and you need to know what it is.

As you're setting your previews, note if any homes are difficult to show. That will definitely affect market value. And frankly, if they are, I'll skip them. Lazy? Maybe, but on the other hand, a difficult-to-show home is not going to be comparable to MY listing because I don't take difficult-to-show listings!

Effective previewing in an urban market entails a lot more than just looking at a bunch of homes. Sure, that's what you're going to do (look at a bunch of homes), but in order to really evaluate the information you're gathering, you need to go in with the heart & mind of a detective.

We'll talk about that next time.

Playing Detective...Pricing Historic Homes in Urban Neighborhoods: Step 3

In the last installment, I talked about how important it is to preview preview preview. The more competing listings you preview, the better sense you'll have of where your listing falls into the mix.

Remember, the houses you're previewing are 1) the competition for your listing and 2) houses that haven't sold.

Why is it important to check out the active listings? Some agents don't preview because they don't think the active listings are relevant. "All that matters is SOLD." Eh, I disagree. First, what's SOLD is not competing with your upcoming listing, and when you're dealing with older homes, buyers don't always have a lot of options that meet their criteria. In many cases, the buyer will only find one or two homes that even come close, so knowing what they're comparing your listing to is critical.

Second, it's important to know WHY that active competition hasn't sold. Especially if it appears to be "priced well." You'll never know for sure why a house hasn't sold by looking at the MLS, although you may have your suspicions. It's not as if the listing agent is going to tell you that the house reeks of cat urine or point out that there's no bathroom on the main floor.

So, when you're previewing, ask yourself...

- [ ] WHY hasn't this house sold?

- [ ] WHAT makes it superior (or inferior) to my listing?

- [ ] HOW could the listing agent do a better job marketing this home?

- [ ] WHO is the ideal buyer for this property and is it the same ideal buyer as mine will attract?

(I can't think of a "when" or a "where," so I'll move on.)

Training yourself to ask these questions at every house you preview makes you a better previewer, and therefore, a better pricer. It also helps you to remember each house so you can speak intelligently about the competition with your seller when discussing pricing, as well as down the road when that home's status changes (sells, withdraws or reduces the price), you'll be able to nod and say to yourself, "Hmmmm, I thought so!"

Speaking of down the road...this is another important reason to preview. If the competition sells before your listing does, you'll be familiar with it in case appraisal problems come up on your property and the appraiser wants to use comparables that aren't appropriate. If you've been IN all the comparables, it's much easier to make a compelling case!

Okay, 'nuff about previewing. Next time, we'll talk about how to evaluate the SOLDs in your CMA to help you price your historic home in your urban neighborhood!

Pricing Historic Homes in Urban Neighborhoods, Step Four: Analyzing the SOLDs—Dealing with the Outliers

The problem with using SOLDs in your market analysis is, unless you've been a previewing mad (wo)man over the last eight months, you probably haven't seen the inside of the properties, and now it's too late. So you have to go off the MLS description—a very risky proposition!

But we'll do our best.

Print off all the SOLDs that seem to be comparable, even if they're much higher or lower than your assumption of the market value of "your" listing. Drive by all of them! Pay special attention to the outliers—the ones that seem to have sold way out of whack to the rest of the market, or whose Days on Market statistic is unusually low or high.

There's a good chance your drive-by will reveal the reason for the out-of-line price or DOM. Perhaps there's a commercial building next door, behind or across the street. Or, common in Denver, a corner lot that doesn't have a private back yard, or any back yard at all. Maybe it's a pop-top done wrong and doesn't fit in with the neighborhood. Busy street with a bus stop in the front yard?

Or conversely, you might see that it has a stellar location with an extra-large lot, a mountain view or around the corner (at a suitable distance) from a popular coffee shop.

If the reason for the outlying price and/or DOM isn't obvious from your drive-by, go line-by line through the MLS listing. Is it missing a garage in a market that expects garages? No basement? One bathroom? Obviously, if the interior photos show that it needs work, that's relevant. Check the showing instructions to see if there are any obvious limitations on access.

If all else fails, and you really feel a particular house is a good comparable, call the listing agent. Hopefully they'll be helpful so you'll understand why the house sold at the price it did. Or, maybe not. But give it a try.

It really is the outliers that give you the most grief when looking at the SOLDs. There probably are some sold listings that fall right in line with what you're thinking the price of your listing ought to be, but the ones that don't give you fits. The more research you do on these outliers will not only make your CMA stronger, but will give you an air of confidence when going through your CMA with a seller.

"Real Estate Is a Relationship Business"— Not Exactly (a rant)

We hear this all the time—heck, I say it all the time! "Real Estate is a Relationship Business"—meaning that the more people who know you and like you, the more real estate you'll sell. As opposed to the good old Numbers Game philosophy that the more people who throw away your monthly marketing postcards or ignore your newspaper advertising, the more real estate you will sell.

And of course, I believe this—at least the part about how the more people who know you and like you, the more real estate you'll sell.

But is real estate really a relationship business?

I say no.

This blog was partially inspired by an episode of the reality show "Million Dollar Listing" (don't get me started. Oops, too late.)

The three twenty-something ~~boys~~ young men ~~drama queens~~ who are the stars of the real estate reality show seem to have an unending supply of "Dear Friends" with gazillions of dollars to spend on real estate (or gazillion-dollar homes to sell). Dear, dear friends. *"After all,"* sez Chad, *"real estate is a relationship business."*

Hmmmmm.

If you've ever watched the show with a critical/cynical eye, you might have noticed that these ~~boys~~ young men ~~drama queens~~ give abysmally bad counsel. Often laughably self-serving, almost always bordering on incompetent. They advise their Dear Friends to make full price offers in a declining market before the house even hits the market. They allow their sellers to dictate the price and terms of their listings, whining all the while that the seller is being unreasonable (but not knowing what else to do). They talk their buyers out of even asking for repairs at inspection because the seller has already come down on his price (again, in a recessionary market).

I don't know anything about agency law in California, but if it's anything like Colorado, these ~~boys~~ young men ~~drama queens~~ are failing in their agency obligations to their clients. Or, if not technically violating agency law, definitely doing nothing to earn their $100k+++ commissions.

Speaking of commissions, a recent episode showed Madison being dismayed when his seller client accepted a lowball offer on her $3.75M listing, which resulted in—get this—a $42,000 decrease in commissions for him! Poor Madison.

So, what does this have to do with real estate and relationships?

Selling real estate is about knowing how to sell real estate. Let's say that differently. It's about knowing how to manage and facilitate the exchange of real property so that the buyer or seller who hired you is satisfied with the outcome.

Sure, building your real estate business may have everything to do with your relationships, but THAT'S NOT WHAT WE DO! Is tax preparation a relationship business? Is dentistry a relationship business? Is dog-training a relationship business?

No, we expect our tax preparers to know how to prepare taxes. We hope our dentists know how to fix cavities. We expect a dog-trainer to be a master in dog behavior. That's their business.

Our buyers and sellers have the right to expect that we know our business. Which is...how to manage and facilitate the exchange of real property. Not how to persuade our Dear Friends to provide us with easy paychecks.

Rant Over.

It's That Time of Year Again...Doo-Dad Time!

Ahhhhhhh...flickering jack-o-lanterns...the changing o'the leaves...the first snowfall...chestnuts roasting on an open fire...and time to order your end-of-year Doo-Dads!

Every year 'round this time, real estate agents open their checkbooks (or, better said, key in their credit card numbers) and spend millions of dollars on calendars and other Doo-Dads designed to be distributed to anyone and everyone who crosses their paths. The goal? Why, to ensure that every human being on the planet knows who they are, what they do and how to reach them, of course!

A worthy goal, indeed.

Even I, staunch opponent of the typical Doo-Dad, am sorely tempted this time of year to spend my few remaining marketing dollars on something of value to throw at my sphere of influence in hopes of drumming up some last minute fourth-quarter business or filling up my pipeline for the spring season.

But sheesh, most Doo-Dads are really silly. C'mon—personalized fly-swatters? Ice-scrapers? Lip balm? Oh, I'm not sayin' that I won't use a free fly-swatter, ice-scraper or lip balm, but I can pretty much promise you that such Doo-Dads are NOT going to make me feel obligated to use the person or company whose name graces said Doo-Dad!

That said...I like magnets. Always have. Not just any old magnet, mind you; it has to be cool if it's gonna go on my fridge. Even more important, it has to be cool if it's gonna get sent out to my precious sphere of influence.

What do I mean by "cool"? Glad you asked.

A "cool" magnet is one that is 1) extremely clever or attractive, and/or 2) contains truly useful information that the recipient will appreciate and 3) reflects my personality or interests.

What are some examples of UNcool magnets? Oh, how about a plain-jane, vanilla business card magnet? Or a list of kitchen measurements? Or, from someone like me, the sports schedule of the local hockey team? (But if you LOOOOOOOVE hockey, this would be totally cool for you).

If you're going to spend your hard-earned dollars on Doo-Dads, put your money where your heart is. If something seems a bit silly to you, it probably is. As with every other prospecting method you evaluate, be willing to listen to what your gut has to say on the matter. If your gut seems to be saying "Eh... we can do better," trust me, you can.

A Real Estate Career Is NOT for the Liability-Phobic*

Been watching a conversation on the web about whether or not to put buyers in your car...as opposed to driving separately. While some of the comments are ridiculously snotty ("They can drive themselves!" or "Let THEM use their own gas!"), the most sincere objection seems to be that putting another warm body in your car creates liability for you.

We hear similar objections all the time to doing things that serve our clients.

DON'T attend inspections! DON'T recommend mortgage brokers! Don't give any advice that might be construed as legal! Don't put buyers in your car! Blah blah blah.

Basically, in order to CYA to the best of your ability, you should, as one instructor put it—"stand outside and smoke" during most phases of a real estate transaction. To avoid liability, y'know.

Well, shoot, I don't buy it. My buyers and sellers paid me darn good money to be intimately involved with every facet of their real estate transaction. And I showed up. Yes, to inspections. I got on the roof and joined the party in the crawlspace. If I didn't know three good inspectors, I recommended only the one or two I liked. I wrote my own addendums that probably bordered on practicing law. And yes, I put buyers in my car.

It was my job. And in my 13 years of doing my job, I can honestly say I was richly rewarded for doing my job and only threatened legally once. By doing my job, I served my clients, which not only led to happy clients, but more paychecks for ME 'cause my deals closed!

I knew what I was doing. And I did it. Even if I risked being sued. This is a liability-ridden business. If you cain't take that heat...go find another kitchen to play in.

By the way, here's my opinion on putting buyers in my car:

In 13 years, I can count on one hand (okay, maybe two) the number of times I rode separately from my buyers. I usually drove, but if my buyer had a kids' car-seat issue, I rode with them. The only times I had a buyer follow me was if we were meeting at the house and only looking at a few others—then it just seemed to make sense.

The time spent driving between houses is great bonding, rapport-building and information-gathering time. I can't imagine not having that time with my buyers as we're getting to know each other and figuring out what they want in a house. It also gives me the opportunity to demonstrate my expertise in the area and for them to ask questions which builds my credibility.

I've shopped for houses in other markets and the agents always drove. I'm trying to imagine them leaving me in my rental car to follow them in an unfamiliar town...and I'm pretty sure I would think they were rude, antisocial, lazy or ashamed of their car. I certainly wouldn't think MORE of them if they made me drive myself.

That said, if I didn't feel safe with someone, I probably wouldn't want them in my car, but neither would I be working with them.

* Nothing written here should be construed as legal advice <grin>

Greatness Doesn't Inspire Me Nearly as Much as Mediocrity Does

We read about Great leaders who have overcome tremendous obstacles to achieve...well...Great things. We hear stories of tippy-top producers who found themselves at some point living in their cars...but today make gazillions of dollars. There are stories like Jack Canfield's where he had to peddle his idea for the Chicken Soup for the Soul book to dozens of publishers before one bit...and it became one of the best-selling books of all time.

Stories like these are supposed to be inspiring. But can I be brutally honest for a moment? I find them more intimidating than inspiring. Call me humble (ha!), but I'm just not sure I have what it takes to reach such Greatness and prosperity. (Besides that, I've never lived in my car, which seems to be a pre-requisite for Greatness, although I have run out of gas a few times. Does that count?)

I find far more inspiration in mediocrity. When I need to rev myself up to work on a chapter in my next book or prepare for an upcoming speaking gig, I seem to magically stumble upon someone in my industry who does their craft poorly, or at least, without Greatness. Many of whom are quite successful, I might add! Just the other day I was reading a fairly popular book about entrepreneurship and was stunned at how superficial and obvious, not to mention poorly edited, the material was. I mean, DUH. This stuff comes straight from Old School Self-Promotion 101—and the book was touted as revolutionary!

Anyway, after reading about half the book, I couldn't wait to get back to working on mine, which I'd back-burnered earlier this year. Heck, if this guy's stuff can be considered "revolutionary," to what heights might MY stuff climb?!

This approach could easily apply in a real estate career. Sure, there are a handful of real estate practitioners who are Great but the vast majority is, by definition, average. Many, of course, are less-than-average, but darnit, if they don't do okay!? Frustrating, isn't it?

Well, take that frustration and be inspired by it. Visit open houses on Sundays and observe how poorly many agents handle them—their signage, their (lack of) knowledge of the home and neighborhood, and their often-uncomfortable rapport-building skills. Eavesdrop on the other agents in your office and hear how unprofessional some of them sound while talking to prospects and clients. Preview listings in your area and notice how poorly they are priced and marketed. Read through several MLS listings and see how many fields are incomplete and the descriptions dull. As you work your own deals, note how long it takes for other agents to return your calls, and how unfriendly or unprofessional their outgoing voicemail messages are.

If you, like me, are intimidated by the Great, look to the mediocre for inspiration. You can do better, significantly so, and in today's world of increasing mediocrity, you might find yourself among the Great!

"I'm Your Friend, so I'll Be Honest with You...!"

Couldn't sleep last night. Got up, turned on the TV, flipped thru channels until I landed on HGTV. When I can't sleep, HGTV tends to be my go-to channel since they usually have SOMETHING on besides "paid programming."

Anyway, I got my first taste of The Property Shop with real estate goddess Tatiana. I'd heard that she wasn't exactly the warmest, fuzziest real estate broker on the planet...and, indeed, I doubt she's ever accused of being a little ray of sunshine.

This particular show's overall theme was the difficulty of working with friends and family. Okay, fine. You have my attention since that's sorta what I preach about all day long.

The first storyline has Tatiana reluctantly listing an over-improved loft in the 'hood. For a friend. Said friend had been trying to sell the loft for a year, priced at $900,000. No luck. Location sucks.

Tatiana comes in and says two things that made me LOL.

#1—"*Since you're my friend, I'll be honest with you. You're overpriced!*"

#2—"*Since you're my friend, I'll list it for you at $895,000, but if it doesn't sell, we'll have to...blah blah blah.*"

Call me fussy, but since when is "friendship" a requirement for honesty in a real estate transaction? And since when do friends let friends overprice because they're friends?

Maybe I'm just punchy from lack of sleep...

Real Estate Prospecting—Turning Cheese into Soul

It's that time of year where thoughts turn to holidays and business plans. What to do, what to do in the new year to make it better than this last one?!

It's awfully tempting to seek comfort in traditional prospecting methods that have worked (?) for decades. Even if it sounds ghastly to you to knock on doors, call up perfect strangers or pester your friends for referrals; even if your bank account can't really handle an expensive mailing or advertising campaign, you figure..."Heck, if it's good enough for so-and-so, it's good enough for me!"

Trouble is, and you know this deep inside, these traditional methods are cheesy. Uncomfortable. And increasingly ineffective as consumers tire of being marketed to. Combine your obvious discomfort in implementing cheesy prospecting methods with the general public's weariness of said methods... and what you have is a colossal waste of your time and money. Neither of which many of us have in great supply these days.

So, what to do instead? How can you, as I very cleverly just coined, Turn Cheese into Soul?

Over the next several episodes, I'll tackle some of the most popular "traditional" prospecting methods (like Expired listings, FSBO's, Open Houses and Newsletters) and show you ways to make them work for you...without selling your soul to do so...yep, it can be done!

Sneak peak—all my Cheese-to-Soul advice will center around stepping out of the Numbers Game of prospecting—to approach your prospecting with a Quality over Quantity mindset...

Stay tuned!

Real Estate Prospecting—Turning Cheese into Soul: Expired Listings & FSBO's

For the record, I have never seriously pursued Expireds or FSBO's myself; however, I have BEEN an expired listing and have appeared to be a FSBO, so I speak from the perspective of a consumer, not a real estate agent or trainer.

And I tell ya—the expired and FSBO campaigns I've personally been the recipient of are pretty darn cheesy. Obviously the agents are taking a shotgun approach to getting business from us poor saps who desperately need their "professional services." The good old Numbers Game—throw enough doo doo against the wall and eventually something will stick. And most of it is, indeed, doo doo.

Here are some examples of the cheesy marketing I've gotten from agents who want my business...

- Daily postcards addressed to "Property Owner."

- Postcards with a hand-written "Call me! I Have a Buyer for Your Property!" (uh, the house was on the market for the last 9 months).

- Envelopes with my name misspelled (at least that's a step above "Property Owner")

- Letters with promised "enclosures" missing (e.g., "Enclosed is a list of homes that have recently sold in your neighborhood!")

- A laughably cheesy series of letters with an insultingly condescending tone.

I've also been cold-called, of course, although not nearly as much as I expected. In almost all cases, the caller was obviously calling from a list and was not in the least bit prepared for a real live human being to answer the phone. They were usually nervous, probably due to the fact that they were not at all prepared to intelligently discuss the specifics of my listing. I guess they were just shooting for the appointment, and didn't bother to "waste any time" in preparation.

Here's the thing.

The owner of an expired listing or a FSBO probably really WOULD like to hear from you...if you have something to offer aside from a cheesy canned marketing piece and a desperate desire to get a listing agreement signed. These people are not the enemy—they're, yes, real live human beings who have a need they'd love you to fill. But no mass-mailing or cold-calling campaign is going to convince anyone you're the right (wo)man for the job.

What to do instead?

Quality over Quantity. Instead of simply shoveling out postcards, brochures and missing enclosures to as many targets as possible, take the time to personalize your approach to a few. Drive by the home. Take a close look at the expired MLS listing or the FSBO brochure. Note any marketing challenges you see and think about how you would address them. See if you can identify why the home hasn't sold—it may be price, but it very well may not be. Try to figure out if the property is a short sale; that will affect your approach. Ask yourself—"*Can I sell this home?*"

That's what your target audience wants to know. Can you sell their home?

If I had received just one personal letter (and I don't mean just a hand-written envelope) from an agent who had taken the time to actually LOOK at my situation and address it specifically, that agent would have had a great shot at my business. If one of the agents who called me actually knew where "Doe Run Estates" is located and why it's special (and challenging), I'd have been impressed. If any of them had indicated they had a clue why my property didn't sell, or even a sincere desire to find out, they might have caught my attention.

But, sigh, no. All attempts to entice me to take the next step were in vain. Hopefully they had more luck with their 99 other targets-du-jour...

Stay tuned for the next episode of turning cheese into soul...

December 2009

Real Estate Prospecting—Turning Cheese into Soul: Newsletters

Next up on the list of ways to turn Prospecting Cheese into Soul...the ever-popular Newsletter!

I probably have enough opinions on the topic of Newsletters to fill up half a dozen blogs...and I may just do that. But we have to start somewhere, so let's start, um, here.

We real estate agents love our newsletters, don't we? I wonder how many companies out there are capitalizing on our affection for the newsletter? Encouraging us to "build relationships" via our newsletter...to stay in touch with our friends via our newsletters...to promote ourselves and our wonderfulness via our newsletter?

I'm on a lot of newsletter distribution lists from agents around the country. Some are...well, let's just say that some are better (less-cheesy) than others. Most are clearly purchased "as is" and distributed at the touch of a button (or click of a mouse). Some display a little bit of customization, such as a spot to write a "personal" note and feature a listing or two. A few appear to be 100% created from scratch.

What are the typical topics covered in a real estate agent's newsletter? Lessee...home improvement tips, gardening ideas, recipes, market stats, Just Listed and Just Sold announcements, mortgage news...sorry...but YAWWWW-WWWN. Not only does every real estate newsletter seem to follow the same pattern, but half the time, the information is so boilerplate as to not even apply to the local market! Even the fully customized newsletters, while more relevant to the audience, still tend to look, sound and feel like templates.

So let's step back a bit.

What's the real purpose of your newsletter? Is it to...

✓ Educate your audience on the average Days on Market or Price per Square Foot in your area?

✓ Impress the reader by displaying your new listings or bragging about your recent closings?

- ✓ Ensure your friends know how important it is to winterize their sprinkler systems?

- ✓ Share your gardening expertise, even though the monthly "tip" is clearly from a different climate?

If you answered "yes" to any of the above, I'll encourage you to think about your answer.

Isn't the ultimate goal of a newsletter to make your audience like you? And remember you?

We can debate all day about what exactly "like" means, but in general, I believe the point of a newsletter is that the person who receives it thinks a little more highly of the person who sent it than they did before it was sent. Which naturally leads to them being just a little more likely to remember that person than they were the day before.

So, what, in a newsletter, might inspire that reaction? Or conversely, what might be the kiss of death?

More next time...

Real Estate Prospecting—Turning Cheese into Soul: Newsletters, Part Deux

In the previous installment of the Cheese to Soul series, I commented that I might have half a dozen posts in me about how to create an effective newsletter. Fortunately, or unfortunately, that might actually be true. We'll see how far I get today.

Remember, the goal of a newsletter is to make the recipient of the newsletter smile and think of you fondly. Which is best accomplished not with gardening tips, Just Sold notices or descriptions of your listings, but rather with interesting content that reflects YOU—your voice, your personality. And the best way to do that is to write the content yourself.

Now, don't freak out on me. Writing interesting content YOURSELF is not all that hard, especially if you work under the principle that less is more. As in—don't feel your newsletter has to be formally formatted with a Volume

Number, Table of Contents and a three-column layout. Nope. In fact, a simple email-style newsletter will work much better. If you're on my mailing list, you've seen my "newsletters" which are nothing more than me rambling about something, hopefully of interest, with my cute little signature logo at the bottom. No sidebars, very few graphics, and only the occasional sales-pitch (which I usually apologize for).

And, by the way, my newsletters are probably the most important (and effective) self-promotion I do.

Write your newsletters with the goal of inspiring your audience to respond. Responses are good. They open the door to ongoing conversations with your readers and you never know where they'll lead. You're much more likely to get meaningful responses to your newsletters if they're done in a casual format, rather than a formal newsletter format. Whenever I get a newsletter that appears to be professionally designed, I might be impressed, but I'm not inspired to respond. And, frankly, I make the assumption that the newsletter is mostly boilerplate or sales-pitchy anyway, and not likely to be of interest to me. If I'm pressed for time (which is most of the time), I hit DELETE.

Make sure your newsletter goes out from YOU—as in, from Your Name. Not from some professional-sounding company or even your fancy tagline. YOUR NAME. Period. I can't tell you how many newsletters I get from people I know, but I'd never know who they were from because the "From" field is a company I've never heard of.

One last tip for today ...DON'T use a program to send out your emails that doesn't allow replies! I was recently added to an acquaintance's Avon drip campaign and right across the top of my daily marketing email (sigh) is the note: "PLEASE DO NOT RESPOND TO THIS EMAIL. This email box is not equipped to handle correspondence." Sheesh.

So...what might you write about that would be "meaningful" to your audience and inspire them to respond?

You know the drill...stay tuned.

Turning Cheese into Soul—Newsletters: The Difference between "Meaningful" and "Interesting"

The other day I got a very timely question from my cyber-friend Ron considering this week's Cheese-to-Soul series.

Ron asked if I knew of a source for good real estate-related newsletter content that would be "meaningful" to his Sphere of Influence. He's frustrated by the material available for purchase, most of which simply feels canned. Moreover, he's uncomfortable using much of it because it relates to topics he's NOT an expert in, such as tax planning, home staging and credit reports.

I agree. As I may have mentioned a time or two, I refuse to use canned, boilerplate material. I think it's cheesy and dorky. (My definition of Dorky is any written, self-promotional communication that is dull, dry, boring or corporate. Most content-for-purchase pretty much qualifies.)

But let's go back to Ron's quest for real estate information that would be "meaningful" to his SOI. Here was my response to him:

"Here's the thing—your SOI doesn't have a lot of interest in real estate on a day-to-day basis. Therefore, there's not much in OUR world that would be generally meaningful to people outside of our world, with a few exceptions that come up from time to time.

You want your newsletters to be interesting to your audience, more so than "meaningful." And you know what's interesting to your SOI? Stuff from YOU. From YOU, their friend, Ron. Maybe an observation about the real estate market, if it's interesting, or to pass on a funny story from your career. Or maybe not related to real estate at all.

I write to my SOI every month in email form, not newsletter form. I want my SOI communications to clearly come from me, not some canned product I bought off a virtual shelf. If newsletters/emails are going to be part of my marketing plan, I'm going to put some effort into them in the hopes of inspiring my friends and acquaintances to think fondly of me, rather than to just simply remember that I sell real estate (and promptly forget)."

Remember that the primary goal of your "newsletter" is not to impress, educate or overtly prospect. It's simply to remind the people you know that you exist and that you're a pretty cool guy or gal.

I recommend that you always have a notebook with you to scribble down ideas for SOI newsletters—and I think you'll be pleased how quickly your list will grow once you get in the habit.

Okay, so that's three blogs on the Art of the Non-Cheesy Newsletter. I think I'll move on now...next up—Greeting Cards! Or...maybe listing presentations...or maybe...heck, I dunno. Just stay tuned!

Turning Cheese into Soul—Send(ing) Out Cards the Soulful Way

Today's topic is about greeting cards. Specifically, a program called Send Out Cards. If you aren't familiar with the product/program, it's a greeting card system where you choose a card from an online selection, customize it, and "sign" it...hit SEND and a real, live greeting card goes out in the mail with what appears to be your signature. You can even provide samples of your handwriting and the system will "handwrite" your personal note in the card so that appears to actually have been written by you.

I've been rather critical of the program for a while now. I did try it a few years ago, had a negative experience—my cards were sent out twice, thus destroying any notion the recipients might have had as to the authenticity of the cards. I've never used or recommended Send Out Cards again.

However, I had a conversation a few weeks ago with my new friend John Lind, who might have changed my mind. At least, sorta. Maybe I should say that he opened my eyes to a better way to use the product/program; one that is much more in line with my philosophies of how such things ought to be done.

John uses his Send Out Cards membership in a decidedly non-dorky/non-cheesy manner. In fact, his use of the program falls right in line with what I teach about staying in touch with your Sphere of Influence. Instead of simply relying on the program to sign and mail a mildly clever but run-of-the-mill greeting card, he takes the time to use the technology offered by the program to create a truly memorable card—one that will almost certainly make the recipient smile; maybe even LOL!

Here's an example of a card John sent me:

John generated this card after our discussion where I explained why I didn't like the idea of Send(ing) Out Cards. He "wrote" a very nice note on the inside of the card; one that was personal to me and our conversation. I am, in a word, impressed. And yes, I did LOL when I opened it. I even kept it!

Here's another card John did at Thanksgiving...

Kim

Wishing you a very

HAPPY THANKSGIVING!

"I know how hard it is for you to put
food on your family."

- George Bush, Greater Nashua, N.H.,
Chamber of Commerce, Jan. 27, 2000

So, what's the punch line? While it's cheesy (IMO) to rely on technology to do your staying-in-touching FOR you, it's not at all cheesy to use technology to make your staying-in-touching memorable!

See the difference? Let me know if you have any cool ideas I can ~~steal~~ admire.

A New "Game" Plan for 2010

As it happens every year 'round this time, New Year's resolutions are being made with a vengeance.

In our world of real estate, these resolutions tend to focus on revving up one's prospecting efforts in hopes of having a Great New Year. Promises to more fully commit to a cold-calling or door-knocking campaign, to more aggressively pursue expired listings and FSBO's, to formally choose a farm area or finally figure out what SEO really means.

All well and good. I wish you luck with that!

But in addition to all these Numbers Games, I submit the following plan for your consideration...

Rather than attempting to contact 100 people a day in hopes of catching the attention of a few, how about trying to impress just a few every day, in hopes of making a memorable impression on every single one? If you were to impress two people a day, at the end of a year, that's over 700 people on the planet who think you're really cool—instead of simply sort of recognizing your name from your mass-marketing efforts.

Instead of pestering your sphere of influence once a quarter with requests for referrals (which I promise you are not welcomed with open arms), try reconnecting with the people you know as a friend or acquaintance first—a friend or acquaintance who happens to sell real estate.

Instead of focusing all your time, energy and budget on hunting down new prospects, spend at least half of that time being a kick-a$$ real estate agent for those clients who have already honored you with their business.

It is possible to run a perfectly respectable real estate business without doing ANY formal prospecting other than what I describe above. If the people in your world think you're a pretty darn cool person AND a terrific real estate agent, they'll take great care of you throughout your career.

No game-playing required.

Appendix

Additional SWS Resources

SWS Books

Sell with Soul: Creating an Extraordinary Career in Real Estate without Losing Your Friends, Your Principles or Your Self-Respect

If You're Not Having Fun Selling Real Estate, You're Not Doing it Right

Prospect with Soul: Discovering the Perfect Prospecting Strategies for Wonderful, Extraordinary, One-of-a-Kind YOU

Learn more and purchase at the SWS Bookstore – www.SWSStore.com

SWS Courses & Programs

The Exceptional Agent Program: Because Competence Gives You Confidence

SOI with SOUL: Building a Sphere of Influence Business Model from Scratch – No Referral-Begging or Pestering Required!

The SWS School for Rookie Real Estate Agents

Selling with Soul for Life: Seven Weeks of Building Your Business...for Life!

Prospect with Soul: The Seven Week Course to Discovering the Perfect Prospecting Strategies for YOU

The Accredited Consultant in Real Estate® Course and Designation

Learn more and purchase at the SWS Bookstore – www.SWSStore.com

The SWS Community

Club SWS – www.ClubSWS.Info

SWS Connect- www.SWSConnect.com

The Accredited Consultant in Real Estate® www.TheConsultingProfessional.com

Index by Category

Compensation

Pay for Non-Performance? I Really Don't Wanna..., 87

The Confident Rookie Series—SECRET EIGHT: Get Comfy with Your Commission, 157

A Perfect Example of Keeping the Monkey...Agents Bickering over Commission to Keep the Buyer and Seller in the Deal, 205

Competence, Professionalism & Old Fashioned Good Manners

Doctors and Lawyers...and Real Estate Agents?, 42

Preview Ten Listings Today and Report Back, 68

What's Your Angle? Do You Really Need One?, 91

Hellooooooooo??? Are You out There, SOI? Yes, Jennifer, We're Here!, 98

"So, What Is a GOOD Real Estate Agent?", 102

Y'think Your Current Clients Are Talking About Their Real Estate Agent? Uh, Yeah!, 111

Breaking up Is Hard to Do...but It Doesn't Have to Be Ugly, 124

Sales-y or Service-y?, 136

I'm Sure She Didn't Mean It This Way...or Did She?, 145

Real Estate Agents—A Better Approach to: "I Return Calls Between x and y...", 148

Always Be Closing...?, 167

"Dear Real Estate Professional, I'd Like to See a House, Please", 170

Even if They Don't Complain...Sellers Notice, 206

Sixteen Ways to Keep Your Seller Happy with You, 207

"Real Estate Is a Relationship Business"—Not Exactly (a rant), 220

Fan Favorites

Real Estate Is Not a Numbers Game (at least, it doesn't have to be), 27

What's the Best Way to Ask for Referrals? Don't., 36

Real Estate Agents: Get Good...or Get out, 64

Gas Prices Too High to "Waste" My Time with Buyers? Oh, Puh-leeeaze!, 100

Can a Single Woman Expand Her Sphere of Influence Without Sending the Wrong Message?, 118

Any Idiot Can Give Their House Away...If Price Is All that Matters, What Do They Need Us for?, 173

Call Me Mercenary...But a Personal Crisis Can Be Good for Business, 189

AVOID BURNOUT! Stop Taking Responsibility for Stuff that's Not Your Responsibility to Take!, 199

Why Did My Friend Hire Someone Else? Oh, Let Me Count the Reasons..., 209

"Real Estate Is a Relationship Business"—Not Exactly (a rant), 220

"I'm Your Friend, so I'll Be Honest with You...!", 225

Introverts

Introverts—Stay IN Your Comfort Zone!, 35

Introverts—Always Offer Your Hand First, 39

A Great Niche for Introverts!, 40

Introverts—Show up When It's the Right Thing to Do, 48

Do I Deserve Your Loyalty?, 49

Introverts—Pick up that Phone!, 50

To Expand Your Sphere of Influence—Be in the Right Place at the Right Time...More Frequently!, 125

Introverts, Always Ask "What's in It For Me?" (and no, that's not a typo), 145

"Mismatched" Spouses—Introverts & Extroverts, 166

Making New Friends to Sell Real Estate to—a Guide for Introverts & Other Reluctant Networkers, 177

Reluctant Networkers—Your Next Biggest Client May Be at Walmart!, 179

Is Shaking Hands Too 20th Century in Today's Germophobic World?, 187

Listing Presentations

What Does a Listing Agent DO for All that Money?, 32

Just Say NO to Price Reductions!, 44

What Your Home Sellers May Not Know...but Need to, 52

My Dear Home Seller: What's Your Plan B?, 110

To Present or Not to Present...I Have My Answer, 132

The Confident Rookie Series—SECRET SEVEN: Let Your Seller Prospect Talk!, 156

The Confident Rookie Series—SECRET EIGHT: Get Comfy with Your Commission, 157

"How Can I Compete with a Minimum Service Real Estate Company?", 161

What if My Seller Asks for a 'Listing Exclusion'?, 168

Okay, Miss Smarty-Pants, HOW Do You Get Your Sellers on Board to Get Their Home Ready for Market?, 175

Mastering Your Market

Yes, a Sphere of Influence Approach IS Enough in Today's Market, if You..., 122

Attracting Real Estate Business by Being a Master of Your Market, 195

Becoming a Market Master—Here's How..., 197

Newsletters

Christmas Card Lemons...to Lemonade, 132

Real Estate Prospecting—Turning Cheese into Soul: Newsletters, 229

Real Estate Prospecting—Turning Cheese into Soul: Newsletters, Part Deux, 230

Turning Cheese into Soul—Newsletters: The Difference between "Meaningful" and "Interesting", 232

Pricing

Just Say NO to Price Reductions!, 44

Average "Days on Market"? Who CARES?, 135

Any Idiot Can Give Their House Away...If Price Is All that Matters, What Do They Need Us for?, 173

Should You Price to Ward off Appraisal Problems?, 184

Adventures in Pricing—Historic Homes in Urban Neighborhoods, 213

Pricing Historic Homes in Urban Markets—Step One: Make like a Boy Scout..., 214

Pricing Historic Homes in Urban Markets—Step Two: Preview, Preview, Preview!, 216

Playing Detective...Pricing Historic Homes in Urban Neighborhoods: Step 3, 217

Pricing Historic Homes in Urban Neighborhoods, Step Four: Analyzing the SOLDs—Dealing with the Outliers, 219

Prospecting

Real Estate Is Not a Numbers Game (at least, it doesn't have to be), 27

Okay, so I Lied...Real Estate IS a Number's Game...Sort of..., 34

Introverts—Stay IN Your Comfort Zone!, 35

What's the Best Way to Ask for Referrals? Don't., 36

SOI—It's More Fun with a Friend!, 45

Is SOI Right for You?, 63

I Was Cold-Called This Morning...and I Was Rude, 83

Sales Pitched at 24-Hour Fitness...and I WON'T Be Joining!, 90

What's Your Angle? Do You Really Need One?, 91

Phooey on Prospecting...I Just Wanna Do My Job!, 127

Today's Market Realities, Part I: When to Venture out of Your Comfort Zone...and When to Stay in..., 129

In Today's World...Sales Pitchee's Just Say No, 135

Persistence Pays Off...? Eh, Maybe There's a Better Way, 176

What You Can Do TODAY to Ensure a Sweeeet Tomorrow, 187

Attracting Real Estate Business by Being a Master of Your Market, 195

Real Estate Prospecting—Turning Cheese into Soul, 226

Real Estate Prospecting—Turning Cheese into Soul: Expired Listings & FSBO's, 227

Real Estate Prospecting—Turning Cheese into Soul: Newsletters, 229

Real Estate Prospecting—Turning Cheese into Soul: Newsletters, Part Deux, 230

Turning Cheese into Soul—Newsletters: The Difference between "Meaningful" and "Interesting", 232

Turning Cheese into Soul—Send(ing) Out Cards the Soulful Way, 233

Rants & Ridiculousness

Doctors and Lawyers...and Real Estate Agents?, 42

Real Estate Agents: Get Good...or Get out, 64

I Was Cold-Called This Morning...and I Was Rude, 83

No Wonder Houses Aren't Selling..., 84

Always Look for the Negative...Yeah, That Works (she says sarcastically), 89

Sales Pitched at 24-Hour Fitness...and I WON'T Be Joining!, 90

Gas Prices Too High to "Waste" My Time with Buyers? Oh, Puh-leeeaze!, 100

It's All About ME (a rant)!, 104

PUH-LEEEEEAZE Don't Use Your Office Email Account!!, 120

"Good for You, Let Me Know if You Need Anything.", 180

Just What a Rookie Agent Needs—CHARM SCHOOL!, 188

"Real Estate Is a Relationship Business"—Not Exactly (a rant), 220

"I'm Your Friend, so I'll Be Honest with You...!", 225

Recession

Real Estate Agents: Get Good...or Get out, 64

Hey! What Happened to the Real Estate Market?, 66

No Wonder Houses Aren't Selling..., 84

Please Tip in Cash (an alternative to Referral-Begging), 101

Is Walking Away the Financially Responsible Thing to Do?, 119

Dave Ramsey Sez: In a Tough Market, Work Twice as Hard. JA Sez..., 123

The Realities of Today's Less-than-Vibrant Real Estate Market, 128

Today's Market Realities, Part I: When to Venture out of Your Comfort Zone...and When to Stay in..., 129

Seriously, Is It Time to Hit PAUSE on Your Real Estate Career?, 131

Referral-Begging

What's the Best Way to Ask for Referrals? Don't., 36

I'll Be Happy to Refer You as Long as It's My Idea...(that is, please don't ask me to), 99

Asking for Referrals Versus NOT Asking for Referrals—Which Is More Risky?, 105

Rookies

Jake's New Real Estate Career, 53

The Saga of Jake Continues..., 54

Jakes Sells a House...or Two, 55

Announcing Our Rookie of the Year...Jake!, 57

Reflections on Jake's Success, 60

Was Jake Lucky?, 61

Should New Real Estate Agents Focus on Buyers or Listings? And Why?, 80

Newbies, Don't Be Intimidated...You Can Do It, 80

Can a New Agent Make It in Today's Market?, 113

Aspiring Real Estate Agents—Can't Go Full-Time Yet? Consider This..., 116

The Rookie Agent Learning Curve...Elongated?, 146

New Real Estate Agents—Get Help if You Need It...Yes, Even if..., 148

The Rookie Series—Ten Secrets to Looking as if You've Done This Before!, 149

The Confident Rookie Series—SECRET ONE: Master Your Systems BEFORE You Need Them!, 150

The Confident Rookie Series—SECRET TWO: Practice with Your Printer!, 151

The Confident Rookie Series—SECRET THREE: Don't Wing It with Your New Buyer!, 152

The Confident Rookie Series—SECRET FOUR: Drive Your Route Ahead of Time, 153

The Confident Rookie Series—SECRET FIVE: Cheerfully Waste Your Time, 154

The Confident Rookie Series—SECRET SIX: Find Your Handyman, 155

The Confident Rookie Series—SECRET SEVEN: Let Your Seller Prospect Talk!, 156

The Confident Rookie Series—SECRET EIGHT: Get Comfy with Your Commission, 157

The Confident Rookie Series—SECRET NINE: Admit that You're New, 158

The Confident Rookie Series—SECRET TEN: What to Say When You Don't Know the Answer, 159

"Good for You, Let Me Know if You Need Anything.", 180

Just What a Rookie Agent Needs—CHARM SCHOOL!, 188

WHY Don't We Care About Training for Rookie Real Estate Agents? Seriously, I'm Asking!, 193

Sphere of Influence

Real Estate Is Not a Numbers Game (at least, it doesn't have to be), 27

Okay, so I Lied...Real Estate IS a Number's Game...Sort of..., 34

What's the Best Way to Ask for Referrals? Don't., 36

Using Reverse Psychology with Your FAMILY SOI, 38

SOI—It's More Fun with a Friend!, 45

Give (Referrals) and Ye Shall Receive!, 46

Introverts—Show up When It's the Right Thing to Do, 48

Jake's New Real Estate Career, 53

The Saga of Jake Continues..., 54

Jakes Sells a House...or Two, 55

Announcing Our Rookie of the Year...Jake!, 57

Life Is Good...Says Jake, 60

Reflections on Jake's Success, 60

Was Jake Lucky?, 61

Is SOI Right for You?, 63

My Friday SOI Success Story, 65

An Excuse to Contact Your Past Clients—for Old Fogies Only!, 72

ANOTHER Excuse to Contact Past Clients—Use that Camera!, 73

Does Your Spouse Refer Business to You?, 74

You Won't Win 'Em All with Your SOI...and that's Okay, 82

My Dear Sphere of Influence, "Thanks, But I Don't Want Your Loyalty!", 83

"Advertising" to Your Sphere of Influence, 88

Helloooooooooo??? Are You out There, SOI? Yes, Jennifer, We're Here!, 98

There's GOLD in Them Thar SOI!, 103

Pretending to Be a Democrat—That'll Teach Me!, 114

Can a Single Woman Expand Her Sphere of Influence Without Sending the Wrong Message?, 118

Is a Sphere of Influence Approach Enough in Today's Market?, 121

Yes, a Sphere of Influence Approach IS Enough in Today's Market, if You..., 122

To Expand Your Sphere of Influence—Be in the Right Place at the Right Time...More Frequently!, 125

Christmas Card Lemons...to Lemonade, 132

SOI 101—What Exactly Is an SOI (Sphere of Influence) Business Model?, 138

SOI 102—The SECRET to a Successful Real Estate Sphere of Influence Business Model, 139

SOI 103—"My Daughter's Best Friend's Parents Just Hired Another Real Estate Agent!", 141

SOI 104: "I Think I've Blown It with My Sphere of Influence. Can I Recover Their Support?", 143

I'm Sure She Didn't Mean It This Way...or Did She?, 145

Does Your Friend Owe You a Courtesy Call when She Hires Someone Else?, 169

Making New Friends to Sell Real Estate to—a Guide for Introverts & Other Reluctant Networkers, 177

Reluctant Networkers—Your Next Biggest Client May Be at Walmart!, 179

Call Me Mercenary...But a Personal Crisis Can Be Good for Business, 189

Can You "SOI" in a Resort Community (that is, can you depend on your sphere of influence for business)?, 190

Nurturing Your Relationships TODAY for Business Tomorrow, 198

"Jennifer, What Do You Think of Client Appreciation Parties?", 212

"Real Estate Is a Relationship Business"—Not Exactly (a rant), 220

Turning Cheese into Soul—Send(ing) Out Cards the Soulful Way, 233

Working with Buyers

My New Buyer Calls at 7:30am on Sunday Morning...Do I Jump? You Betcha!, 96

Gas Prices Too High to "Waste" My Time with Buyers? Oh, Puh-leeeaze!, 100

The Confident Rookie Series—Secret Three: Don't Wing It with Your New Buyer!, 152

The Confident Rookie Series—Secret Four: Drive Your Route Ahead of Time, 153

Working with Sellers

Being Up-Front with Our Sellers, 30

What Does a Listing Agent DO for All that Money?, 32

Just Say NO to Price Reductions!, 44

What Your Home Sellers May Not Know...but Need to, 52

Preview Ten Listings Today and Report Back, 68

My Dear Home Seller: What's Your Plan B?, 110

To Present or Not to Present...I Have My Answer, 132

What if My Seller Asks for a 'Listing Exclusion'?, 168

Any Idiot Can Give Their House Away...If Price Is All that Matters, What Do They Need Us for?, 173

Okay, Miss Smarty-Pants, HOW Do You Get Your Sellers on Board to Get Their Home Ready for Market?, 175

Even if They Don't Complain...Sellers Notice, 206

Sixteen Ways to Keep Your Seller Happy with You, 207

Ten Ways to Show Your Seller You Don't Care, 210